Situatedness

Post-Contemporary Interventions

Series Editors: Stanley Fish and Fredric Jameson

Situatedness,

or, Why We Keep Saying Where We're Coming From

DAVID SIMPSON

Duke University Press   Durham and London 2002

© 2002 Duke University Press   All rights reserved
Printed in the United States of America on acid-free paper ∞
Typeset in Quadraat by Tseng Information Systems
Library of Congress Cataloging-in-Publication Data
appear on the last printed page of this book.

In Memoriam

TONY TANNER

March 18, 1935–December 5, 1998

ARTHUR SALE

August 7, 1912–April 18, 2000

now permanent as stars

The shadow-side of the liberated subject is its degradation to something exchangeable, to something that exists merely for something else; the shadow-side of personality is the "So who are you?"

THEODOR ADORNO, "On Lyric Poetry and Society"

So what is this *situating?*

JEAN-PAUL SARTRE, *Search for a Method*

People situate themselves because they can't go home.

TED TAYLER, in the hallway, April 1996

Contents

Acknowledgments

Situatedness has proved to be the most perplexing topic on which I have ever tried to write, and for long periods I have doubted whether it is a topic at all. So it is with gratitude well beyond the usual that I thank those who have assured me along the way that there is something worthwhile here, whether by convincing me that I am making some useful sort of sense, or by sending me to important sources and arguments I had not known of or had forgotten: Georges van den Abeele, Lauren Berlant, Arif Dirlik, Kevis Goodman, Alan Grob, Karen Jacobs, Martin Jay, Marjorie Levinson, Helena Michie, Rob Nixon, and Paul Rabinow. My thanks also to audiences at the University of California at Davis, the University of Cape Town, Columbia University, the University of Natal (Durban and Pietermaritzburg), Muhlenberg College, Rhodes University, Rice University, and the University of Saskatchewan who have listened and responded to parts of what here is now published. Jane Beal helped prepare the bibliography. An early draft of the manuscript produced a rigorous response from Mary Poovey that I found most helpful, although I am not sure that she will entirely approve of what I have made of it. Christopher Herbert and Fredric Jameson have been an inspiration both in their own work and in their wonderful attentions to mine; every bit of their advice has seemed pertinent, and I have tried my best to follow it. My first, last, and most constant reader has been Margaret Ferguson. She has been a star and ever-fixed mark to every wandering thought; her worth is happily not unknown.

Introduction

Let me situate my argument. . . . This call for permission to situate, at once modest and aggressive, figures prominently in the rhetoric of our time, the time around the year 2000. What does it tell us? What is its history? How has it come into speech, and what work is it claiming to do? The popularity of the word might suggest that it really does refresh the tired language of subject specification, breaking with precedent and offering a newly respectable accountability and self-advertisment; or, alternatively, its usefulness might be that of obfuscation, of masking a familiar compulsion to self-justification by a new term. Can we hope to tell the difference? Might it perform both of these functions?

Questions

There is something comforting in talking about a *situation*, whether one's own or another's. We contemplate our situation in life, perhaps with complacency ("I am happy with my situation") or perhaps with anxiety ("the situation is out of control"), but mostly with a sense of knowing what it is, or supposing that it might be knowable. In trying to formulate the questions raised by the "final solution to the Jewish question" Inga Clendinnen (who in this respect stands for many) remarks that "large theories may generate good questions, but they produce poor answers. The historian's task is to discover what happened in some actual past situation . . . not to produce large truths." [1] To invoke the "actual past situation" is to sound the ring of reality, to conjure up the aura of presence, most urgently to be desired in the case of this most exigent of actual pasts; desired even as it is feared (for what might we discover?), because *not knowing* is the most terrible of predicaments for those who have come after. The "actual situation" promises to free us from the spider web of theory and from the disabling kinds of self-consciousness that have been the demands of theory. Speaking to the matter of one's own situatedness holds out a similar allure, that of being in place and knowing one's place, and of sharing the good news (even when it is bad news). We all know or think we know about the limitations of "large theories": this knowledge is one of the defining articles of faith of the condition called postmodern. Situations, in contrast, are appealing for their apparent implication in the local, the empirical, the visible, and the tangible: *let me tell you where I'm coming from.*

Kenneth Burke, who also stands for many in this respect, once supposed that literature could perform this task of specifying situations. He described it as a kind of "*correct* magic, magic whose decrees about the naming of real situations is the closest possible approximation to the situation named," thereby allowing us to "come closest to a correct gauging of that situation as it actually is." [2] These situations are "real" and intersubjective, belonging to the species and not just to idiosyncratic individuals (p. 3). They are as close as we can get to lives that we do not live in ourselves. Once again, in a fragmented world, they are comforting, offering "universal relevance" (p. 3).

Such assurance is also and above all important to the desire to judge, to render a verdict. Clendinnen again: "My own view is that there is a great distance between those who do what they must do to survive in an imposed situation, and those who design or participate in the imposition of that situation" (p. 65). Indeed. And yet the handing down of judgment has mostly been a fraught experience for the more reflective spirits who see themselves as in retreat from various forms of absolutism. We often admit that all situations are exceptional and unrepeatable, "that our understanding of our fellow human beings will not and cannot be complete" (p. 112). How then to judge? How to estimate the adequacy of evidence? The law, as I later show, has been much concerned with situatedness, and with trying to tell the difference between what is imposed and what is willed. Despite the promise that "thick description" has held out and perhaps even sometimes delivered, we are haunted by a sense of how difficult it is to know others and also to know ourselves. Cultural and subcultural commonality can induce a fantasy of true knowing and hold out the possibility of adequate judgment, and this may be one reason (although only one) why we are possessed by the legacies of the "final solution" and not so much by those of atrocities identified as more remote and perpetrated by persons less undeniably like us. But there is no getting around the slippage into indefinite speculation, into a gathering of evidence that is unstoppable once begun.

The Enlightenment knew this even as it proposed the task of specifying the nature of situations. It knew that to speculate about situatedness is to think about everything that is around one, synchronically, even as it supposed or pretended that only some things mattered or mattered most (climate, political structure, occupation). It began to know, in its evolution toward what Michel Foucault has nominated the "sciences of man," that what mattered was not only what is but also, diachronically, what ever has been and is becoming: the whole world and its history along with its tendencies to a future.[3] When it comes to explaining why anything is what it is and where it is, and not something or somewhere else (or why anyone is as they are and not otherwise), all that is or has been in the world is potentially part of the case. To trivialize an example made famous by the chaos theorists: it is not likely that the butterfly that flapped its wings ten years ago in Sumatra affects my choice from today's lunch menu. Dietary habits, my level of hunger, and/or whimsy will probably matter more in deciding for or against the shrimp. Indeed, an expressed belief in the butterfly effect might well qualify me for psychiatric attention. But it is very hard to prove that effect to be impossible, even as it is not very useful to search out how it could be plausible. Some evolutionary psychologists think that our important preadaptations, with and by means of which we are still living, were developed during the Pleistocene.[4] Others, mostly social scientists and humanists, believe that what matters most is derived from short-term cultural determinations. But what is culture? Everything? Including perhaps the Pleistocene and the butterfly? Endgame.

This is not a book about everything, although it is about how people have tried and still try to set limits, to make claims, and to find comfort. Trying to cope with everything does not make for a manageable life, so that despite what I have just said people do continue to situate themselves, either voluntarily or in response to someone else's request that they do so. The academic version takes the form of *let me situate my argument*; the more casual and widespread locution is *let me tell you where I'm coming from.* The invitation to *situate your argument* can sometimes earn the response *I hear where you're coming from.* We often find ourselves giving a role to *situatedness*, to a location and embeddedness that can be described and specified. My first thoughts about this habit were irritable ones, in the manner of a poor man's analytical philosopher: I found these declarations to be either without meaning or pointedly ambiguous, making knowledge claims that could not be cashed in. But of course the common language is often like that, and in its more compulsive locutions it tells us something about the social and personal relations that are being managed by way of such phrases. So I have ended up with a rather long account of this language and its arguable provenance and purpose. Sartre asked himself the question "just what is this *situating?*" some time ago, and he probably thought he had answered it. But no one much goes back to Sartre (whom I discuss at some length in chapter 5) as an authority for the claim to situate oneself: the philological history of the term is erased in its common usage, and necessarily so because that history would call up all sorts of questions that the usage itself is designed to evade. The common language is largely designed to keep things moving along, to enable social exchanges to occur without long detours into their underlying complexity. It is a tool for those who seek to manage our energies and imaginations, as well as for our own efforts at resisting such management or adapting it to preferred outcomes. Its function makes it resistant to analysis, but much can be learned when that analysis takes place. Because the history of the common language is erased in the interests of efficiency, that history has much to teach us about why some kinds of efficiency rather than others are on offer.

Coming before Sartre there was the larger project of what we may still call the Enlightenment, not just in its well-known form as a coherent body of thought aiming at the production of rational universals but in

4

its conflicted identity as seeking coherence out of the intuition of radical disparities ascribed to the importance of situatedness itself, to the different influences of time, place, and person. Versions of this concern had always been around and are visibly coincident with the very earliest efforts at describing individuality and subjectivity in theological and philosophical terms. For Christians such as Augustine, Calvin, and Luther the priority was always to get out of or beyond the world, so that in being thus desituated one might be closer to God. For pure materialists such as Holbach and Helvétius in the eighteenth century, when the word *situation* began to become commonplace in its modern sense, the absoluteness of our being limited to life in the world made our situatedness both all-important and radically indescribable. No two persons could ever share the same situation in life. Microscopic differences always inform the evolution of individuals even when they seem to share a general situation — identical twins apparently raised under the same conditions, for example. Strictly construed, the same conditions are never really the same conditions, and the tiniest difference (for example, one twin falling over while the other remains standing) affects the development of life forever after. The task of describing or controlling this, or of proposing and believing in a standard, shared situation, is then impossible. This was one version of Enlightenment. What it offered to a would-be social science could only be a world governed by noncomputable chaos. Helvétius might well have worried about that butterfly in Sumatra.

But there was another tendency that has been called Enlightenment, and it was the one that became dominant in the social science disciplines that have figured so importantly in the self-descriptions and management techniques of complex modern societies. This second Enlightenment sought to produce describable constants out of the morass of idiosyncrasies that the pure materialists proposed as all-powerful and beyond control, and whose terms seemed to legitimate nothing beyond absolute hedonism and libertinism. It largely erased the body as the impossibly complex site through which all data are mediated, and focused instead on a stripped-down mentalist self interacting with an equally reified set of objective world conditions. Its two major forms were rationalism and culturalism, each of which presented the problem of theorizing some sort of fit between something called *mind* and something else called *world*. The hypotheses whose credibility has not survived well, such as the belief in the power of climate over character as theorized by Montesquieu, now tend to appear as charming historical curiosities. But that is only because the curiosities have been created as such by the culturalist emphasis of much modern thinking (outside the medical sciences) about how we are situated, about *situatedness* (the word I will be using, and which I explain in chapter 1). We assume, that is to say, that the power of society, of occupational or political affiliation, or (increasingly at the present time) of ethnic identity is what matters most in making the self what it is. We do not see these understandings as curiosities. We believe in them. They are the things we most often refer to when we situate ourselves. The invocation of situatedness draws heavily on the habits of culturalism, but also leaves open an option for other, more classically materialist, accounts of what we are. It is, as the occasion demands, all over the place, which is why I think it is interesting and symptomatic.

On the one hand, invoking situatedness permits us to have faith in our powers of modification, in our ability to design the world conditions that best promote human or personal happiness, while at the same time it remains available as an excuse for behavior we cannot, or say we cannot, control. It is in this sphere of self-definition that many of the most rancorous disputes occur. Left-thinking persons are committed to the value and integrity of such terms as *agency* and *praxis*, whereby individuals and groups can operate on what they are given to effect positive transformations, but they also recognize *ideology* as a coercive form of situatedness that prevents many or most people from seeing the truth about their lives. Right-thinking persons have a very similar belief in agency, except that it is usually called *free will* and is affiliated with various sorts of religious and moral traditions and outcomes. Both kinds of thinking have been under stress, very evidently in the recent past and also I would say in the subjectivity-theory of the long-durational period of modernity, but both have continued to subsist as the alternatives between which we are most often given a choice. They entail very different kinds of politics, of course. Belief in rampant freedom of the will is usually used to legitimate a designated elite, those who have made the right choices, so that it calls for a reciprocal disciplining of errant individuals (most others) by strong institutions or traditions. Left-thinking models tend on the other hand

6

to make a priority of commonly produced new standards that are more open to modification because that is how they were produced, even as they are shadowed by the residue of an ideology that they are seeking to pass beyond. Both models, left and right, believe in the power and usefulness of changing our given situations, whether in the cause of restraining or of expanding the possibilities for human happiness and pleasure, individual or collective. They disagree mostly about how many and what kinds of conditions are deemed capable of positive modification, about whether people will respond predictably when they are thus modified, and about whether the available rewards are to be had in the material or ethical-spiritual spheres. The conservative Edmund Burke, for example, thought that the binding powers of habit and tradition are what makes us adequately human, so that to remove them is to threaten psychic and social disintegration. His radical opponents supposed that the human mind was flexible enough to profit from the creation of new habits and traditions quite different from those already in place. Both convictions depend on a faith in the power of situatedness.

There is no simple evidence that this general cultural formation is about to change completely. But I do think that the simultaneously more hyperbolic and incrementally commonplace present-day use of the rhetoric of situatedness is an indication that the system is under stress. The appeal to situatedness is indeed only the latest version of a very traditional effort at locating and explaining subjects and objects, an effort that has made use of such terms as *society, culture, milieu, ideology, instinct, habit, reason, will, choice,* and so forth. But what seems to me to be new about *situatedness* is its emphasis on the availability of self-specification in reference to categories that have previously been deemed largely involuntary. Thus I can cheerfully offer to situate myself, making use of a reflexivity that the other terms (such as *culture*) do not provide. It is as if I can will or choose or define my form of embeddedness. Situatedness is at once something given and something created or interpellated. It projects as an option (let me situate myself, my argument) what is also predetermined (occupation, subculture, ethnicity). It finesses or fudges, in other words, the longstanding problems arising from a vocabulary in which we choose between freedom and determination, elective and involuntary affiliations. Other currently popular terms belong in the same rhetorical field but inflect it differently. To speak of *subject positionality*, for example, is also to imply a knowledge of where one stands, along with (I would say) a supposition of one's successfully achieved intention to stand there. To speak of the *locatedness* of persons or things, on the other hand, seems to suggest a more objective embeddedness, a condition that is less open to alteration or choice, although it often signals a pride of place or condition of comfort. The orientations are, respectively, active and passive, even as each conjures up the echo of the other. *Situatedness*, I think, holds open a position between the two. Sometimes it seems as if the insoluble questions generated by the self-other vocabularies of modernity are about to be subsumed in an epidemic of self-specifications: *let me tell you where I'm coming from.*

But this move has not yet been made, and cannot be made without visible stress. In the condition of stress some things become more apparent than before, and one can at least speculate about the possibility of new or different forms of self-accounting (and of accounting for the self in the first place) that might be about to be invented or discovered. I am not going to suggest that we simply do away with the rhetoric of situatedness, for there is nothing yet available to put in its place and language reform doesn't work like that anyway. But I do think it is important to monitor the rhetoric and to try to make some sense of its historical and contemporary functions, which I have found to be not at all simple or self-evident. In particular, the odd duality of empowerment-disempowerment to which the rhetoric of situatedness commonly speaks is not so odd when it is seen for what it is: the authorized, flexible subject position of most of us living in the so-called liberal-democratic societies. (I should admit that these are the ones I am writing about, and among them chiefly the United States. There is nothing "global" to be assumed here, although we should be aware of the degree to which the rhetoric of American English is itself being exported and assimilated elsewhere.) Once we see that the rhetoric has conflict built into it, then we can begin to ask why and to what ends rather than fighting the old battles about an essential experience of control or the loss of it. Once we see that the claim I make about situating myself cannot be strictly defended or explained, then we can ask what else I am doing when I make it, and we can wonder whether I might make different claims that are in fact defensible or that produce different outcomes.

Why is the specification of subject-positions under exceptional and notable stress now, if the expression and naturalization of stress has been its unavowed function all along? That it is so is suggested not just by the poor fit between the term *situatedness* and the concepts or gestures that it seeks to embody or to pacify—nothing less than the entire predicament of being in the world—but also by the very visible conviction among western intellectuals (especially the anglophones) that his majesty the subject is in a more than usual state of crisis or rhetorical insecurity. The one is not necessarily the same as the other: we could be dealing with a smokescreen whereby the avowed instability of the subject is its very mechanism of self-insurance, its strategy for holding on to its gains and privileges, so that the anglophone construction of crisis becomes itself ideological, a pathos of imagined dispossession that signals the exact opposite: a gestural participation in self-abnegation that works mostly to help us convince ourselves that we are suffering as we should, and with those whom "we" have made suffer. Leaving this question open, as it must remain open, it is nonetheless apparent that in attending to such categories as schizophrenia, deterritorialization, and nomadism (Deleuze and Guattari), or mimicry and hybridity (Bhabha), or masquerade and performance (Butler), among others, we are bidding ourselves to study or inhabit complex identity forms that have in common a commitment to not being or seeming simple or whole. Homi Bhabha says it very well in paraphrasing hybridity as *"neither the one nor the other"* and mimicry as *"almost the same but not quite."* [5] What might be behind and around this commitment to partial and provisional subjectivities?

First, we are being told over and over again that the major new developments in our economy and culture are toward globalization, and that along with globalization there comes a diminishing of the nation-state and of the forms of identity that it has seemed to provide. There is much argument about whether nation-state functions are indeed diminishing and about whether or not it would be a good thing if they did. But the discussion itself already calls into question some of the kinds of embeddedness that have been around for a while, such as *being* British or being or *becoming* American. Questions such as *what am I? who am I? where do I stand?* and *where do others think I stand?* become newly mystifying when the global component of identity and affiliation requires attention and description. Manuel Castells sees a world made up of "historically emptied nation-states" and "fundamental identities," with very little in between, so that "instead of autonomous subjects, there are only ephemeral situations, which serve as support to provisional alliances supported by capacities mobilized for each occasion." [6] This condition generates "defensive identities around communal principles" that are outside traditional forms of association (2: 11).

Thus, second, and going along with the above, there has been a visible disaggregation and refiguring of some of the so-called traditional rhetorics of affiliation, such as family, locality, occupation, and ethnicity. Whether or not these were ever stable enough to be called traditions, many now believe them to be less efficient forms of management and self-management than they once were. Enlightenment, while it offered some people a position of radical independence of mind (Kant's famous *sapere aude*), also held out the belief that such acts of independence might emanate from a common reason. For those not yet ready for reason there were the affirmative forms of situatedness that made up the ideological cement in building (as in Germany) or in maintaining and expanding (as in Britain and the United States) the nation-state—*becoming* German, *being* British—along with the more predictable and enduring kinship and group affiliations. Many are now telling us that these options are gone. Reason is no longer an incipient universal and societies and subgroups are no longer bounded systems. The demand for accountability has not disappeared and may in fact have become more acute as the older terms wither away without there being any agreed-on new terms to replace them.

Third, and again related to the two previous conditions, there is a frequently described move away from bureaucratically and hierarchically organized norms for working and living and toward loose networks forming and dissolving through time, changing as the nature of tasks themselves change, and thereby generating or exacerbating a high degree of the reflexivity (knowing and saying what one does as one does it) that is already in place as the result of a popularly disseminated hermeneutic consciousness — for Schiller and the romantics a property of elites but now increasingly typical of ordinary social interactions. These "network" developments do not of course displace hierarchies in any complete way but subsist along with them, so that the whole matter of self-recognition (do I already know my place or do I have to establish a place for myself?) is rendered nontransparent and labile. The rhetoric of situatedness is placed under particular stress in such circumstances.

Fourth, and finally for now (although this is by no means a complete analysis of the situation of situatedness, which is after all one of the major topics of this book), there is some evidence that the credibility of the culturalist-objectivist social science model may be on the wane, and it is very unclear what if anything is coming along in its place. This is above all why I think it matters to initiate a discussion of the rhetoric of situatedness. Internationally, the breakup of the old Eastern bloc and the difficulty of finding viable examples of successful state socialism elsewhere have led many to pronounce a victory for capitalism and the free market, which has traditionally associated elaborate social-scientific planning with communist or socialist governments. Within the capitalist states — Britain and the United States especially — governments have been mostly cutting back on the rational interventionism that typified, for example, the New Deal and the War on Poverty, allowing the initiatives they represented either to disappear or to be spontaneously reincarnated as the results of voluntarist affiliations generated by a rebirth of some proposed ideal civil society (this last being a completely separate topic requiring skeptical attention, but not here). Making the world better to make better people has not been a high priority in recent years. If there is at the same time a diminished language or no language at all for describing anything between atomic self (and its chosen groups) and global everything, then we will have been collectively made over by the forces and interests that (I still believe) govern much of our lives and that prefer to maintain an evacuated rhetoric in the sphere of social description. If, in other words, we no longer have available or give credit to any term for social interactions and determinations that is not already a pastiche (*community* is a good example), then we cannot give voice to the conditions of individual and group existence that are objective and not subject to self-specification, to people situating themselves. Not only will the social science project be a thing of the past but the needs it was so often meant to address will no longer be recognizable.

The notion that there is no society other than that constituted voluntarily by acts of civility or modeled subjectively in individual ethical behavior (with the family as a traditionally endorsed supplement) may be nothing more than a holdover from the vigorous conservative revolution of the 1980s carried through by the forces known familiarly as Thatcher and Reagan. The acquiescence that has taken the subsequent form of a belief in globalism, something too vast and complex to be apprehended, and rendering all previous forms of embeddedness inefficient or redundant, with its attendant recourse to the self-situating subject, may in turn then be a largely ideological figuration. It is important to worry over this because, of course, the declaration of one's situatedness has also been endorsed by a "leftist" thinking that considers accountability to be an obligation and declaring situatedness to be a way of fulfilling it. That assumption cannot be taken for granted because it is possible that in so doing we are participating in a terminological simplification whose effect is to trivialize the realm of the social.

The culturalist emphasis that has typified so much post-Enlightenment thinking, according to which the important thing to do is to create a positive environment, has also recently been challenged academically by new forms of biological determinism (sociobiology is a famous example) that promise to give us segments of something called human nature that we can exclude from the modifying forces of short-term environments and so think of as building blocks for very long-term (although never immanent) forms for human relations. This is to restore the "body" and "nature" emphasis to the description of the self that culturalism displaced, and to find there not the chaos that Helvétius and others proposed but a set of describable long-durational adaptations (effectively constants) among human needs and motives. Few if any biologists argue for the absolute independence of nature from nurture, but in giving more space to nature and to an evolutionary timescale indifferent to the effects of short-term planning than many traditional social scientists have done they have made the rhetoric of situatedness murkier than it already was by pressuring it to acknowledge or at least wonder about inertial "human" characteristics in relation to determinations that are more obviously historical and contingent. The biological-cultural synthesis that describes many current assumptions about how we exist in the world, whereby what we bring to experience is from the first modified by what we find around us and so back and forth, does not make the rhetoric of subjectivity any easier to specify. If anything it increases the range of what we might mean when we claim to situate ourselves, so that we are much less sure than we thought we were about where we stand and are coming from. Artificial intelligence in particular and cognitive science in general also offer serious challenges to the inherited vocabularies of agency, will, and choice.[7] They also therefore add to the sense of panic that sponsors situatedness declarations in the first place, and makes them seem to work as affirmative avoidance strategies.

For all of these reasons, and no doubt for others, we may be about to see a shaking out of the rhetoric of situatedness, a new range of do-it-yourself efforts (always of course using premachined parts) at knocking together an accountable self. Cultural situatedness may well have claimed too much—although we will see that in the founding texts of the social science project there was commonly a clear awareness of the difference between probability and certain knowledge—but it has been used to sponsor a number of social initiatives that we may still want and for which we have no other rationalizations. There is some risk, then, that we will lose much more than we gain in deciding to ditch culturalist rhetoric just because its logic is almost always fuzzy and at times even implausible. There remain some benign uses for this fuzziness once it is understood as such. At the same time, and more cynically, I shall argue that this same fuzziness is purposive for a mature and late capitalist society that must leave unspecified any precise boundary between individual opportunities and criminal or reprehensible behavior of the sort that one would prefer to blame on one's situatedness. The rhetoric of situatedness has always generated antinomies. John Stuart Mill was worried about too much conformism, so he championed the rights of entrepreneurial individuals to disobey rules and conventions; in late-twentieth-century America many are worried about the opposite problem, an individualism too much indulged and rewarded to the detriment of communal values. Shifts in the rhetoric of situatedness can then look like business as usual, and indeed they have mostly been just that—verbal expansion joints designed to shift weight while preserving the structure of the whole. But we cannot know for sure in advance whether something more radical than business as usual is beginning to show up. This is one of the questions I will raise again and again.

One situatedness condition that may not be business as usual is the sort of ecobiological conglomerate described by, for example, Ulrich Beck's *Risk Society*, whereby manmade changes to the world return in the form of invisible, unpredictable, and threateningly nondiscriminatory life changes for humans themselves (Chernobyl and Bhopal come to mind).[8] Worked-over nature has always fed back the results of its disturbance to, for example, industrial workers in mines and factories. But now the effects seem limitless and invisible: no one anywhere can be sure of ever being safe. Neither culture nor nature describe what is happening here, nor is the synthesis of the two a happy or positive one in the tradition of progressive dialectic (which may explain the appeal and indeed the urgency of a "pure nature" movement among radical ecologists). This means that when I claim to be situating myself I have to be all too aware that I may not know how I am most critically situated, or how I am affecting others around me. And if this uncertainty has always affected the self-knowledge of the workers in mines and factories, its pervasiveness now among the relatively affluent intellectual class may indicate the validity of Beck's thesis that no one now thinks himself immune from radical threat.

Cultural situatedness is therefore inevitably now a muddle and less open to rationalized description than ever before. Because culture now includes everything that we know and do, every bit of our lives has the potential to explain every other bit. Christopher Herbert's *Culture and Anomie* (first discussed in chapter 3) explains how this has come to be so. A similar dilution of the term *ideology* has troubled those working in the marxist tradition: now there is nothing that is not somebody's example of ideological thought. Unlike *culture* and *ideology*, *situatedness* is not yet a household word but it is similarly omnivorous and prone to slippage and may indeed be the term of the moment for describing some of the territory that *culture* and *ideology* (but also *individual* and *agent*) have previously sought to map out. In chapter 1 I discuss both its popularity and its slipperiness. There is an ungainliness to *situatedness* that dramatizes the degree to which the term and the concepts it gathers up do not quite fit together, an ungainliness that I hope can still be exploited to reveal how and why that might be. This task will become more difficult when the term has been deadened by familiar repetition, as is the case with *culture, ideology, freedom, choice,* and a number of others that come to mind. This happening term *situatedness,* whose voicing is now so often the *imprimatur* of state-of-the-art thinking and approved moral seriousness, signals the extent to which we have all become social scientists. I am writing this in June 1999, just over two months after the shootings at Columbine High School in Littleton, Colorado, which have led to an orgy of explanations about why the violence happened and how it could have been prevented. These explanations range from fairly obvious and commonsense ideas about gun control to the more unusual example of the man who believes that had the Ten Commandments been posted on the walls of the classrooms these deaths could not have come about. I will have more to say about these responses in chapter 6, where I show how the slipperiness of arguments invoking situatedness tends to be acknowledged when it is in people's interest to do so and ignored when it is not. Sometimes it can seem as if the decision to situate oneself is a sort of desperate release from the anxiety of knowing that everything can be explained by anything; a way of affiliating yourself before someone else does it for you. Sometimes it is a function of opportunistic self-interest. At other times those who invoke arguments from one kind of situatedness do so in order to discredit others.

These are some of the issues that will be raised and rehearsed in the following pages. In chapter 1 I offer a more extended introduction to the current popularity of situatedness as a rhetoric available for the subjectification of individuals in late capitalist democracies. I argue that this rhetoric is antinomic and/or aporetic rather than knowledge-based or knowledge-producing; it gestures at the specification of something that mostly cannot be known fully if at all but that is still felt as critical and unignorable and that must therefore be constantly mentioned by oneself and demanded by others. I begin here to try to lay out the key features of the rhetoric of situatedness and its function in contemporary culture. Chapters 2 through 5 discuss exemplary instances of the treatment and theorization of situatedness in four key disciplines: legal theory, social science, literature, and philosophy. I use the term *exemplary* because I do not pretend to be offering detailed or adequate histories of these disciplines, but representative examples. Chapter 2 looks at the ways in which the legal system has handled the matter of situatedness, which has figured prominently in arguments about mitigation, extenuation, and liability. Bentham's probability calculus, Oliver Wendell Holmes's "ideal average prudent man," Morton Horwitz's account of the history of tort, the Loeb-Leopold trial, and Alan Dershowitz's complaints about implausible defense pleas and jury decisions all reflect the centrality of the situatedness problem to the justice system. Chapter 3 describes the oscillation in the social science tradition between objectivist efforts toward (or phobias about) the totally managed situation and a more restrictive attitude to general statements and to the possibility of rationally administered societies. Here I attend in some detail to the paradoxes of a cold war social science that saw as its major task the controlled production of freedom.

Chapter 4 looks at literature as the licensed alternative to objectivist social science, both in its nineteenth-century incarnations and in its contemporary invocations by (for example) Nussbaum and Rorty. I propose that literary and objectivist social science adumbrations of human situatedness represent two ends of the spectrum along which various kinds of subjectification were and are imagined, and that they thus function together in preserving the rhetoric of situatedness as immanently antinomic and aporetic. In chapter 5 I turn at last to Sartre and to his major effort (after Heidegger and Jaspers) to make situatedness a philosophically weighty concept that is able to respond to the inescapably biographical tendency apparent in philosophy itself that threatens to put it out of business as an independent discipline. Finally, in chapter 6 I attempt to set out some of the consequences of taking seriously the inconclusive or fuzzy nature of arguments from situatedness for a new "culture of ignorance" (Niklas Luhmann's phrase) or skepticism not based on either a refutation or an endorsement of some of the current claims made for and about those arguments. There I give various examples of the misuse and exploitation of situatedness claims, both in real life and in best-selling books about it. Readers who are interested principally in a contemporary account of the limits and opportunities pertaining to the rhetoric of situatedness might first read chapters 1 and 6 together; but the historical focus of chapters 2 through 5 is I believe only part of their point. In other words I find that the past forms I there describe are still very much latent and operative in the present. This is not a history that has been laid to rest, nor has it been adequately remembered.

1. Self-Affiliation and the Management of Confusion

What Is Situatedness? If and when the next round of dictionaries is compiled, *situatedness* will show up as one of the buzzwords of the late twentieth century. Its meaning is not yet quite commonplace or self-evident, but it is creeping into familiar use in academic and professional language and may well spread more widely. It has a lot to do with the much more familiar locution I have taken for my subtitle; people are always telling us where they are coming from. But the gesture is as puzzling as it is familiar. It is used mostly as a prelude to telling us where someone is going with their opinions and pronouncements. The claim to be coming from somewhere is usually a precursor to going somewhere else, getting somewhere or something. No one ends a sentence by saying where they are coming from. The declaration works teleologically: it says "let me tell you where I am coming from in order that I may pursue the goal I am about to articulate." So we are seldom invited to ponder very deeply where people are coming from when they tell us where they are coming from. This has something to do with the intuition that we really do not know much about it even as we assert that we do. The phrase is common but not at all clear.

If *situatedness* is not quite a familiar word, then its aura of approximate signification is surely apparent. It has to do with being in the world, in place and time, in a way that is at once unignorable but also a bit provisional. The situations that give rise to one's situatedness can be counted as outside forces that influence subjectivity and one's view of subjectivity, elements of what is otherwise called determination, ideology, environment, history, discourse, and so on. But they are also open to the sorts of responses or reactions that can change one condition into another, act back on the world in the way that has sometimes and traditionally been described as a gesture of freedom or agency. Situations, and the dwelling in situations that is situatedness, then denote a measure of the unstable and indecisive, in descriptive and philosophical terms, at the same time as they signal a measure of comfort and manageability. They are given to us but also open to amendment; we occupy a situation but can move on or imagine moving on to others. The term *situation* appealed to Jean-Paul Sartre in just this way, as something between the doggedly empirical, about which very little can be said, and the general or social-historical, about which too much had been said.

I will take up Sartre later in some detail. For now I want to register *situatedness* as a slippery term, whose slipperiness I hope to expound. I take it to designate an instability or obscurity in the language describing our way of being in the world. It is meant to preserve rather than to resolve the tension we experience between being in control and out of control, between seeing ourselves as agents of change and as passive receivers of what is already in place. This imprecise and somewhat ungainly word *situatedness,* almost but not quite familiar, can be read as the designation of an antinomy or aporia. In other words I want to question the integrity of the solutions that arguments from situatedness have claimed to provide to problems in epistemology, jurisprudence, social science, and other spheres in which people have set out to prove or deduce the nature of their relation to the world. For reasons that will become clear enough I have no privileged vocabulary to put in its place, so that I write propaedeutically, to clear the ground, hoping that we might be at the point where other rhetorics might be almost visible and sustainable by other dispositions of forces than those traditional to the definitive triad of capitalism, individualism, and liberal democracy, which is not to predict imminent escape from or clean passage beyond those terms, as if in pure revolution, although it is to ponder intimations of alternatives and critical rearrangements. Moreover I have no wish to discredit many of the policies that arguments from situatedness have been used to legitimate. The idea that we are significantly made by impersonal circumstances and not by free will has been crucial to the justification of the interventionist programs that I fully believe in and would indeed wish to see expanded.

Similarly, the compensatory notion that we can indeed do something about our place in the world is not to be lightly disregarded. But the strains and stresses that are becoming increasingly apparent in the use of arguments from situatedness suggest that the model may be on the point of falling apart, imploding into its own aporetic logic. If this should happen then the policies that have been explained by way of those same arguments will become vulnerable to attack and perhaps displacement for lack of a better way to formulate them. The radical Right has long been waiting in the wings and has not infrequently occupied center stage with its simplifying notions of moral choice and simple identity as alternatives to the dream of a benevolently administered society. I will argue that the rhetoric of situatedness holds together these antagonists in a persistent dialectic wherein the hyperbolic statement of one enables the reentry of the other. I see signs that this unholy but very intimate alliance is undergoing some strain, and that it may be time to anticipate other ways of making and explaining decisions that have significant consequences.

So it is very much to the point that the word *situatedness* is not to be found in the second edition of the *Oxford English Dictionary*, which was first published in 1989 and reprinted with corrections in 1991. The word is just about recognizable without yet being exclusively (if still always provisionally) defined. The OED does give *situate*, *situated*, and *situation*, in both first and second editions. And the various senses there listed are significant in their differences. A *situation* can refer to a permanent location of a place or thing, in itself or in relation to its surroundings, as in the situation (or siting) of a city or a building; but it can also describe a place where something or person "happens to be for the time," impermanently, or a "position in life" held by a person "in relation to others" or "with regard to circumstances." This is the sense in which we look hopefully to the newspaper for "situations vacant" and in which we think of improving our situations. This same application of the word has taken on a pejorative spin in the black English of South African townships, which according to the dictionary uses (from 1963) *situation* to denote "an educated or professional black person, esp. one considered to be a social climber."[1] A tension or difference of emphasis between the permanent and the provisional is built into the uses and definitions of *situation* and *situated*. The same tension and the same difference is apparent in *situatedness*.

But familiarization may be imminent, not least because of our fondness for the word *situation* itself. Kenneth Wilson's *The Columbia Guide to Standard American English* notes just this fondness: "We have built this generally useful word into a number of cliché phrases, such as *a conflict situation* . . . or *a no-win situation* . . . and we also find it an easy-to-use, nonspecific, all-purpose word . . . as a result, we now overwork *situation*."[2] Wilson also lists the linguistic definition of *situation utterances*, dating from 1952. The OED second edition also includes a new crop of compounds coming into use since the first edition: *situation comedy*, *situation report*, and *situation(s) room* (in military use), and *Situationist International*. This last, a revolutionary movement founded in Paris in 1957 by Guy Debord and others, took up precisely the activist, opportunist sense of the word *situation*, so dear to Sartre, in calling for an alternative to the passive consumption of the spectacle by way of "the construction of situations, that is to say, the concrete construction of momentary ambiances of life and their transformation into a superior passional quality."[3] A much more domesticated alternative appeared in the anglophone *situation ethics*, which emphasized a pragmatist openness to revising one's attitudes and practices in the face of new experiences.[4] More recently, in 1983, Jon Barwise and John Perry initiated a project in *situation semantics* as a prototype for a more general *situation theory* bringing mathematical, philosophical, and linguistic methods into mutual relation, one governed by the view that "finds meaning located in the interaction of living things and their environment."[5] They declared that "reality consists of situations — individuals having properties and standing in relations at various spatiotemporal locations" (p. 7). Since then, the province of situation theory has come to include information modeling and artificial intelligence research along with linguistics and mathematical logic. In the words of one writer, "in situation theory an organism's way of understanding the world is modeled by a *scheme of individuation*" inducing "a classification of different parts of the environment, called *situations.*"[6] The analysis includes a "scheme of individuation" and a "collection of constraints" as well as the invocation of a "perspective" (pp. 148, 151). It seems to describe, in other words, albeit in very technical language, the same pattern of predictable and unpredictable opportunities for being in the world that Sartre and others intend to describe in using the same term. It offers an apparently describable and manageable segment of experience to make up for the ungraspable complexity of the whole: "Situations are contrasted with worlds; a world determines the answer to every issue. . . . A situation corresponds to the limited parts of reality we in fact perceive, reason about, and live in."[7]

Situation was one of the keywords of eighteenth-century literary and philosophical diction in both English and French, from whence it made its way into German. Indeed, the word appears somewhat obsessively in late-eighteenth-century writings (novels for instance) describing the place of persons in the world. And it is a word concerned above all and originally with the specification of *place.* According to Edward Casey's important book *The Fate of Place,* this preoccupation has not been typical of the more technically philosophical self-projections of modernity, so that its emergence from latency in the common language to rhetorical prominence in contemporary philosophy may be taken to indicate an important shift of emphasis. According to Casey we have long been governed by "site-specific models of space stemming from the early modern era" and effecting a reduction of place to simple coordinates of space and time; at last, in the postmodern moment, "space is being reassimilated into place," with its local and particular profile now emphasized.[8] In this narrative, Aristotle maintained a sense that "*where* something is constitutes a basic metaphysical category" (p. 50). This understanding was steadily eroded as place was reduced to point, *situs* to position, in a mathematicization of experience: points have position but no place, just as souls and minds aim to have no body. The corresponding category is that of space, unlimited and open-ended, with no relation to boundary or location (p. 77). By the end of the eighteenth century place "vanished altogether from serious philosophical discourse in physics and philosophy" (p. 133); it has become "a reduced residuum with no inherent ability to alter the course of things in the natural world" (p. 141). To situate something is to give it simple location as a point in space and time. Leibniz's "situation," for example, "does not really *situate*; it merely *positions* in a nexus of relations" (p. 183). The refiguring of this constraint occupies much of twentieth-century philosophy through Heidegger and Merleau-Ponty and into the postmodern. Place is brought back to life as an unignorable condition of being, albeit never as "simple presence" (p. 337) but always in its "stubborn, indeed its rebarbative, particularity" (p. 338).

Casey's book makes a learned and comprehensive argument for the disappearance and reappearance of place. It thus offers a crucial context for any effort (such as mine in this volume) at plotting the history and function of our current fondness for situating ourselves.[9] But the story Casey tells about the history of philosophy does not work or work in the same way for other language registers. The novel, for example, as we will see, shows in the late eighteenth century a huge commitment to specifying situations as local, embedded predicaments that are by no means reducible to punctilious definition; but at the same time it can be argued that the pressure of the philosophical vocabulary, especially on the Jacobin novel, does contribute to a high level of confidence that the situations of characters can be accurately specified, almost as if they were simple space-time locations. The term, in other words, is definitively labile and unstable, and goes in different directions. In our late-twentieth-century vocabularies an affinity for *situations* has become very apparent in the social sciences and of course in the humanities. In these fields there has been a visible emphasis on solving, or seeming to solve, residual problems in the epistemology of subject-object relations by the invocation of an in-place and in-time practical attitude to living in the world, something that can be assumed or defined by ostension. This is the language of "let me situate myself / my argument" and "let me tell you where I am coming from." It commonly comes with an embrace of the rhetoric of action, of change, of political progress. Donna Haraway's influential essay "Situated Knowledges" is in this sense a classic of its kind.[10] Here, situated knowledge is a knowing that is at once contingent and objectively real, in that it can be "partially shared" (p. 187). Being located or "situated" in the world allows us as much access to objectivity as is needed for changing the world and keeps us at a distance from the temptation to subscribe to outright relativism. At the same time it confesses and apprehends its own partiality; indeed, only "partial perspective promises objective vision" (p. 190). In this "embodied objectivity" (p. 194) Haraway finds prospects of "rational conversations and fantastic imaginings that change history" (p. 193). She gives us permission to see ourselves, once again, as agents and progressives.

Here the invocation of the term *situation* has become methodologically affirmative, a way of preserving or reinventing a function for agency, for human effort, in the face of all the familiar forces—the state, ideology, the sex-gender system, the economy—that have seemed to threaten such agency with extinction. And it is, I think, typically the intellectuals on the Left who find it helpful or obligatory to keep on situating themselves and appealing to situatedness. There is a longstanding pressure at work here. Sometime after the French Revolution the rhetoric of place and patriotism, locality and belongingness, was taken over by the conservatives. Edmund Burke was the most important figure in this capturing of in-placeness conditions for the political Right. He quite brilliantly identified a static or slowly evolving rural England as the last best hope against rootless cosmopolitanism and detraditionalizing radical republicanism; only the true-born Englishman was adequately situated, leaving the opposition looking for a home. And to this day one is unlikely to hear many if any of the denizens of the conservative think tanks appealing to their situatedness. The pathos of the Left is that it is committed at once to a celebration of the liberating functions of theory, of universalization, and of freedom from origins and disabling traditions—all the things we call Enlightenment values—while at the same time suspecting the unwholesome applications of these same values and gesturing toward a locatedness that prevents them from becoming sublimely impersonal and destructive. In short, an unstable situation.

Explaining every detail in the long historical origins of the rhetoric of situatedness is not my aim in this book, although I will attend to some of the most important developments. But for the modern left-thinking intellectual it is safe to speculate that the influence and example of Habermas has been paramount, to the point that history before Habermas (in Sartre, in Jaspers, and elsewhere) risks being forgotten or undiscovered. It is Habermas who takes up the usefulness of the *situation* as something tending toward closure while always remaining open, as a term that can mediate between the equally indefensible extremes of reification and formlessness, thus offering a bewildered left-thinker the opportunity to imagine agency without culpability. Habermas's theory of "communicative action" is founded on a "cooperative negotiation of situation definitions" in such a way that all participants are deemed *capable of mutual criticism*."[11] The inherited "lifeworld" provides a repository of previously agreed on situations so that we do not have to begin in some sort of primal confrontation (p. 70), but within this nexus of the inherited and the new everything is negotiable. Individual needs and desires are thus bound to encounter and come to terms with what is in place and up for inspection, so that persons must "harmonize their plans of action on the basis of common situation definitions" (p. 286). The process is interactive and democratic, task-oriented and tending to consensus, so that its very exercise contributes to the social norming process on whose previous results it also depends.

There is much to say about Habermas, and much to suspect in his status as fashionable authority figure; at the very least one must ponder the degree to which this conversational model premises its democratic credentials on equal access to speech and equal ability to speak when one has access. Here I shall only record the qualifications that Habermas himself records, which are so often omitted by those who make use of his positions. Although it is true that "the very situation that gives rise to the problem of understanding meaning can also be regarded as the key to its solution" (p. 120) — so that there is an appealing air of problem solving at work here — it is also clear that the ideal communicative interaction event is either trivial or utopian. In other words it works best when it is least noticed, in routine exchanges where nothing much is at stake, or it shows up as most necessary when it fails, when consensual situations are not successfully negotiated and differences remain unmodified. And Habermas says that the more "decentered" and detraditionalized the world becomes, the more stress is attached to communicative action, because there is less that is given and more to be negotiated (p. 70). Even in ordinary interactions he does not assume a resultant stability, but rather a "diffuse, fragile, continuously revised and only momentarily successful communication in which participants rely on problematic and unclarified presuppositions and feel their way from one occasional commonality to the next" (pp. 100–1). Again, "under the microscope *every* understanding proves to be occasional and fragile" (p. 130).

This said, then the stability of outcomes must seem to depend on a belief in some psychological motivation toward the *creation* of stability, a compulsion to normalize of the sort that Adam Smith long ago proposed in his *Theory of Moral Sentiments*. And the analysis of what really is the case, under the microscope, looks very much like that of a number of other popular cases in the world we know: flexible employment patterns, short-term contracts, temporary emotional alliances, gender identities, and so forth. But it could be that human nature can in fact put up with this fragility and uncertainty when it is persuaded, economically and ideologically, to do so; and that it can even be made to celebrate it, as it does in various contemporary theories about various things. Hence the appetite for invoking and referring to "situated action," as Jerome Bruner calls it (*Acts of Meaning*, p. 19), tends either to obscure the fragility of the situation (as qualified by Habermas) by sheer terminological assertiveness, the way in which it can so readily be named, or to propose it in a tone of pragmatist bluster as the way the world really is, and oneself in it.

So it is a positive message we get from Haraway's situated knowledge, one that is very appealing on moral and practical grounds. But it resolves rather too neatly the muddle and indecisiveness I want to preserve in my use of the related term, *situatedness* — the term that is not yet in the dictionary. Situatedness, as I see it, does not give rise to a method. Nor does it yet deserve, if it ever can deserve, invocation in a litany of approved vocabularies, as if to pronounce someone or something as "situated" is somehow to answer the questions one might have or to resolve the uncertainties one might experience. We are all under various pressures to produce solutions, to direct or defend social policies, to offer "outcomes" with actual or imagined empirical consequences, and ultimately to authenticate ourselves. The pressure is both external and self-imposed. It is not to be denied (for who does not want to be thought of as making a difference?) but it is to be monitored at those points where we find ourselves too hasty in proposing solutions. Take the following claim by the editors of a book of essays appealingly titled *Situated Lives*: "We view our own knowledge as critical feminist ethnographers as partial and situated, and, in analyzing women's and men's lives, we view our subjects as positioned actors who forge 'situated knowledges' in order to act within their material circumstances." [12] The implication here is that the declaration of one's own situatedness gives permission for an account of the actions and agency of others, and sets acceptable limits on the claims made for this account. But the "situated" lives of others seem to acquire an objective status, open to inspection. It is not clear what is being claimed or by whom. To position someone seems to be to pin them down, even when their position might be temporary or unrepresentative. The declaration of one's situatedness is often an admission of one's limits rather than a claim to authority. But its language of easeful (even when stressful) exculpation can then itself become a covert affirmation whereby the subject secures itself precisely in confessing its insecurity. Here is Dominick LaCapra, describing the difficulties of deciding who gets to talk about the Holocaust: "Certain statements or even entire orientations may seem appropriate for someone in a given subject-position but not in others. (It would, for example, be ridiculous if I tried to assume the voice of Elie Wiesel or Saul Friedlander. There is a sense in which I have no right to these voices . . . Thus, while any historian must be "invested" in a distinctive way . . .) . . . not all statements, rhetorics or orientations are equally available to different historians." [13] Being situated, then, places limits on what one can say, or on one's credibility in making certain statements. LaCapra is understandably sensitive here to what is surely one of the most morally fraught inquiries open to the historian. But what does it mean to say what he does say, that some things cannot be said by him? And to imply that what is said by him is credible as long as it does not replicate or imitate what others, such as Friedlander and Wiesel, are saying? The confession of situatedness seems to be at once denying LaCapra some kinds of authority but permitting him other kinds — those not said by Friedlander and Wiesel. What kinds of statement are preempted by the admission of not being a Holocaust survivor, and what other kinds are permitted? And why? Why does a moral discrimination ("I have no right") transform itself into an epistemological one ("not . . . equally available")? Why are so many of us willing to agree with this type of statement?

Most obviously, in our willingness we are thereby on or off the hook, all sorts of hooks, rather than being left puzzled and somewhere in between. We think we know where we stand. Grander versions of this knowing keep coming back even as they are widely recognized as dangerous and not to be desired. So Derrida writes of an *ontopology* that is "an axiomatics linking indissociably the ontological value of present-being [*on*] to its *situation*, to the stable and presentable determination of a locality, the *topos* of territory, native soil, city, body in general," and he hardly needs to spell out the affiliation of all of this with the very state of mind that helped the Holocaust itself into being.[14] But there is the ghost of this in LaCapra's machine, which is all the more troubling in its commonplaceness (for it is not his alone). And if there is not a ghost, if here I am being too harsh, is there then anything more than an emptiness, a withholding of meaning, of the sort that Elspeth Probyn has so astutely discovered in the language of localization: "Local, locale, and location become abstract terms, cut off from a signifying ground and serving as signposts with no indication of direction"?[15]

The contemporary feminist debate about localism and locality in which Probyn here participates is perhaps the most important interrogation we have had since Sartre of the rhetoric of situatedness, although the term is not always used. Feminist writers were of course crucial in introducing the scrupulous gestures of self-positioning that is now commonplace in left-liberal gatherings, and the feminist critique of tacit universalisms was significantly carried out by insisting on the limits of all interpretive pronouncements and on their existence in place and time. This critique is by no means redundant, so that one of the difficulties of understanding the rhetoric of situatedness is the sense that we cannot do without it, and the awareness that if we try to do without it then we risk sliding back into the very complacencies that feminists have done so much to unsettle. At the same time feminist writers themselves have been very aware of the potential of self-location gestures for taking the place of the old assurances and becoming just another version of untroubled and affirmative identity. Saying where you're coming from can turn out to be just as inadequate and restrictive as pretending that you don't have to think about it. The prominence of autobiography in feminist writing, for example, has at once challenged the unsituated rhetoric of much analytic writing while also providing various examples of "telling life stories in the name of history." These words come from Gayatri Spivak, who has for some years kept vigilance over our collective tendencies to a "meaningless piety" by way of "calling the place of the investigator into question." [16] Her own now rather famous response to the exigencies of subject-specification — hard to live with but hard to do without — has come to be known as "strategic essentialism," an identity claim that is made because one has to have a "mobilizing slogan" but which remains "ideally, self-conscious for all mobilized." [17] For Spivak it is the temporary specificity of the "situation" that saves this strategy from collapse into true essentialism (p. 4) and makes it, when properly understood, actually a "deidentification of oneself" (p. 6). But as I shall show, and as Spivak herself has often implied, this rather scrupulous existentialist use of the term "situation" is by no means standard in our current lexicon, which all too often finds consolation in the illusory concretions of being situated.

The historical coordinates of this controversy about subject-specification are not easy to grasp. Nancy Hartsock, writing in 1987, lodged a notably dissenting opinion about the prevailing skepticism she saw becoming familiar around her: "Why is it, exactly at the moment when so many of us who have been silenced begin to demand the right to name ourselves, to act as subjects rather than objects of history, that just then the concept of subjecthood becomes 'problematic'?" [18] A timely and reasonable question, but one that comes directly face to face with the widely held conviction that having the right to name oneself does not automatically make one into a subject of history, and that such subjectivity might itself be the problem and not the solution. Others have criticized the habit of speaking for oneself, and the recourse to location as a means of projecting a self to be spoken. Like Elspeth Probyn, Caren Kaplan has taken up the suspicious assurances that a rhetoric of locality provides, and which she finds to be at work in some well-known essays by Adrienne Rich. Locale, Kaplan suggests, is not at all the sign of something stable and intrinsic, but signals only "the construction of bundles or clusters of identities in and through the cultures of transnational capital." [19] Location, then, is "discontinuous, multiply constituted, and traversed by diverse social formations" (p. 182). In a similar spirit Doreen Massey has questioned the reliance of locality studies, which she explains as coming to the forefront (in Britain at least) as a specific response to Thatcherism in the early 1980s, upon stable and unproblematic identities.[20]

Even Massey, however, is not immune to the comforts of situatedness claims as she explains the function of her introductions to previously published essays and talks: "The reason for including them in this way is that I want to present the context *as I saw it* in order to explain where the papers were coming from, why it was that I was trying to say *that, then*" (emphasis added). The rhetoric of disavowal—these papers were situated in place and time and are not to be taken as eternal verities—is indistinguishable from the claim, weak to be sure but visible nonetheless, that there is a reliable self-knowledge about these occasions. Limited certitude goes along with the declaration of limits, in a way that is absolutely typical of much of our state-of-the-art theorizing. The following paragraph by James Clifford is exemplary:

> "Location," here, is not a matter of finding a stable "home" or of discovering a common experience. Rather it is a matter of being aware of the difference that makes a difference in concrete situations, of recognizing the various inscriptions, "places," or "histories" that both empower and inhibit the construction of theoretical categories like "Woman," "Patriarchy," or "colonization," categories essential to political action as well as to serious comparative knowledge. "Location" is thus, concretely, a *series* of locations and encounters, travel within diverse, but limited spaces.[21]

The density of scare-quotes alone indicates that we are in the hands of a highly self-conscious writer aware of all the hesitations that an educated mind must now maintain about a whole set of terms and concepts. But it is the terms that do not earn quotes or italics that require notice, terms like "political action," "serious comparative knowledge" and, above all "concrete situations" and "concretely" (not coincidentally one of the favorite verbal icons of Modernist literary criticism). These are the terms whose unquestioned visibility anchors and resolves the uncertainties of the others, which are indeed only rendered uncertain in order to legitimate the integrity of these concretions. Skepticism about making one's location fixed or consensual is only a prelude to the verification of a miniaturized form of empirical experience (or, more exactly, of the language of empirical experience).

I discovered this paragraph in Kaplan's *Questions of Travel* (p. 168) where it is quoted approvingly and without demurral. One can guess why this is so, since the claim we make to a politics or a history is almost always dependent on some invocation of the concrete, the actual, the experienced, that which remains in place after we have gone through the ritual of retraction and qualification that governs so much else. Nor is it easy to imagine how things might be otherwise. Here it is useful to bring Althusser once again to mind.

I am going to talk about the "as" locution, used by the editors of *Situated Lives* ("as critical feminist ethnographers"), in some detail later on. It mostly functions as simultaneously avowal and disavowal. It says that because we are *x* we can claim *y* kinds of knowledge because we also understand the limits of what we claim as pertaining only to *y* kinds of knowledge; and on *y* topics we really do know our stuff. The famous Althusserian account of "interpellation" emphasizes the passivity and ready-made quality of social designations or subjectivities. It is ideology that makes the subject see itself in the ways that it does: "The existence of ideology and the hailing or interpellation of individuals as subjects are one and the same thing." [22] Althusser's notorious example is that of a policeman hailing a person in the street with "hey, you there" (p. 174). This is an instance, he says, of how individuals are transformed into subjects, persons who have social and self-signification. We do not control the process—others do—although the most common form it takes may well be that of self-interpellation, whereby we make the "gestures and actions of subjection" all by ourselves (p. 182).

Althusser's example, and his thesis, are a useful and continually pertinent corrective to the notion that in declaring one's situatedness, perhaps now the most fashionable form of subjectivity, one is justifying a claim to some sort of knowledge or agency. But in its own way it is just as absolute and extreme as the rhetoric of self-invention or self-fashioning that traditionally constitutes the liberal-democratic subject. So sure is Althusser of its efficiency that he strains at least my belief in his expansion of the example of the policeman (one that is itself already begging the question of typicality). He goes on to say that "experience shows that the practical telecommunication of hailings is such that they hardly ever miss their man: verbal call or whistle, the one hailed always recognizes that it is him who is being hailed" (p. 174). Nor is this, he says, to be attributed simply to everyone having something on his or her conscience. Every subject, in other words, knows that it is him or her who is being subjectified, every subject acknowledges the interpellative act as the ritual calling of him or her and no other. This suggests a fantasy of the opposite kind to the one that liberal humanists are likely to indulge in as the justification for their doings—a fantasy on Althusser's part of passivity or mechanical compliance, and ultimately, like the other, a fantasy of self-understanding, of knowing our place, now defined as passive rather than active and self-determining. I think that my own response to a "hey you" in the street would indeed be to turn around; but not (unless I knew the voice or had just stolen a purse) in the knowledge that I am the one who is being hailed. I think I would be looking to see if it might be me, and in ordinary circumstances my assumption would be that it isn't. So I would be checking, and perhaps deciding if this is a person whom I might wish to be hailed by. My response, in other words, would not evince any certainty, but some confusion. It might be me that is being plucked from introspection or anonymity, or it might not. I would not know if I am the one being subjectified in this way at this time. I would not know, that is to say, the terms of my present situatedness, although I would indeed feel at risk.

Antinomies and Aporias Perhaps the example given above is a suspiciously homely one, but it leads happily to the point I want to make. We do not know much about our situatedness. Returning to the quotation from Adorno that stands among the epigraphs to this book, we do not know how to answer very comfortably the question "so who are you?" But we also know (recalling another quotation) that we can't go home. We have to say something. My aim in this book is to try to offer an account of how and why we know so little. And my hope is that after such an account we may know more about why we don't know more, and about why we keep asking the questions in the same way and running into the same dead ends. If there are solutions or new models on the horizon, they cannot be had without exploring the terms of the antinomies and aporias we currently live with; or, if they are had, they will not last, given all the evidence for the persistence and apparently continuing (ideological) rewards and false comforts for leaving things just as they are.

Antinomies or aporias? These terms denote somewhat different traditions, although they need not finally stand as mutually exclusive. The antinomy, although traditional in rhetorical and jurisprudential argument, became a key word in Kant's *Critique of Pure Reason*. Antinomies are the contradictions that human reason necessarily encounters in its coming to self-consciousness; they cannot be avoided.[23] Only the "skeptical method" can produce certainty out of these contradictions, and it does so by bringing to light the misconception whereby reason mistakes the conditioned for the unconditioned, thinking itself free from the rules of experience while still in fact remaining within the conditions of experience (p. 422; A 462). This is an inevitable illusion, given that "reason is by nature architectonic" and "regards all our knowledge as belonging to a possible system" (p. 429; A 474). The impasse forces us to redefine the problem at the transcendental level, to get beyond the empirical world conditioned by the understanding. The need to solve the problem, it seems, is what shifts us to the transcendental, in which domain all problems are solvable, because open to redefinition as, finally, not dependent on the categories of the (empirical) understanding (p. 431; A 477): "The critical solution, which allows of complete certainty, does not consider the question objectively, but in relation to the foundation of the knowledge upon which the question is based" (p. 435; A 484).

The third of Kant's antinomies concerns the question of freedom and determination, the question of freedom of will, both as it pertains to arguments about first causes for the existence of the world (for or against "God") and as it informs interpretations of human volition, routine and otherwise. This is the one that most pertains to the question about situatedness, of which it is indeed an exemplary precursor. Are we the makers of our world, the active agents and forgers of situations that some of us imagine ourselves to be, or are we the passive receivers and reproducers of what is given, as is the interpellated subject described by Althusser? Kant wants to show that the whole question is misconceived, that it can only be understood by redescribing the conflict at the transcendental level, at which point the conflict disappears even as it is understood to have been inevitable and to be inevitably recurrent. But the perplexed left-thinker cannot make this move away from the material world. Can we then hope to deliver ourselves, as Kant thought that we could, from "a great body of sterile dogmatism, and set in its place a sober critique, which as a true cathartic will effectively guard us against such groundless beliefs"? (p. 436; A 486).

No one who now feels compelled to a rhetoric of situatedness is going to feel comfortable invoking a model of transcendental subjectivity, not because it will not work — actually it works very well — but because we no longer, for the most part, find it helpful to resort to that which is by definition out of the world (even if it is thought to be that which makes the world possible) as a useful solution to any of our particular problems. The debates within which questions about situatedness arise are mostly very much within the world, questions about how one estimates the responsibility for a crime, for a cultural condition (sexism, racism), or for an economic position (poverty or wealth), or indeed about why one is entitled to an opinion about anything at all. Because these matters are to be adjudicated within the same empirical world in which they themselves occur, the transcendental move is not commonly deemed helpful, and is bound to be vigorously contested in a democratic culture with an ambivalent attitude to expertise and a lively distrust of universals. So while the antinomies continue to occur and recur, most of us are a lot less confident than was Kant about a significant way to solve them, a way that matters as well as being technically or formally coherent. Kant felt himself under desperate pressure to solve the subject-object question, and he found the transcendental method a way to do it for a generation still visibly preoccupied with the tension between theology and science. Most of us today are driven by different conflicts.

The complicated reconciliation Kant performs between freedom and necessity, allocating one to the intelligible world and the other to the sensible world, will then not solve (although there is no doubt that it has something to say about) our current experience of the antinomies of situatedness. Our problem is not so much one of deciding between absolute agency (I make my world, create my situation) and complete passivity (I am forced to be what I am), although some might still put it this way; it is more a matter of figuring out how to respond to the acceptance that we are always in both positions at once. That we are, as I have said, ineluctably in a muddle. The same muddle informs the specification of kinds and degrees of objectivity and relativity: Stanley Fish, for one, has spent much of his career pointing out how the acknowledgment that "we are always and already interpretively situated" tends to appear as the prelude to some ruse or another whereby we and we alone see things as they really are.[24] Claims about the degree to which we are active and/or passive thus tend to become opportunistic rather than properly descriptive. We say what suits us, or what we think suits the moment. I shall come back to this.

Antinomy, then, remains a useful word for describing how our thinking about situatedness conducts itself. Others have certainly found it so. Anthony Cascardi has analyzed the "self-contradictions of the rational subject" as a key component of the "legitimizing context for modern culture in the West," and his findings are very much congruent with the terms of my inquiry here. He too finds modernity antinomic, with Descartes and Nietzsche not so much alternatives as recurring extremes within a single historically structured paradigm: the presence of each inevitably calls up the other.[25] Fredric Jameson invokes antinomy as the trope of postmodernity—evidence perhaps that we have not changed as much as we sometimes think we have—and makes it symptomatic of a nonprogressive moment, something different from the "contradiction" that always presupposes that progress beyond contradiction can be made.[26] And before them there was Lukács, who made the "antinomies of bourgeois thought" constitutive of Kant's separating out of the thing in itself (unknowable but necessarily to be supposed) from the thing as it appears in empirical life. Lukács regarded the antinomic structure of "rationalist formal systems," that is to say the definitive modern (bourgeois) systems, as itself the "logical and systematic formulation of the modern state of society." [27] All the wranglings about the priority of subject over object and object over subject, all the dilemmas of situatedness, are to be understood as symptoms of a historical false consciousness that takes as its premise the distinction between the representation and the thing in itself. The "situation of bourgeois man in the capitalist production process" (p. 135) is to know that he is situated, but not how or why. The solution is not to be had by another version of formal philosophy, of the sort that Kant tried, but by a turn to history: "In the case of almost every insoluble problem we perceive that the search for a solution leads us to history" (p. 143). But who then can see "history," so long as we are all in it up to the top of our heads? Lukács's famous suggestion is that some of us are only in it to just below the eyeballs; that the proletariat, as the embodiment of the newly emergent truth of history, can be supposed to represent the coincidence of self-consciousness with knowledge of the world. The bourgeoisie can only apprehend "unresolved antinomies" (p. 148); the proletariat, in its furtherance of its own class interests, is actually the energy of objective historical change, no longer speculative but practical, and is thus no longer obliged to take seriously or to replicate the demands of antinomic consciousness. The predicament of reification that governs "all the social forms of modern capitalism . . . can only be made fully conscious in the work-situation of the proletarian" (pp. 171–72). Only the "standpoint" of the proletarian can provide the "self-knowledge of its own social situation" (p. 159).

Let us note the rhetorical sleight of hand or double expression that invokes the objectively known situation (of the proletarian) with the solution of the ideological problems of situatedness (of bourgeois man). Perhaps this has something to do with Lukács's own later (1967) understanding of the "overriding subjectivism" with which he had tried to overcome subjectivism itself, the "purely contemplative nature of bourgeois thought" (p. xviii). And of course the problems are not solved—in their own terms they are not solvable—but simply displaced and rendered redundant. They disappear, they are no longer problems. This leaves Lukács (the author in 1922) open to the irony of a history that has not yet and in the opinion of many today may never bring about this objectification of the consciousness of the proletariat or indeed of anyone else, so that his argument stands now as visibly utopian rather than obviously predictive. I shall want, as I have said, to hold on to this faith in history as the most profitable testing ground for the dilemmas of situatedness, not because I think I stand outside everyone else's history with a fistful of new answers, but because I think that the recurrence of the same old imponderables masquerading as certitudes is under visible stress at the moment and might more openly expose its confusions as we set sail into what we think of as the broad ocean of the postmodern, with its imagined and perhaps imaginary new ways of being and thinking. I shall, then, try to hold on to the notion of a history that is useful despite its not having the imprimatur of a confidently declared objectifying interest of the sort that Lukács (in 1922) found in the proletariat. If it is still true that "only the dialectics of history can create a radically new situation" (p. 188) then we cannot confidently either affirm or foreclose on the imminence of a moment at which the very term *situation* will become either clear or redundant.

Which brings me back to the other word, *aporia*. This word might better satisfy Jameson's notion of that which offers "nothing in the way of a handle" (*The Seeds of Time*, p. 2) than his preferred *antinomy*, which as we have seen has in Kant and indeed (although in a quite different way) in Lukács the implication of a solution waiting in the wings. *Aporia* too has a history, beginning with the Greeks, but it is to Jacques Derrida above all that we owe its currency in the contemporary rhetoric. Derrida's interest in the aporetic began at least as early as 1968, in his early work on Heidegger.[28] He has restated and redeployed the same concerns in his volume *Aporias* (1993), a restatement necessitated not just by the continued relevance of the underlying concept but perhaps also by the somewhat lazy enunciation of the term as denoting, in the common critical rhetoric, more or less any old difficulty, leading Derrida himself to acknowledge the apparent limits of "this tired word of philosophy and of logic." [29] The ἀπορία invokes being at a loss, being stuck, in a muddle, experiencing difficulty in getting at, passing through; ἄπορος indicates "without means" or "unprovided for." One might say, then, that it is the most complete alternative to the "contradiction" as Jameson describes it, with its lurking sense of imminent solution or mediation, a sense also informing the *antinomy*. Both terms taken together, each invoked as the shadow of the other, are for now as close as I can come to sketching out the place of *situatedness*, a description of which does require a confession of muddle, of not seeing the way, of feeling unprovided for (by one's parent philosophers?), as well as of a glimpse of or hope for a future in which the muddle might be seen to have been antinomic all along, simply a matter of misunderstanding or false consciousness.

This effort at the introduction of an as yet unexhausted but already about to be exhausted term such as *situatedness* also requires my avoidance of some of the more familiar terms that will have already come to the reader's mind as describing similar questions about our place in the world. The most obvious of these terms is perhaps the two-in-one of "freedom and determination," sanctioned by generations of philosophers and theologians as that which most needs to be posited and brought to resolution (are we the one or the other?), while it is itself, I would say, more a symptom of the unknowing that surrounds our place in the world than it is the means to any clear knowledge. This is a consciousness-based terminology that presupposes clear decision making even as it insists in its own very expression that the citation of one word will inevitably raise the specter of the other, so that what ensues is an inexhaustible swinging back and forth, but one carried out all too often with an absolute conviction of the correctness of whichever item is on the table. Even to speak of freedom *and* determination holds out a prospect of some computational formula for specifying where one begins and the other ends. *Situatedness*, on the other hand, holds on to a singleness of experience and description that is not of itself elucidatory, although it remains faithful to the intent to call up for inspection everything that is the case in a given place and time. Its definition is thus phantasmagoric or utopian, because no one can call up or track down everything. It remains in this way wedded to the aporetic and (or) antinomic rather than to the conclusive. It is not yet quite the comfort term that *situation* has become, although it is fast becoming one.

Now in calling up everything that is part of the case for describing a thing or person's place in its world, *situatedness* will inevitably gather around it the whole family of other words that are already familiar (such as freedom and determination, ideology and agency) for doing some of the same work. They all belong together in the collection of words Kenneth Burke analyzed in *A Grammar of Motives* (first published in 1945). He found that there is "something essentially enigmatic about the problem of motives," leading to "inevitable ambiguities and inconsistencies among the terms for motives." Instead of trying to resolve the ambiguities, which is a hopeless task given the irreducible specificity of all acts and situations (no two are alike), we might better take the time to clarify their "resources." [30] Every time a description is reduced to any one of these words—let us say "freedom"—then all of the others come flooding in because "no one of them is enough" (p. xxi). This provides for the opportunistic refiguring of all critical priorities involved in the attribution of motives. Burke's five basic words, *act, scene, agent, agency,* and *purpose,* can be used to generate all statements assigning motives (pp. xv–xvi) and can be mutually assimilated and prioritized to reflect all sorts of preferences. The words, that is to say, communicate with each other, so that the mention of one sets off a chain of associations that requires being made up to some standard of coherence. Burke invokes *situation* as an example of a "scene" word:

> Political commentators now generally use the word "situation" as their synonym for scene, though often without any clear concept of its function as a statement about motives. Many social psychologists consciously use the term for its motivational bearing (it has a range extending from the broadest concepts of historical setting down to the simplified, controlled conditions which the animal experimenter imposes upon his rats in a maze). The Marxist reference to "the objective situation" is explicitly motivational, and the theorists who use this formula discuss "policies" as political acts enacted in conformity with the nature of scenes. However, the scene-act ratio can be applied in two ways. It can be applied deterministically in statements that a certain policy *had* to be adopted in a certain situation, or it may be applied in hortatory statements to the effect that a certain policy *should be* adopted in conformity with the situation. (p. 12–13)

The word, for all its comforts (or perhaps because of them) is slippery. What we are seeing now in the popularity of the not quite cognate *situatedness* is a process wherein this newer scene word has the same tendency to digest or assimilate all the other scene words, as well as the other terms in the vocabulary of motivations—agent, agency, act, and purpose. As an agent acting for a purpose, one acts within the terms of one's situatedness. But to say this is to invoke (by the bravado of such an empty specification) the readmission of all of those other terms as competitors for the status of primary term. Burke says it well in saying that "all thought tends to name things not because they are precisely as named, but because they are not quite as named, and the name is designated as a somewhat hortatory device, to take up the slack" (p. 54). *Situatedness*, then, is not naming anything precisely but sheltering a whole range of other terms that are themselves equally approximate. Every so often this society of underdescribers elects one word from its membership to stand in for but not to "represent" the others, so that the very act of speaking it ignites the campaign for its recall. The chapter of Burke's from which I have just quoted is aptly titled "Antinomies of Definition."

Speak Before You're Spoken The spirit and method of Burke's account is one I hope to exemplify in this study, which aspires to contribute to an understanding of some key words in the rhetorical culture of late capitalism, not so much for what they "say" as for what they purposively do not say, or say badly or loosely. Burke, along with William Empson, offers one of the most sophisticated models for this task, although his effort is of course itself an event in place and time, as Frank Lentricchia has made clear: "Burke's wager in 1935 . . . was that the adhesive force of bourgeois nationalist symbols of allegiance was entering a state of decay, that other symbolic agencies were competing to take their place: that, indeed, this very situation of fluidity signified an unstable or revolutionary period in which people were in the process of shifting their allegiances from one myth to another. It was a situation of maximum opportunity for the literary intellectual [who] might have found himself in strategic leadership as director of a rhetorical war." [31] Does the array of tendencies at play around and within the rhetoric of situatedness suggest some comparable opportunity, and therefore historical shifting, in the postmodern present? It is possible. It is also possible that the compulsion to shifting allegiances has become normative and commonplace, a feature of ordinary life always with us, so that it becomes even harder to perceive or imagine a point at which quantity shifts gear into quality, a point at which "things change." Let us ponder what may be a significant example in the sphere of ordinary language, of commonplace rhetoric.

As a middle-aged white male . . . This is what I want to call the *azza* sentence. Its name is legion. It signals countless self-interpellations uttered here in the anglophone United States in the 1990s, and it is so far showing no signs of ceasing as we enter the new millenium.[32] The *azza* sentence is ubiquitous in the popular diction governing social encounter and debate. It is especially prevalent in contexts in which we are aware of having limited space and time, as in the "letters" column of newspapers and journals. It is a way of establishing one's credentials as authoritatively and efficiently as possible. It preempts the Althusserian "hey you!" by an upfront "here I stand," a self-interpellation that tries to beat the other to the draw. With such sentences we subjectify ourselves in a way that signals the urgent insecurity of democratic culture and at the same time declares a temporary invulnerability and a goal-seeking purpose. No one utters sentences such as "as a middle-aged white male I would like to know what is on TV tonight." There are still many situations in which our credentials are not at issue. But there seems to be a growing number of situations in which they are. So we find sentences such as "as a middle-aged white male let me tell you how I feel about feminism, or multiculturalism, or the tax rates. . . ." We can add in the appropriate qualifiers to address different topics. So the white or other male becomes gay, straight, able, or disabled, anglophone or not, according to the topic and the audience for his opinion.

Some people don't have much need for this gesture of aggressive-defensive self-affiliation. Thus one can generate innumerable likely sentences beginning "as a John Wayne fan," while the likelihood of Wayne ever having introduced himself "as a leading Hollywood actor" in anything other than a spirit of irony is very remote. To achieve name recognition and/or authority as a one-of-a-kind person (president, pope, and so on) is largely to be able to dispense with these sentences; fewer and fewer situations occur in which one is not already adequately subjectified. The rest of us are stuck with it. My guess is that in its incarnation as a compulsive identifier, the phrase is quite recent. By way of contrast, here is the first sentence of Darwin's introduction to *The Origin of Species*: "When on board H.M.S. *Beagle*, as naturalist, I was much struck with certain facts in the distribution of the inhabitants of South America, and in the geological relations of the present to the past inhabitants of that continent." [33] The information passed on here is much the same as it would be in a sentence beginning with "as a," but Darwin does not say it that way. The authority claimed in his introductory phrase is first temporal and informational, and only then occupational. The statement of credentials is embedded, not (as the linguists say) "fronted." And the emphasis on the "I," when it comes, is slighter than it would have been in a sentence reading "as the naturalist on the *Beagle*, I. . . ." Darwin's sentence stresses the words "much struck," not the word "I." In other words we go directly to the topic, the scientific matter, without being detained by any hyperbolic self-interpellation.

I cannot say that I have discovered the first instance of the *azza* sentence: the earliest example I have found occurs in Mary Wollstonecraft, toward the end of the second chapter of her *A Vindication of the Rights of*

Woman. There the author identifies herself first "as a philosopher" and then, in the same sentence, "as a moralist," by way of expressing her critique of the contemporary sex-gender system.[34] As a founding feminist in a contentious historical situation, Wollstonecraft understandably expresses a certain anxiety about her authority in saying what she says. The fronted self-affiliation is the perfect expression of her anxiety, as well as of her claim to credibility. An interesting instance occurs in Mary Cholmondeley's novel *Red Pottage*, first published in 1899. In this passage, Hester is speaking to Rachel of what she might have become: "You . . . might have become like Sybell Loftus, who never understands any feeling beyond her own microscopic ones. . . . People, like Sybell, believe one can only sympathise with what one has experienced. That is why they are always saying 'as a mother' or 'as a wife.' If that were true, the world would have to get on without sympathy, for no two people have the same experience."[35] This is a rather profound observation, making the connection between the *azza* sentence and the prevalence of identity politics, one that is very much still with us. Cholmondeley focuses not on the power of the claim but on its limits, its usefulness for disclaiming any necessary attention to the condition of others whose identity one does not share. Here, speaking for oneself is simultaneously a denial of the need to speak for others who perhaps cannot speak for themselves, an element of the situation that has only become more prominent since *Red Pottage* first appeared. The rhetoric of self-assurance is also that of self-insurance and self-insulation; it has become endemic in recent years in part because the capacity for sympathy itself has come under massive scrutiny and critique as something that is always and already contaminated, narcissistic, and self-projecting. One cannot speak for others because one cannot feel with them, one can only feel for oneself. Paradoxically it is the expression of damage limitation, the self-interpellation that claims only to speak for oneself and one's own limited kind, the attempt to leave space for others to speak their lines from where they are coming from, that is also the most damaging symptom of the antinomic rhetoric of situatedness to the extent that it discourages us from even engaging the problem of thinking and feeling ourselves into the position of the other. I am suggesting that we have earned neither the assurances of self-interpellation nor its self-excusing corollary. It is time to initiate some fresh thinking about the assumptions that come with the rhetoric of situatedness that is currently in place.

There are undoubtedly plenty of other examples of the *azza* sentence in the more distant past of modernity, perhaps some even predating Mary Wollstonecraft in 1791. I shall suggest that the syndrome out of which such sentences are generated is in fact fundamental to modernity, but also that the implications and incidence of the syndrome have become especially acute at our present moment — hence the commonplace nature of sentences of self-affilation. Much of what follows consists of an effort to describe the syndrome, in the hope that a convincing investigation of something that goes largely under the sign of normality is the first step toward new and perhaps more efficient, accurate, and even compassionate rhetorics. And let us not forget Lukács: to speak of modernity, as I just did, is to speak of bourgeois modernity and its insecurities. Much of what goes on in the rhetoric of self-affiliation is distinctly middle class, indeed often professional. The most predictable among such sentences for someone like me would be "as a middle-aged (white) college professor." I may not be the pope, president, or John Wayne (or Sting, whom I would rather be than any of those), but neither do I feel myself to be a complete nobody, one who has nothing to affiliate himself with by way of a marketable or recognizable identity. The radically oppressed or unfortunate presumably do not experience the same insecurities of self-interpellation because they have less to be unclear about and perhaps less to fear from a change in their condition. They may know all too well where they are coming from, and such knowledge can include the understanding that they are not expected to speak and to tell us about it. A sentence beginning with "as an unemployed, homeless person" can be heard, but it signals a discomforting element of mimicry or pastiche. Mary Wollstonecraft knew that she was writing for and about the middle class, those above subsistence and below unquestionable distinction. The middle class is also the natural medium of the rhetoric of self-affiliation. That we now hear so many self-interpellating sentences may indicate the relative consolidation of bourgeois culture in anglophone Anglo-America; it may also speak for the degree to which that always unstable condition of middleness is more than before threatened by its own contradictions and by what it senses or positions as coming from outside, beyond and below. Certainly we must grant that it is no longer plausible to restrict the specifications of one's situatedness to the old analytic warhorses of class and occupation: their name is now legion.

So I think that Andrew Sullivan's critique of the *azza* sentence (see note 32) as the confident emanation of a triumphant identity politics is only half the story, perhaps less than half the story. The ubiquity of such sentences is, I believe, much more accurately understood as evidence for a deeply sensed anxiety about the available categories of identity, and their sufficiency for supporting the arguments or self-inscriptions that we seem compelled to use them for. Our bourgeois-democratic culture does not have access to the genealogical rationale of the Biblical and Homeric heroes, *a* son of *b*, the son of *c*, prince of *x*. Our legitimacy can never be assumed but must always be claimed afresh. This puts considerable pressure on social exchanges with persons we do not know and who cannot be assumed to trust us—that is, most people most of the time. Our common language has devised fairly complicated forms of deferential assertiveness, of which the *azza* sentence is one. The familiar statement "if I have offended anyone here I am sorry" is another example. It indicates that there are so many forms of offense that we cannot be sure that we have not committed one of them. But it is also a statement of self-insurance, a preemptive apology that robs those who really are offended of the rhetorical high ground from which they might express their outrage effectively. Such a statement can allow us to give ourselves permission to say things we perhaps should not be saying. It is an opportunistic gesture of self-positioning; by the time we have pondered how to react to the preemptive apology the speaker has moved on.

One could go on. The declarative "I have a question" signifies a similar balance of deference and assertiveness. It warns the hearer that what is coming is one sort of statement and not another—not an attack, lecture, or observation, but yet not innocent of confrontational possibility. The hearer can prepare to receive the question; he or she is not left needing to interpret the function of the utterance. At the same time the speaker signals a potentially antagonistic event, saying "on guard," "prepare yourself," "account for yourself." The statement "what I am saying is . . . ," logically bizarre in that it says what it is saying while it is saying it, is a conventional mode of restatement assuming that the message may require translation or at least restatement, that transparent communication cannot be assumed. And the dreary formula drummed into the brains of frequent fliers, "at this time we do ask you . . . ," again combines deference and provisionality—we are asking you now but we won't always ask you—with a more emphatic command, we *do* ask you, now and in this place. (Compare also the hyperbolic "at this moment in time.") The language of democratic culture is constantly looking for ways to negotiate the balance between control and permissiveness, between imposing order and allowing for personal preference or the appearance of it. In this way it is (and we are) constantly shifting the emphasis within the description of situatedness according to whether the coercive or permissive component is deemed more appropriate. Democracy is uncomfortable with expressing relationships as anything other than volitional; this is why waiters want to share with us everything on the menu except the check/bill. It is uncomfortable also with the expression of the self's desire; hence "I need" replaces "I want." Uncertainty about the proper and effective limits of agency and responsibility means that the expression of mere desire ("I want") is harder to justify than the claim to life-supporting materials in a world competing for potentially scarce resources ("I need"). All "want" sentences thus now tend to be translated into "need" sentences.

The rhetoric of contemporary middle-class life thus tends to be at once assertive and provisional, and provisional in both demographic and temporal senses. When I begin a sentence with "as a middle-aged white male" I am invoking my identity as such only for the statement that I am about to make. I am saying that I might choose other identities to make other statements, for instance "as a tax-paying dog owner" or "as the parent of nine school-age children." I am also admitting that I might have other identities chosen for me. Anthony Giddens and Ulrich Beck have characterized modernity as a "risk culture," which means that we live with "a calculative attitude to the open possibilities of action . . . in a continuous way." [36] Some of these look as if they are self-selected—partner choice or place of residence, perhaps—but others are imposed or have clear constraints placed on choice. We are never quite sure which is which. The rhetoric of reskilling or retooling, to take an example that is banal precisely because it is of such urgent concern to so many, is a good example. At best we are allowed to choose a new occupation, but the choices are not

46

infinite. At worst we are simply bamboozled into believing that losing a job is a failure of willingness to learn new skills: a failure to make the best of our situation. Within the rhetoric of the "lifestyle," the image of choice is being extended to other and more personal components of ordinary life, among which, as Giddens eloquently remarks, "we have no choice but to choose" (p. 81). The *azza* sentence registers the provisionality of one's group affiliation, and suggests that one might choose or find imposed other groups on other occasions; but it also preserves the sanctity of the ego, the "I," over and against all groups. Whatever I designate myself I will still be I, open to other future affiliations. In other words we are not at all sure that I will still be I. The ego identity is not felt as a certitude, so that it generates hyperbolic and compensatory forms. When I begin a sentence with the phrase "as a middle-aged white male" I can be understood quite seriously to be revealing that I am very unsure indeed of who and what I am and for how long. This matters because we often find ourselves speaking and acting out certitudes where we might more usefully and generously admit our ignorance, not so much in routine situations, where a high degree of predictability and identity is both assumed and required (it is not usually pertinent to wonder whether the I who says he will meet you at noon tomorrow is the same I who is making the promise), but in such contexts as those of judicial, interpretative, and analytical decision making that govern or aspire to govern critical social events.

Dreams of Management Sociologists have described, in terms that are very helpful and insightful for my present argument, the antinomic and aporetic characteristics of the rhetoric of situatedness (although they do not use the term). In his 1959 study *The Presentation of Self in Everyday Life*, Erving Goffman showed a precise understanding of the mixture of "cynicism and sincerity" in the habits of self-presentation that he saw around him.[37] Individuals engage in "performance" in order to project themselves into situations; they employ a "front," which Goffman describes as "expressive equipment of a standard kind" employed to legitimate performance (p. 22). The aim is "maintenance of expressive control" (p. 51) and "impression management" (p. 208), made necessary by the degree to which "everyday secular performances in our own Anglo-American society must often pass a strict test of aptness, fitness, propriety and decorum" (p. 55). Because interactions are fraught with risk, and because "full information" about a situation is never available (p. 249), individuals find themselves preoccupied with trying to minimize "performance disruptions" (p. 243), unpredictable and uncontrollable circumstances and responses. Self-affiliation sentences, although not discussed by Goffman, are a perfect example of the rhetorical effort to accommodate the various tensions he identifies as typical of social interaction. Indeed, his book can be read as a brilliant analysis of the kind of situatedness pertaining to the moment at which such sentences are, if my hunch is correct, about to emerge into full platitude, into the commonplace. Goffman's emphasis is not, however, contextual or historical; although no claim to universality is made, there is no exploration of limits, no sense of things not always having been as they seemed in 1959. One could even say that there is an instrumental dimension to Goffman's work, which specifies its special applicability to "the kind of social life that is organized within the physical confines of a building or plant" (p. xi). In the spirit of efficient corporate management he as much as admits that there are "practical reasons" for acquiring expertise in "impression management," so that we can come to know better how to call forth a "desired response" (p. 1).

This element of Goffman's work is on the edge of a collapse (although it never does collapse) into management studies. And that road has indeed been subsequently taken by others, for instance by Tom Peters and Robert Waterman, whose In Search of Excellence was, for some time after its first publication in 1982, the bible of the American business community. In this book the authors argue that the informal and hard-to-quantify elements of the workplace, traditionally reduced to mathematical or utilitarian formulas, can in fact be "managed," and indeed are managed in the so-called excellent company. These companies are the ones that can "manage ambiguity and paradox," realizing that we "will sacrifice a great deal to institutions that will provide meaning for us" and that people do well when they are told that they are doing well.[38] Excellent companies, that is to say, know how to control their employees' sense of situatedness; they know that "if people think that they have even modest personal control over their destinies, they will persist at tasks" (p. 80). The successful corporate leader is concerned with minutiae, "with the tricks of the pedagogue, the mentor, the linguist—the more successfully to become the value shaper, the exemplar, the maker of meanings" (p. 82). With barely a shred of circumspection on the part of the authors, what is adumbrated here is the world of Orwell's *Nineteen Eighty-Four.* There are no Big Brothers, just excellent companies. And it is important that these companies are not in the business of suppressing the sense of freedom, but of cultivating it within limits that can be controlled.

This should be evidence enough that any pedagogue, mentor, or linguist aspiring to exercise a critical intellectuality is obliged at least not to fall too far behind the corporate vanguard in its conscious and articulate effort at manipulating the antinomies of situatedness in the service of profit. Tom Peters has by now produced several updated versions of "state of the art" corporate theory. His 1992 *Liberation Management* makes euphoric sense of the instability and insecurity of the subject, now translated into a rhetoric of constant opportunity. Here, traditional (and visible) management disappears, to be replaced by "self-contained" work groups doing everything in an atmosphere of "necessary disorganization" and dissolving after each completed task "never to exist again in the same form." The appropriate metaphor is now that of "carnival." [39] One imagines a string of sentences such as "as the person temporarily responsible for the initiation of *xyz*," which are perfect examples of the important case made by Arif Dirlik about the use of culture in management practice "to make increasingly engineered lives appear as the epitome of empowerment." [40] This is surely not new, and it represents an alliance between corporations and the intelligentsia that was made famous in F. J. Roethlisberger and William Dickson's *Management and the Worker* (1939), where every "concrete situation" is explained as the result of complex and overlapping contributory situations: "personal situation," "work situation," "social situation," "output situation," "supervisory situation," and so forth.[41] The social scientist's task is to assist in the designing of a happy and productive whole based on the understanding of all these situations. What is perhaps new, or newly critical since Roethlisberger and Dickson's landmark study, is the obscuring or disappearance of hierarchy and the dispersal of responsibility among nominally equal work partners in a process Castells has called "the individualization of labor in the labor process" (*The Information Age,* 1: 265). This is only empowering for those able to market an expertise for very high rewards, for those who can command positions in the "core labor force" (p. 272). The rest become ever more disposable, thereby "shrinking the middle" of the occupational structure (p. 279). This same always ideological and only occasional autonomy appears also in the sphere of consumption, with specific market slots devised according to a highly segmented array of "ideologies, values, tastes, and lifestyles" (p. 340) wherein one can choose anything except the option of not choosing.

An important, critically contextualized account of some of the antinomies of situatedness informing the working class is offered by Richard Sennett and Jonathan Cobb in their 1972 book *The Hidden Injuries of Class*. The authors note the tendency of American working-class speakers to use passive constructions when describing their own successes in the workplace, demonstrating a "protective alienation of the real person from the performing individual." [42] The real self is not involved at work; it is thus not subject to the vagaries of workplace disciplines and rewards. Thus one young plumber reports that he received a raise when "the south wall mess was straightened out" (p. 193), refusing to take the credit for having been the one who did the job. This is a suppression rather than an avowal of self-affiliation. It is protective in a context where the employer's response is not predictable; but, say the authors, it has a downside, whereby "the person does not come to exercise control over his situation, transforming the conditions of his or her life, but instead simply moves from one set of circumstances to another" (p. 271). At its most extreme such behavior is prone to theorization as a personality disorder. Sennett and Cobb instead suggest that it is an intelligible response to the specific conditions of the working life in midcentury America. In his larger study of the evolution of the culture of privacy, intimacy, and disclosure, *The Fall of Public Man*, Sennett summarizes this same syndrome as "a logical way to feel in a society whose logic is to absorb people into questions of self-adequacy." And he notes once again the rhetorical profile of the response: "The self at work is split into an 'I' and a 'me.' The 'I,' the active self, is not the self the institution judges; the 'I' is the self of the worker's motivations, his feelings, his impulses. Paradoxically, the self which accomplishes and is rewarded is described by passive language, by reference to events which happen to the 'me.' " [43] Sennett's account of the purposive decision to use "I" and "me" in this way is reminiscent of Samuel Taylor Coleridge's description of what happens when we make a "bull" — a statement apparently coherent but involving an incongruity of ideas. Coleridge's example is the statement "I was a fine child, but they changed me." He analyzes this as an unnoticed slippage from the *ego contemplans* to the *ego contemplatus*, from the self imaged as identity or agent to the self imaged as object.[44] This, he says, is what happens when we are so absorbed in the moment at the moment that we do not sense any incoherence between the parts of the statement that we are making. Coleridge seems to think of this as some sort of logical slip, and perhaps one that contributes to theological slips, wherein we misunderstand the proper relation between the self and the will. But there are, as I shall hope to show, many and profound social-historical reasons why it is so hard to understand the transitions between the *I* and the *me*, and so useful to obscure them or have them obscured. The history of this relation is part of the history of situatedness, and it is a history whose function has been not to encourage understanding but to perpetuate confusion. The middle-class postmodern subject's compulsive and hyperbolic embrace of the rhetoric of self-affiliation has brought that confusion into the foreground.

Sennett and Cobb remind us, if we need reminding, that we live in a complex and divided society whose forms of increasing complexity are accompanied by radical rhetorical simplifications in a process of bait and switch between agency and passivity that can seem to be impossible to follow. Statements are indeed made within situations and about situations, but the exact messages and intentions do not simply become clear because situatedness itself is so imprecise. Bronislaw Malinowski made a famous case for what he calls "context of situation" as a principle for understanding language statements: "Utterance and situation are bound up inextricably with each other and the context of situation is indispensable for the understanding of the words." [45] Notice the way in which one "scene word" (to use Burke's term) is made to serve another: context is situation, situation is context. Malinowski writes as if by calling it a context one might choose or not to refer to the situation, while saying at the same time that the situation is more than an example of *a* context, it is *the* context. More pertinent to my case, though, is the anthropologist's confidence in reaching "positive, concrete conclusions" (p. 308) about language by recognizing the context of situations. He can feel this way because his example is that of a "primitive" society (which we must now understand as one he is making primitive) organized by clear and simple division of labor: "The whole group act in a concerted manner, determined by old tribal tradition and perfectly familiar to the actors through lifelong experience" (p. 311). Analogues invoked in western culture are similarly simplified—the crewing of a ship, soldiers in battle, playing a sport (these are examples of what Sartre calls "groups"). None of this works as a description of the social or labor experience in late capitalism, which is marked by the nonavailability of single, simple roles and indeed by their demarcation, where they do occur, under the signs of alienation and reification. Durkheim took exception to "those excessively mobile talents that lend themselves equally to all uses, refusing to choose a special role and keep to it." [46] But this is exactly what is being increasingly recognized and recommended as the labor pattern of late capitalism.

Situatedness, then, is a scene word that nominally gathers to itself an unpredictable set of synchronic and diachronic apposites and opposites, almost always those pertaining to the *subject*, and rendering it simultaneously (or opportunistically) subject *and* object. Notwithstanding the efforts of many writers and critics at questioning or displacing the credibility of foundational models of human subjectivity, it is apparent that the majority culture reflected in politics and the media and enshrined in what we call common sense has never really given up on the forms of assurance that the subject has traditionally provided. This is not surprising in light of the common perception that the world has now been won for liberal democracy, for which the subject has been something of a sacred cow—an entity to be first of all cultivated wherever it might appear as other than utterly original, and thereafter to be protected from all assaults while being (just as important) held accountable for all misdeeds. It remains to be seen whether we are experiencing a collective emergence from a period in which some of our most persuasive intellectuals have been describing the "death of the subject" (and thus the hegemony of the social sciences) as the rationale for our access to new spheres of political and cultural freedom and openness. There is some evidence for specifying our present moment as one marked by "the death of the death of the subject" (a cumbersome but apt phrase that should signal that we are not really in the business of bringing anything back to life), although what now governs much up-to-date theorization is not the metaphysically secure and essential subjectivity that is imagined as traditional, but a much more provisional entity, one that is tenaciously held to as long as it is useful but that can then be traded in for some newly useful and even quite unrelated identity that happens to come our way.

Why might there be a newly intense anxiety or uncertainty about how to describe or cope with the incompatible perspectives that come from continuing to understand ourselves as subject to imposed conditions while possessing some capacities to change them? This is, after all, the standard predicament of the subject for as long as it has been theorized *as* a subject. But the responsibility for and obligation to establishing the terms of one's situatedness has not always devolved so completely on the alerted and defensive individual, who is now faced (if he or she inhabits the middle class) with making some sort of choice, informed or otherwise, about almost everything, with fewer and fewer in-place, choice-assisting habits and authorities to which to appeal. Alain Touraine found that "at the beginning of the eighties no representation of social life prevails . . . there no longer obtains a recognized model of analysis of social agency. In the strict sense, sociology no longer exists." [47] Goffman again is invoked as the prescient observer of this new world in which people become actors, playing "social roles without any need to believe in them, seeking primarily to position themselves vis-à-vis others, no doubt in the expectation of achieving . . . advantages but frequently entering into relationships based upon misunderstanding, avoidance or whatever" (p. 24). I will be proposing that obscurity and slipperiness have always characterized claims made about situatedness, as Kenneth Burke has demonstrated at some length, but that there have been times when it was less of an issue than it is now, a fact that should promote some reflection on the middle-class way of life in late capitalist democracies, for it is surely not an issue everywhere. I will also suggest that there have been moments in our past when influential numbers and kinds of people thought that situatedness could be precisely described, predicted, and beneficially manipulated. This view still holds today in some quarters, and supports all sorts of agendas that we probably cannot do without. But these agendas are very much threatened by their own internal contradictions, which leave room for and indeed invite extreme alternative convictions about the importance of individual will or character over and above anything one might attribute to circumstances. The stakes in this discussion are very high. What is involved is finally nothing less than the legitimacy of all interventionist social planning and the credibility of any rational predictability of human behavior.

I am going to suggest that we are under the influence of a rhetoric that seems to promise certainties where there are only ambiguities; that the rage or disappointment at this outcome can lead us too far in other directions (toward strident individualist or identity claims, for example); and that the ambivalence itself can be and has been exploited and maintained within the system of constraints and opportunities that make up our culture or way of life, permitting us to maintain certain strategic fudges in our collective and individual self-descriptions. In the sphere of situatedness these fudges have had a very long life: it appears that they are at least coincident with the long modernity taking form in the sixteenth century. But they have become urgent again in the late twentieth century. My intention is not to do away with the fuzziness but to show why it is what it is, and what may be gained from understanding situatedness *as* obscure instead of just replicating the obscurity or reducing it to reified and mutually sustaining alternatives.

Parts of this task were very capably performed by Thomas Nagel in his 1985 book *The View from Nowhere*, which took up the impossibility of a "naturally unified standpoint" between a third person (objective) and first person (subjective) view of the world.[48] He too saw a condition in which each perspective was either undervalued or overvalued and he sought, as I do, "not to assign victory to either standpoint but to hold the opposition clearly in one's mind without suppressing either element" (p. 6). He set out to tolerate fuzziness in order to explore the degree to which "absurdity comes with the territory" (p. 11), and he took the risk of being judged to have nothing, after all, to say. He accepted that what we call truth is not to be had by either strictly subjective or strictly objective standpoints, and that what we get from seeing the two together in a "dual aspect" theory cannot comfortably even be called truth. Nagel was principally interested in the implications of a dual-aspect model for moral theory, and offered a "reconciliation" that was not a "solution" by way of an "essentially incomplete objective view" (pp. 126–27). Ethics appeals as "one route to objective engagement because it supplies an alternative to pure observation of ourselves from outside" (p. 136), which is of course impossible. But the turn to ethics is as much a feature of the situatedness problem as an alternative to it. It restores the question to the sphere of the individual, and can do little to prevent a "situatedness ethics" from running into all the old problems as soon as it seeks to legislate or prescribe forms of behavior for anyone else, even those within what is arguably the same social-cultural grouping. Insofar as it is a self-focusing discipline, ethics might seem more likely to provide satisfactory compromises than the more bluntly instrumental and other-oriented forms of inquiry that I will attend to for much of this book—law and social and political science—along with the epistemologies that they have assumed or invoked in justifying their practices. But ethical satisfaction cannot easily be transposed into policy recommendations or even adequate descriptions of complex groups. It cannot become an epistemology, and I do not believe that we have overcome the need for an epistemology.

What does appeal to me about Nagel's analysis is its readiness to take on the description of problems it cannot solve and finds to be insoluble. We are to take him very seriously when he says that the solutions to the questions he raises "require an order of intelligence wholly different from mine" (p. 12). He does not mean that we should just wait for a smarter philosopher to come along, but that the very terms of a satisfactory answer are as yet unavailable. An "integrated theory of reality" may never happen, or may take "centuries," and if it does happen it will "alter our conception of the universe as radically as anything has to date" (p. 51). In the meantime, "when we acknowledge our containment in the world, it becomes clear that we are incapable of living in the full light of that acknowledgment" (p. 231). Something of the same insight can be found in Darwin, which means that he has to be ignored or rewritten by those who are in a hurry to pin down the terms of our situatedness, our "containment in the world." I will be exploring some of the panic reactions to the absence of full light on this matter, some of the manipulations of the shadowy areas, and some of the disabling consequences of thinking that the darkness has been dispersed. I think that it matters to do this at a time when *situatedness* is entering the lexicon as a positive term with an avowed content, a term that legitimates arguments made from it instead of provoking attention to its inadequacies. Quite commonly, the claim to situate is a claim to justify. Skepticism, in the face of this kind of affirmation, indeed of mutually conflicting affirmations, should have its say; and at a time when the rhetoric of affirmation is as confused, hyperbolic, and self-undermining as ours so often is, a measure of skepticism may even be a kindness. The same skepticism was coincident with the very first efforts at specifying the terms of human situatedness undertaken by those who publicized and analyzed what we call modernity. To propose that it has a history is to pose the question of why it keeps on repeating itself, if that is what it is doing. If ours is indeed an age that has forgotten how to think historically, as Fredric Jameson says it is, then one way to break the spell might be to ponder the long-durational success of what looks like an ahistorical rhetoric .[49]

Let it be clear, though, that I am not aspiring to produce a thickly described history, one that claims to stand for all versions of the situatedness question in all of modernity. I am not even offering a comprehensive survey of the disciplines within which it has occurred and recurred. I am making selective use of legal theorists, philosophers, social scientists, and literary writers to illustrate my argument, but I am not setting out to represent these disciplines in any exhaustive way. Other disciplines — most obviously history, anthropology, and psychology — are hardly invoked at all. But I try to cover enough of the territory to persuade the reader that covering more of it would not produce major contradictions to my claim that most attempts to define situatedness are embedded in failure and confusion. Nor am I intending to write the history of an idea, of a paradigm that sails imperturbably through times and places bestowing on them a language for self-knowledge. There are in fact several and various ideas at work in the rhetoric of situatedness, and all of them are confused and confusing. They too have a history that could in principle be written, a history that is outside and beyond themselves and that has ensured their continuing appeal. As such they call for a critical history, a speculation about their noninevitability and contingency. This is the history to which I hope to contribute, although I shall by no means complete it. The big picture that looms behind my account of the aporetic functions of the rhetoric of situatedness and its precursors has the general features of a longstanding political and economic culture that requires for its legitimation an opaque or illegible category called subjectivity, one that appears to be neither convincing nor dispensable. Thus I suggest that the issue about subjectivity is not, as some would have it, so much one of removing it from the picture, as if it were already there, but of seeing through the rules of the game that make it impossible or implausible in the first place as a satisfactory solution to the demands it is called on to answer to. The peculiar thinness and fragility of the rhetoric of situatedness in its current forms suggests that we can at least imagine ourselves to be at a point where the rules of the game can be seen for what they are—or, as some would say, that we might be at the moment of subscribing to the rules of some other game that allows the current one to appear exhausted or at risk. But if that is the case, then it must be said that the credibility of claims made from declarations of situatedness is being quite heroically defended and publicized at the present time, which gives me some hope that the work of critique is still worth doing.

2. Mitigating Circumstances: Secular Situatedness and the Law

Uses or Abuses? In *The Hidden Injuries of Class* Sennett and Cobb's insights into the social and occupational varieties of the relations between the active *I* and passive *me* might lead us to think about the classically received philosophical formulations of the subject-object dynamic in a philosophically untraditional way, one no longer based in an assessment of the internal coherences and contradictions of purely formal systems (the Cartesian cogito, personal identity in Locke and Hume, the phenomena-noumena distinction in Kant, and so on) but rather in a consideration of the local functions of those systems (and indeed of their contradictions) in time and place. To do this would be to produce one kind of a history for the rhetoric of situatedness and its significant analogues. Such a history would explain subjectivity and situatedness as pseudoconcepts rather than as foundational insights or breakthroughs; and the recurrence and repeated dramatization of the pseudoconcepts would suggest, I think, that their traditional function has not just been one of solving or healing theoretical or practical divisions but also one of maintaining them *as* divisions by offering up rhetorical do-it-yourself kits for the temporary performance of gestures of identity and attributions of responsibility that can always be reversed under pressure.

Disciplines and institutions, however, tend not to see themselves as operating in this way. They tend to believe or at least declare that they are functioning according to defensible and consistent principles. Among the various institutions organizing our social lives it is perhaps the legal system that faces the most intransigent problems arising from the rhetoric of situatedness, and at least since Jeremy Bentham these problems have been at the forefront of its efforts at rationalization and legitimation. The sustained attack mounted by the eighteenth-century materialist necessitarians against the concepts of will, choice, and responsibility threatened to establish radical idiosyncrasy as the norm for human experience. According to Helvétius, for example, no two persons can ever share the same situation, "precisely the same positions and the same circumstances." Because, for example, no two children ever fall down exactly the same number of times in learning to walk, all events are nonrepeatable and nontransferable.[1] No two biological-historical organisms are the same, so they cannot be imagined to bring to any one common experience the same capacity to respond to it. The same stimuli must then produce different responses, none of which are the responsibility of their bearers. Whatever laws govern such responses are beyond the reach of human intelligence. Identity and accountability are alike fictions.

This extreme recognition of the aporetic character of the rhetoric of situatedness, and of the way that it dismantles any precise meaning for I and me either separately or in manageable conjunction, threatens the credibility of any legislative standard and any jurisprudence that does not tend toward privileging arguments for exoneration. Helvétius's conviction that our lot in life is largely determined by chance did not however lead him to methodological despair but to an intensified social interventionism: education and environmental control can and should do their best to compensate for the effects of social-biological contingencies by creating conditions that are as far as possible the same for all. Social planning can then proceed according to the criterion of probability, which will not be able to predict every or indeed any one idiosyncratic response, but will conform to the law of averages.[2] A defensible legal practice is, however, harder to establish in the light of this knowledge, given that its job is often to respond to precisely the idiosyncratic events that a calculation of probable outcomes and averages can ignore. This is the challenge faced in an exemplary way by Jeremy Bentham, whose efforts at theorizing situatedness would provide the most important model for subsequent attempts to produce manageable policies out of unmanageable epistemologies. Social scientists and legal theorists commonly continue to operate in the traditions that he put into place. It was Bentham who worked out a fully modern recognition of the aporetic nature of situatedness claims, while hanging on to a belief in the availability of a working taxonomy for making them friendly to planners and policymakers and to judges and juries. His belief in situatedness as generating infinite numbers of idiosyncratic events that could yet be reduced to common or compatible models leads him to some remarkably optimistic projections: "Legislators who, having freed themselves from the shackles of authority, have learnt to soar above the mists of prejudice, know as well how to make laws for one country as for another: all they need is to be possessed fully of the facts; to be informed of the local situation, the climate, the bodily constitution, the manners, the legal customs, the religion, of those with whom they have to deal. These are the data they require: possessed of these data, all places are alike." [3] Bentham does not mean that the laws are literally the same, but that they will be in effect compatible and comparable — and thus justifiable — when the competent legislator has adjusted for the conditions of variability, which are therefore assumed to be knowable and measurable. Organizing an empire as well as an internally complex nation-state according to legitimate principles was presumably the condition governing the need for such a rationally positive outcome. But at other times Bentham is more than a little circumspect about the prospects of ever becoming thus "fully possessed of the facts." Climate and geography might be reasonably described as general terms, as they had been by Montesquieu, Herder, and others, but religion and manners could be no simple things in societies projecting any degree of complexity or diversity, and the play of any and all of these on individual "bodily constitution" was, as Helvétius and Holbach had argued, exactly the hole in the bucket through which all efforts at objective and standardized description must dribble out like so much dry sand. But the effort is made nonetheless.

"Of Circumstances Influencing Sensibility," the important sixth chapter of Bentham's major work *Principles of Morals and Legislation*, is at once a tour de force and a deconstruction of the rhetoric of situatedness. There he lists the factors that may affect the "quality or *bias*" of our sensibility. There are thirty-two such factors ranging from the general (government and religion) to the minutely idiosyncratic (bodily health and strength) and seemingly inviting the proliferation of an infinite number of categories and subcategories between them.[4] Only by the most flagrant resort to overlapping general terms can Bentham assert that he can "sum up all the circumstances which can be found to influence the effect of *any* exciting cause." An item such as number 9: "bent or inclination," seems very hard to keep separate from "moral biases," "religious biases," or "sympathetic biases" (numbers 11, 13, and 15), and all of these potentially devolve from numbers 19 and 28: "habitual occupations" and "education." All of these factors govern the degree of pain or pleasure a person may be thought to experience from a given cause: it is the degree of pain that must be made equitable between different punishable individuals, and because of their different situations equal pain will probably not arise from the same punishment. In his presentation of the kinds and sources of different situations Bentham offers up the prospect of a complete accounting. The judge or legislator should sit with this list before him or her, along with another list of the kinds of punishments available (p. 67). He or she should then tailor some sort of fit between the two as it applies best to the individual case or cases under consideration.

Bentham is here less interested in assessing the nature and degree of the various forms of situatedness as applied to culpability than he is in devising an accountable ready-reckoner for the distribution of punishments after judgment has been rendered. He wants to be sure that two persons convicted of the same crime feel as far as possible the same degree of pain when they are punished. But the same conditions pertain to the attribution of criminality in the first place. Bentham knows that each person's original character or "idiosyncrasy" (pp. 56–57) is open to so many and various modifications that we can only hope to specify a "very small number," and this by "the utmost exertion of the human faculties" (p. 79). So the term "disposition" comes into play as a "kind of fictitious entity" (p. 131) to attach motives to individuals for the purposes of judgment. Whether assessing motive or distributing punishment, what we have is a "detailed estimate" (p. 67) and not an objective specification.

The more this estimate can be derived from a printed calculus, the less it is open to misdirection by the prejudices and idiosyncrasies of judges and juries themselves. But there is nothing more consoling than probability at work here. Even the calculus cannot guarantee a completely adequate fit between individual and sentence: there are too many factors involved and too many of them are unknowable. Adam Ferguson, a short time before Bentham, was quite clear about the inadequacies of the rhetoric of situatedness. He thought that we could have no way of explaining, for example, "the manner in which climate may affect the temperament, or foster the genius, of its inhabitants," and that the simplest intuitions about all such relations must remain mysterious and unjustifiable. We are at a loss "how to connect the cause with its supposed effect" and we will remain so until "we have understood what probably we shall never understand, the structure of those finer organs with which the operations of the soul are connected." [5] Problems arise, of course, when someone claims or is given the responsibility to make decisions affecting others based on the assumption that we do have or can achieve such knowledge, and that we have to have it to make fair and proper assessments. The Humean categories of probability and constant conjunction are quite adequate as long as I am making my way through the world in an everyday, uncontested environment, and Bentham's list of the thirty-two items affecting our sensibility is innocent enough as long as it does not become the basis for decisions that have serious consequences either for myself or for others. But as soon as it becomes part of a legislative or judicial apparatus, the conditions become more stringent and the failures or omissions more critically consequential. In the rest of this chapter I will address the role of situatedness in theories of justice and punishment, which cease to be mere theories as they impinge on courtroom practice and on the details of sentencing.

Questions about situatedness have always been significant for the law, because the law is so frequently obliged to investigate and decide on matters of motivation, intention, and blame. The continuing and perhaps increasing urgency of these questions has been recently highlighted by Alan Dershowitz in his 1994 book *The Abuse Excuse*, which warns of the dangers threatening the criminal justice system as the result of juries giving way to arguments made from attributions of situatedness. People are no longer conventionally responsible for their actions as long as their lawyers can convince juries that circumstances obliged them to do what they did. This is what Dershowitz calls the "abuse excuse," and he finds it so prevalent that it completely collapses the traditional distinctions maintained in law between justifications, excuses, and mitigations.[6] According to this account juries have responded to some patently implausible cases made by defense attorneys for the inevitability of behavior that would otherwise be deemed criminal. The list of abuse excuses that Dershowitz presents (pp. 321–41) looks very much like a postmodern version of Bentham's thirty-two items influencing our sensibility, now pursued even further to the point of parody. It includes some obviously reasonable and agreed-on scientific conditions such as fetal alcohol syndrome—forms of situatedness that have behind them strong material and experimental credentials. But there are also some highly opportunistic specifications such as "meek mate" and "fan obsession" syndromes. It is not so much that juries believe these explanations to be definitive and completely convincing, it is rather that they can be persuaded that there is at least enough credibility to such syndromes to cast the shadow of a doubt over the attribution of complete individual responsibility. The viability of some of these coinages in the courtrooms suggests at least that the norm of contemporary cultural commonsense has moved significantly in the direction of giving credit to arguments from situatedness that might formerly have been deemed absurd. Along with this there goes an attention to situatedness conditions that are not at all absurd but that seem to be unknowable and implacably aporetic. Ian Hacking, for example, has described the recent legal history of child abuse, which was not defined as a condition until 1961 and came to be applied to sexual abuse only in 1972.[7] He points out the pattern of recursivity whereby the definition of the syndrome assists in determining and proliferating the symptom; but it is the attention to the symptom itself that interests me. Of course child abuse, sexual and general, has existed and still exists, but it is equally obvious that it can be and surely has been invented or imagined in retrospective memory. The point is that one can hardly ever know for sure which is which and (given its implication in the culture of privacy) that there is mostly no prospect of a way of telling the difference. In other words an event that can often produce only a critically inadequate investigation has become central to the culture of contemporary life, so that one has to wonder, notwithstanding the very real sufferings of many persons, about the motives informing our current attraction to inquiries that must always remain aporetic, so much so that even genuine cases are likely to command a high level of general disbelief. Legal and therapeutic procedures have different functions (there are few truth requirements in therapy) but seem increasingly to overlap and conflict.

Dershowitz's list includes, as I have said, a number of conditions (for example, fetal alcohol syndrome or multiple personality disorder) that most of us would expect to take seriously and to factor into decisions about motivation. It includes other syndromes that are very much under debate and hotly contested, such as attention deficit disorder. But it includes many others that would be visibly outrageous to many or most people, such as "superjock," "fan obsession," and "football widow" syndromes, but that defense lawyers presumably invent with some hope of winning over a jury. No one, it seems, can be sure of being sure that even the most apparently occult and unlikely determinations are not at work in the complex operations of human situatedness. Everyone can think of something to blame in his or her situatedness. After the "Twinkie defense" (where mental incapacitation was attributed to the consumption of junk food) and other such anomalies one can see why Dershowitz is worried, but it is too easy to blame what he calls "a national abdication of personal responsibility" (p. 41), as if the antinomy can be dissolved by a simple recourse to moral character. The retreat on the part of juries from attributing strict responsibility might indeed itself be a reaction against the perceived excessive emphasis on moral individualism encouraged by Protestant and Puritan theology as well as by liberal economic theory.[8] It may also reflect a sense that we are, as individuals, being increasingly deprived of the social and economic support systems whose existence would alone justify stringent standards of personal responsibility by a general agreement that we really might all be starting from the same place in life. If government does nothing (or less and less) for our collective well-being and self-maintenance, why should we fault each other for not meeting its standards for abiding by the law? To immerse oneself in a group defined according to an implacable situatedness may be a psychological relief as well as a hardheaded protective strategy. One thinks again of the workers studied by Sennett and Cobb in *The Hidden Injuries of Class* protecting their inner selves from any implication in the dynamics of the workplace, with its unpredictable sequences of rewards and punishments. At the same time the specification of a biophysical cause for an apparently voluntary act presents the mind or self as betrayed by its situation in the body. This has been the pattern of much religious rhetoric and it fits comfortably with an inherited cultural habit. Dershowitz's description in *The Abuse Excuse* of the critical expansion of the category of mitigating or extenuating circumstances and diminished responsibilities in the minds of contemporary juries has been a crisis waiting to happen in the letter of the law as well as in its spirit, at least since the law became obliged to incorporate the dynamics of atomic individualism in relation to social contract. Nor is it without precedent. In the introduction to this volume I introduced a frivolous instance of the butterfly in Sumatra flapping its wings and affecting my choice from a lunch menu. Bentham himself said something not dissimilar in refuting the absurdity of connecting the cackling of the Capitoline geese with the murder of Henry IV two thousand years later.[9] Bentham, of course, can point to a chain of events. But none are definitive although all are arguable. In what follows I will try to set out some of the terms and (pseudo) solutions of the antinomies of modern British and American law as they pertain to attributions of situatedness.

The formal terms of the debate have changed little since they were announced at the beginning of the third book of Aristotle's *Nicomachean Ethics*: "Since virtue is concerned with passions and actions, and on voluntary passions and actions praise and blame are bestowed, on those that are involuntary pardon, and sometimes also pity, to distinguish the voluntary and the involuntary is presumably necessary for those who are studying the nature of virtue, and useful also for legislators with a view to the assigning both of honours and of punishments."[10] Compulsion and ignorance are the two categories of involuntary behavior, but when compulsion involves some subjective action, as when one is made or persuaded to do something, then the action is "mixed" and can have a voluntary component (p. 965) even when such action is not in the strict sense "chosen" (p. 968). Producing a principle of judgment here is very difficult because there are "many differences in the particular cases" (p. 965). Moreover if voluntary behavior is based on a sense of the good that comes from an act, then we have to deal with the degree to which "different things appear good to different people" (p. 971).

Aristotle here sets out the problem of discriminating between voluntary and involuntary actions, one that has continued to perplex theorists of jurisprudence through succeeding centuries, as it still perplexes us today. At what point do the pressures and circumstances affecting a person's action become so irresistible that it can be said to be involuntary, and thus potentially immune from legal or moral condemnation? When does one's situation become the effective agent in one's behavior, putting aside all considerations of a strictly personal responsibility? Are there such things as strictly personal or plausibly impersonal responsibilities? Traditionally, "children, fools, and madmen" (in the words of Thomas Hobbes) have been deemed nonpersons under the law; that is, they are not held responsible for their actions.[11] These categories are themselves troublesome, for any precise specification of any one person's place on the scale running from sanity to insanity is difficult if not impossible, and while an age of majority can be specified it cannot prescribe every particular instance of a young person's psychological development that falls within it. English common law has tended to deal with these issues as specific instances open to judicial resolution and, occasionally and for many years, to the monarch's discretionary right of pardon. At the same time, acts of passion (rather than premeditation) have been implicitly classed as committed in a state of temporary insanity; they have tended to argue for at least extenuation if not excuse, in reference to "the common infirmity of human nature" (p. 199). According to John Locke, the sane man and the madman are two persons, even when they happen to inhabit the same body, "which is somewhat explained by our way of speaking in English, when we say such an one *is not himself*, or is *besides himself*." [12] How does one put into practice a theory of punishment founded in notions of individual responsibility—and thus requiring complete and partial exemptions (excuses and extenuations) for those not responsible—without inviting abuse and misapplication? How can we be sure that we are not punishing the innocent and acquitting the guilty because of an ignorance or overadmission of situational criteria and mitigating circumstances?

The answer is of course that we never can be sure, although this knowledge has not always caused the same degree of anxiety in all who have pondered it in different times and places. William Blackstone was not hopeful about a scientific scale of crimes and corresponding punishments: "But, if that be too romantic an idea, at least a wise legislator will mark the principal divisions, and not assign penalties of the first degree to offences of an inferior rank." [13] In other words, the judge must live by his professional wits. All "pleas and excuses" are to be estimated according to "want or defect of will," for without a "vitious will" there can be no crime (4: 20–21). Thus, notwithstanding an accepted age of majority, "one lad of eleven years old may have as much cunning as another of fourteen" (4: 23) and should be judged accordingly. Blackstone makes an explicit address to the argument from situatedness in relation to drunkenness. It has been suggested (by Montesquieu), he says, that drunkenness is a function of climate. Northern Europeans drink because of "custom" and "constitutional necessity," southern Europeans out of "choice" and an inclination to luxury, so that there is less criminality attached to drunkenness in Germany than in Spain. Blackstone is not sympathetic to this position: "The law of England, considering how easy it is to counterfeit this excuse, and how weak an excuse it is, (though real) will not suffer any man thus to privilege one crime by another" (4: 26).

Situatedness, then, can be a factor in judgment insofar as it impinges on the attribution of "want or defect" of will, but only within a limited series of categories: defects of understanding or the presence of elements of chance and compulsion. The same logic governs Sir Robert Chambers's case for exemptions from punishment, and it remains conventional in criminal law to this day.[14] As there came to be increasingly less reliance on the use of pardons, mitigation clauses seem to have become more specific and more important to the written law;[15] but Blackstone's categories seem to have survived more or less intact. There lurks behind and within them an instability that always impinges on decisions relying on intuition and circumstantial evidence. This instability was maximized by the necessitarians of the eighteenth century, to the point of proposing a doctrine of complete extenuation in the spheres of motive and intention. Holbach (under his nom de plume of Mirabaud) saw man as "nothing more, than a passive instrument in the hands of necessity," so that those we call "wicked" are compelled to act after a different mode, whether or not they maintain the appearances of choosing and willing.

The criterion for judgment, if there is to be such a thing, must then be different: "Nature does not make men either good or wicked: she combines machines, more or less active, mobile, energetic . . . they can only be called bad or good, relative to the influence they have on the beings of his species." [16] It becomes, in other words, utilitarian.

The utilitarian project, as we have already seen in Bentham's foundational account, was significantly engaged in an effort to cope with the consequences of the radical situatedness it recognized as fundamental to human behavior: fundamental, but ultimately indescribable. Utilitarian theory took up the task of justifying a maximally diversified, complex society within which more and more subcultures emanating from different occupational sectors and kinds of situatedness were requiring political, economic, and statistical recognition. The impossible complexity of causes determining human acts had been one factor persuading Bentham to focus instead on trying to describe their probable effects. All punishment is regrettable, even evil; it can only be justified by the greater good accruing to the whole than would result from its omission or remission. So, in order to avoid executive anarchy, Bentham came up with a probability criterion: we should seek out those punishments least likely to be radically affected by individual variations among those to be punished. It is not a perfect system but it is one with a defensible rationale. It is rendered even less perfect because, despite the emphasis on effects rather than motives and intentions, some reckoning with these items is necessary in order to convince the public that the punishment does in some way fit the crime and that motive and intention are part of any calculation about the nature and degree of the crime. The problem of situatedness thus reappears and continues to inform both judgment and sentencing. Later in this chapter I will look at the topography of the aporia into which Bentham is reluctant to descend, in the form that it appears in the career of Clarence Darrow and more generally in the American legal tradition. Before I do so, however, it is important to register another and different response to the seemingly insoluble problems presented to legal theory by a strong awareness of situatedness of the sort that Bentham articulates: the alternative or analogue discovered in morality by Kant and the German idealists.

Morality and legality are different doctrines with different traditions.

Moral inquiry emphasizes motives and their qualities, and it can be carried on with relatively little concern for actions. Legality, on the other hand, is principally interested in actions and their consequences. But the two concerns overlap, most of all in a culture whose legal decisions are carried out in reference to a category of subjectivity that is also closely described in the language of moral worth. (Dershowitz's emphasis on personal responsibility can be seen as part of the contemporary displacement of politics by ethics, which I will discuss in chapter 6.) Utilitarian theory moved a long way away from any basis in morality. William Paley provides an extreme statement of the distance traveled in opining that punishment is not about "the satisfaction of justice, but the prevention of crimes." Crimes are not to be punished in relation to a standard of guilt, "but in proportion to the difficulty and necessity of preventing them." [17] Much more bluntly than Bentham, Paley dismisses the tendency toward excuse or extenuation that comes along with a sense of the power of situatedness as it informs any decision about guilt, arguing against the "over-strained scrupulousness, or weak timidity, of juries, which demands often such proof of a prisoner's guilt, as the nature and secrecy of his crime scarce possibly admit of; and which holds it the part of a *safe* conscience, not to condemn any man, whilst there exists the minutest possibility of his innocence" (2: 297–98). Paley wants us to avoid giving way to the "uncertainty that belongs to all human affairs" (p. 298), and thus to extricate ourselves from the morass of imponderables that faces us when we are trying to adapt punishment to exact moral judgments. His advice is that we consult circumstantial evidence and the preponderance of evidence.

At the same time, as we have seen, morality and legality overlap even for Bentham insofar as the credibility of punishment depends at the very least on its not operating in direct opposition to moral opinion. For example, only outrage would follow a decision to punish someone just because the crime needs a punishment, notwithstanding the perceived innocence of the particular person accused. And given the connection between morality and legality in the culture of modernity, with its interest in atomic individualism, one can see that there is available a response quite different from the utilitarian, a response based on strengthening rather than weakening the link between law and personal integrity. Punishments (legal judgments) might then appear all the more appropriate

and justified the more consonant they are with a moral judgment, insofar as there is a working communal standard for moral behavior. But this
will only work as long as moral judgments are as far as possible kept clear
of the insoluble problems presented when one tries to assess guilt in an
environment conditioned by belief in the strong power of situatedness.

This alternative is articulated in Kant's writings on punishment. For
Kant, the (human) subject must first be habituated to a notion of morality
before any legal decisions can be rendered functional and intelligible.
At the same time, legal decisions can reflect back on and help publicize
moral behavior. The mutual goal of both is the cultivation of the sense of
a sphere of freedom, most readily intuited in one's struggle against one's
natural inclinations. Kant is indecisive about the degree to which this
moral intuition can be understood as universal rather than as cultural-
historical. He sees the Gospels as making recognizable the "full purity
and holiness of the moral law," implying the necessary context of a Judeo-
Christian culture for its growth, but he adds as a qualifier the phrase "although indeed it dwells in our own reason." [18] Generally he is emphatic
about the foundational status of the moral instinct as "an involuntary and
irresistible impulse in our nature, which compels us to pass a judgment
with the force of a law upon our actions, visiting us with an inner pain
when we do evil and an inner pleasure when we do good, in accordance
with the relation our actions bear to the law" (p. 69). Thus we are our own
judge and jury, "condemning or acquitting ourselves" (p. 69).

This is of course exactly the sort of culture-bound reasoning against
which Nietzsche will produce the counterexample of the pagan Greeks,
among others. If ethics is itself a historically situated practice, then the
appeal of Kant's argument as an attempted solution to the imponderable
problems of situatedness is radically qualified. For him the task is, as it
had been for Calvin and Luther, one of desituating oneself from the persuasions of contingent circumstances and inclinations, which Kant will
often call "habit" (for example, p. 64). Situations are an inhibition on the
proper exercise of the moral law; far from being an excusing or extenuating condition, they are completely contrary and hostile to its emergence.
Thus we are to struggle against situation-generated inclinations, rather
than invoking them as mitigating clauses in explaining bad behavior. To
the degree that we succeed, we are in the moral sphere. And by effectively

doing justice on ourselves within this sphere, we preempt the need for legal response in the first place, detaching ourselves also from the contingent decisions of other judges and juries who are susceptible to their own empirical interests and constraints.

Kant's philosophy is famously dependent on gestures aimed at desituating the self. Proper aesthetic judgment, like moral judgment, is only possible in a pure space of nonempirical contemplation. It is a Stoic ethic, according to which we can be a source of happiness to ourselves (and minimal competition for others) only as long as the scope of our needs and desires is narrowly regimented. Whereas Bentham and Paley moved away from the language of morality in order to defend the realm of law, Kant works to minimize the need for law by playing up morality. Both sides, however, pitch their cases against the deviations that are latent in arguments appealing to situatedness conditions. Both recognize the problems posed by such arguments for any workable jurisprudence. Bentham allows for the authority of the situated judiciary insofar as it embodies the required standards for the common good, within and with reference to which all acts occur. Only then can the judge and jury be deemed independent of the pressures resulting from their own particular situations (which the modern critical legal studies movement, for example, has argued to be impossible). Kant seeks to displace all external judges and juries to the point of maximum redundancy.

Kant's priorities are further argued out and tightened by Fichte and Hegel. Fichte insists that all gestures of self-foundation and postulation entail assumptions about the similar status of others, to the degree that we can only *think* our own freedom as already necessarily restricted by the rights of others to the same freedoms.[19] This is a legal relation, and it is binding as such even as it remains self-apprehended (pp. 63–67). Violation of the laws is thus a violation of that element of self which makes us free beings; such actions then bring about an abrogation of rights (pp. 343–46). Evils done against others thus become evils done against the self (p. 358). The atomic individual's most critical situation is that within the society of others which is the state, and not his or her idiosyncratic relation to local and particular determinations of the sort listed by Bentham as capable of modifying sensibility. Because freedom is defined as freedom from exactly these sorts of contingent determinations, the person who invokes them as excuse is in fact arguing for a heavier rather than a lighter punishment. Thus the habitual drunkard (to take the standard instance) is, in pleading this condition, confessing that "he changes himself into a beast on a fixed principle, and that he is, therefore, not fit to live among rational beings" (p. 351). The argument from situatedness becomes exacerbating rather than extenuating. The more it is invoked, the heavier the punishment deserved. Claiming the power of habit or compulsion is by definition removing oneself from the properly human characteristic of freedom.

The same goes for Hegel, who also works to diminish the operation of extenuating circumstances, seeking to limit their consideration to the sphere of pardons and to exclude them from that of rights. One should not, he argues, allow a tolerance for crimes of passion as somehow mitigating guilt, because to do so means "failing to treat the criminal in accordance with the right and honour due to him as a man; for the nature of man consists precisely in the fact that he is essentially something universal, and not a being whose knowledge is an abstractly momentary and piecemeal affair." This said, we should not worry whether a criminal has a clear idea of the nature of his crime. The claim that he does not only seems to "preserve the right of his subjectivity," while it actually "deprives him of his indwelling nature as intelligent." [20] Implicitly, his failure to divorce himself from the persuasions of his situation, whether momentary or customary, renders him less than properly human. Punishment restores his humanity in that it is to be understood as "the reconciliation of the criminal with himself, i.e. with the law known by him as his own and as valid for him and his protection" (p. 141). Even bad luck, within this position, must, for example, be understood and anticipated by me as "an embodiment of my own willing" (p. 251), to the degree that I have failed to prepare for the inadvertent consequences of my acts. My task is always to isolate the universal element within the particular situation; when I fail to do so I am failing as a human being.

This strong conjunction of the moral and the legal in Fichte and Hegel must appear to the contemporary liberal a rather harsh doctrine. It is a maximization of the responsibilities of an ideal atomic subject and a minimization of the "human" failures of that same subject, especially those for which it might be claimed that one is not responsible, including all the pressures of situatedness. In its very extremity it is a clear antithesis to the options embraced by the juries about which Alan Dershowitz writes, and which he fears are increasingly typical of the contemporary legal climate.[21] The majority of those claiming Dershowitz's "abuse excuse" would simply be, for Fichte and Hegel, less than fully human and deserving of pity or exile but not of legal extenuation or excuse. But the Kantian tradition has not proved significantly constitutive of late-twentieth-century anglo-American judicial practices. If Kant had ever introduced himself "as a rational philosopher functioning in the Pietist culture of northern Germany" it would only have been to dismiss such situating rhetoric as irrelevant. (Hegel famously tried to have it both ways by suggesting that the moment of nineteenth-century northern Europe was also the moment of the emergence of the universal; and Lukács would say the same of the "perspective" of the proletariat on and in history.) No one in the liberal-individualist tradition can afford to be as comfortable with the dismissal of situatedness claims as Fichte and Hegel (especially) seem to be. Indeed, the pattern in the United States in the nineteenth century was quite different, as we will now see.

Situatedness in American Law Alan Dershowitz's polemic is an American polemic, perhaps even a Californian polemic (it being a convention of cultural commentary that what happens to America happens first in California). American law has worked to privilege situatedness in one simple and functional sense. The fact that an act committed in one state can be interpreted differently from the same act committed in another inspires a very primary sense of the importance of situations. A contrary tendency may be imputed to the operations of the Supreme Court, and to the national emphasis on codification rather than common law, along with the efficient distribution of legal records between the different states. But the United States, for whatever reasons, does seem to have generated a high awareness of the claims of situatedness as determining or modifying behavior. The visible diversity of a traditionally multicultural society and the positive validation of entrepreneurial freedom, along with many other conditions to which I will be referring throughout this inquiry, seem to have produced a rhetoric acutely sensitive to the conflicts and paradoxes of being an individual in a collective, so that the limits of freedom and constraint are open to (and arguably insist on) the sort of constant renegotiation of which the instability of the *azza* sentence is but one example. This issue seems to have become especially urgent in the postwar–cold war period, as we will see in the next chapter. But it was alive and operative long before that.

Morton Horwitz has described the American legal system after 1776 as an evolutionary practice responding to the changing economic needs or preferences of entrepreneurial capitalism. After a postrevolutionary period marked by suspicion of the English common law and a fear of the power of judges, which in turn lead to a strong desire for codification, Horwitz finds a new notion of the law becoming current around 1820 and marked by a sense of its usefulness for "promoting socially useful conduct." [22] He identifies such broad tendencies as the erosion of strict liability, the displacing of nuisance by negligence decisions, and the incorporation of the legal profession into the political-commercial establishment, along with the appearance of laws favoring the principle of competition and embodying a high valuation of individualism. In legislation relating to insurance, Horwitz notices a tendency to "conceive of a greater and greater portion of activity as appropriately within the realm of chance" (p. 228), thereby allowing corporations to absolve themselves of obligations for which they might otherwise have been held responsible. Thus, for example, bankruptcy claims began to be tolerated as a means of writing off debt, with such failures being deemed the result of "uncontrollable" forces rather than of any personal imprudence (pp. 228–29).

In other words, and to apply Horwitz's argument to the matter of situatedness, it became allowable to make reference to circumstances outside of one's control as a legal defense against acts for which one might otherwise have been held responsible, and this happened as a means of minimizing the inhibitions on both corporate and individual risk-taking on which the economy in general and even the legal profession were becoming increasingly dependent.[23] Risk at this point was a positively validated cultural energy, one that could be accommodated more readily than the extended and massively complexified present-day category about which Ulrich Beck and Anthony Giddens have written so well. Horwitz here provides the beginnings of a history for situatedness in

American law, and perhaps in American culture more generally. He suggests that the general profits (or "good") of an undefined or ambiguous accountability model were proving well worth the inconveniences of an occasional, visibly inadequate test case. If he is correct then he goes a long way toward explaining why our culture continues to require the display of legal and pseudolegal cases (such as the Hill-Thomas hearings) which seem designed *not* to produce clear resolutions and decisions. These displays (and they include a number of the notorious criminal cases of the twentieth century) work to involve the general population in the gesture of apparent decision making. Even as the displays divide that population, they incorporate the ordinary person into a process of confirming the legal system as accessible and accountable to us all. If the outcome appears to be often a matter of chance and even of vested interest, then the effect on a society saturated with the rhetoric of democratic opportunities and freedoms is ultimately confirming, even when it also generates an inevitable cynicism. In other words, when "they" are seen to be corrupt or incompetent or simply limited in basic human ways, then "we" are justified in being no better. We can thereby give ourselves permission to participate even more enthusiastically in the risk-taking culture than we do already. The personal morality tradition represented by Kant and his followers remains as an alternative to the implicit directives of the legal establishment; but because it is not integrated with or adjusted to that system (or to the social contract in general, in the manner that Fichte and Hegel recommended), it can only appear (in verdicts) as the punitive application of an ideologically fantasized common standard or (among defendants) as sheer idiosyncrasy, just another version of the vigilante syndrome. That is one of the dangers of turning to a rhetoric of personal morality as the proper solution to the perceived current excesses of arguments from situatedness.

Situatedness, in light of Horwitz's historical explanation, necessarily comes to be available simultaneously either as a power to be appealed to for excuse or as a hostile pressure to be resisted, according to one's needs at any given moment. Cultural coherence seems to require logical contradiction: one can claim either passive obedience to situations or heroic resistance to them, and sometimes both at the same time. Thus we are regaled with images of persons trodden down by their circumstances as well as those of persons rising above them, in about equal proportions. Neither of these options is itself fully "the" American way; the American way is in fact the insecure embrace of both at once, the dramatization of antinomy. The degree to which arguments privileging situatedness occupy this purposively unstable and malleable position within the culture makes them more readily available for polemical and opportunistic uses than for philosophically sustained, coherent rationalizations. The investment of institutional rhetoric in presenting the one as if it were the other opens up the sorts of stresses that are handed down to individuals as they try to articulate what it is to be a subject.

Legal theorists have wrestled with this antinomy but only occasionally to the point of facing the aporia. Oliver Wendell Holmes's *The Common Law*, first published in 1881, follows a utilitarian emphasis in defending the law's relative indifference to situational considerations in favor of the requirements of the "general good." [24] Holmes's standard is that of prudent and reasonable persons, average persons, so that in liability determinations "minute differences of character are not allowed for. The law considers, in other words, what would be blameworthy in the average man, the man of ordinary intelligence and prudence. . . . If we fall below the level in those gifts, it is our misfortune" (p. 87). The duty of juries is to normalize themselves to this standard: "The theory or intention of the law is not that the feeling of approbation or blame which a particular twelve may entertain should be the criterion. They are supposed to leave their idiosyncrasies to one side, and to represent the feeling of the community. The ideal average prudent man . . . is a constant, and his conduct under given circumstances is theoretically always the same" (pp. 88–89). Holmes's position has much in common with Adam Smith's use of the persona of the "impartial spectator";[25] something in common with Bentham's commitment to a use-value criterion; and something very loosely analogous to Kant's emphasis on self-generated moral propriety. But it specifies none of these options to the point where it might exclude anything of the others. Holmes is, in the traditional way, anxious to exclude radical claims for the mitigating function of situations. He is not at all, for this reason, an apologist for the juries described by Dershowitz— quite the opposite, in fact. But because the "ideal average prudent man" defines himself in relation to a "community" standard rather than to a posited universal or at least translocal standard, any jury members seeking to form themselves along these lines in any literal fashion are going to find themselves facing problems rather than solutions. Holmes's invocation of the "community" is an instance of the very problems that a legal system in a highly diversified culture must solve; it cannot function as a foundational intuition for further decisions in a world where the "community" is itself a localizable and disputed part rather than the whole that Holmes presumably intends it to be. The model is thus tautological. In order to offset the problems posed for legal judgment by radical or strong individual or group situatedness, Holmes invokes the authority of the situatedness of the jury. Insofar as he requires the jury at least to attempt the gesture of self-production, he might persuade them to shed their idiosyncrasies as mere individuals. But that cannot guarantee that they can become an adequately representative "community." Their collective situatedness is more general than it was for each of them as individuals, but it can be neither universal nor empirically (locally) comprehensive. Twelve persons, however good and true, cannot represent or apprehend the complex divisions of interest, occupation, and affiliation that have preoccupied the theorists of modernization.

In a second book covering the period up to 1960, Horwitz describes a move in Holmes's thought away from attempted objectivism and toward a compromise with what he describes as the irresistible pressures requiring a recognition of the pragmatic and political (or as we would now say "ideological") operations of the law.[26] In "The Path of the Law," written in 1897, Holmes concludes that the only meaningful definition of the law is a prediction about "what the courts will do." They do not obey the logic of a pure system; they are historical creatures, creatures of their situations, and as such must be studied historically if they are to provide the basis of a prediction.[27] This shift from the attempted objectivism of The Common Law fits the profile of the larger movement Horwitz describes, a movement toward understanding the law as a means of conflict resolution in situ (pragmatically) rather than ex cathedra. In response to this tendency there were renewed efforts at codification, especially between 1870 and 1900, so that the resulting legal practice was one of checking and balancing.[28] Commentators such as Nicholas St. John Green and jurists such as Francis Wharton understood the slippery slope that stretched before the courts as soon as they did away with their dependence on finite, objectivist arguments.[29] But the need to pay attention to a bottomless and insoluble situatedness had become a prominent part of the American legal imagination.

Holmes is a model of rationalist ambition when he is set beside Clarence Darrow. Darrow is quite rightly a hero of the liberal tradition for his opposition to the death penalty and his stand on behalf of the common man. He inherited from the necessitarians a firm belief in the power of physical attributes and external environment in determining acts and the mental states behind them. Punishment, he found, had no effect in lessening crime because crime itself derived from circumstances beyond the control of its perpetrators. Criminals, he believed, tended to emerge from the poorer classes and to be mentally and physically weaker than other persons.[30] Physical constitution and environment together determine criminal behavior. Because neither element is within the control of individual will, no responsibility can be adduced for criminal acts: thus we should not "hang or pen" anyone for "having not grown as large, as tall, or as symmetrical as the ordinary man"; and because crimes are "indigenous to the particular soil that gives them birth," it is the soil rather than the individual that must be changed (pp. 88–89). As to the individuals, we had better try love and charity rather than punishment if we are to hope to affect them in positive ways (pp. 178–79).

Darrow emphasizes two kinds of situatedness, materialist (the mind in the body) and culturalist (the person's in the world), to cast doubt on the propriety of any punitive decision. No one can know enough about another to pass judgment, because too much information is missing. Darrow restates Bentham's problem, although not in the spirit of Bentham's attempt to pass it by: "To understand fully another's life would require infinite pains and such research as no judge could give or pretend to give" (p. 107). It is exactly this missing information that "bears upon the real character of the man and should go to show whether, on the whole, he deserves blame or praise, and the extent of each" (p. 108). In other words, the complexities of situatedness are such as to deprive judgment of any authority. Moreover, the judge himself is limited by his own situation: "At his best he takes with him to the judgment tribunal every prejudice, bias and belief that his education surroundings and heredity have left on him" (p. 109). The "ideal man" he constructs in order to normalize his standards of judgment is a figment of himself and his kind. Holmes's "ideal average prudent man" must be understood as nothing more than a distillation of the qualities aspired to by the socially established and affluent.

Clearly, any complete acceptance of Darrow's arguments would mean the end of all punishment and prosecution, as well as a complete reorientation if not dismantling of the law as it had existed for many centuries. Total understanding would prescribe total pardon; interim or partial understanding, which is all we have, can therefore not support punishment. As polemical gestures against, for example, the common-sense approval of the death penalty, Darrow's positions are powerful and I believe persuasive: they make both clear and compassionate sense. Because the law is, however, still motivated to recognize the opportunities for critical decision making by atomistic individuals driven by moral character or mere prudence, it has not yet gone over to any complete embrace of Darrow's arguments.[31] Their force is fully apparent in his famous plea of 1924, in defense of Richard Loeb and Nathan Leopold, who were on trial for murder in Chicago. Loeb and Leopold were eighteen and nineteen, respectively, at the time of the crime (to which they confessed), and thus were positioned in the grey area of the minority-majority distinction. Darrow always calls them "boys," and they are not technically adults; but neither are they at an age where some rational self-control or voluntary will would be deemed implausible. Darrow does not argue for acquittal but for the nonimposition of the death penalty. He is not seeking to prove innocence but rather something less than complete culpability. His arguments are therefore uninhibited in their opportunism, and they articulate various declarations of cultural and biophysical situatedness in a very pure and extreme form.

Darrow invokes an "infinite number of causes reaching back to the beginning . . . working out in these boys' minds."[32] Richard Loeb becomes the product of "the infinite forces that conspired to form him," which would take "infinite knowledge" to describe (pp. 55–56). His very wealth is seen to have conspired against him by depriving him of ordinary pleasures and ordinary human conduct: "Wealth has its misfortunes" (p. 63). (And in this Darrow anticipates something like what Dershowitz and others will call the "superjock syndrome"!) Or perhaps Loeb read the wrong books. In summary, "he was not his own father; he was not his own mother; he was not his own grandparents. All of this was handed to him. He did not surround himself with governesses and wealth. He did not make himself" (p. 71). The other defendant, Nathan Leopold, is described as having read too much Nietzsche at an early age, from which he acquired a belief in the "superman" (p. 80). It is one of "life's infinite chances" (p. 83) that this "boy" came into contact with these books; the publishers that produce them and the professors who teach them must be held just as responsible as the accused (pp. 84–85). And it is a further chance that the two boys came together, because neither would have committed the crime without the other.

Darrow's plea uses radical situatedness arguments in the necessitarian mode almost *ad absurdum* not to prove innocence but to instill the shadow of a doubt about complete culpability in the traditional sense that assumes voluntary will. He mixes long-durational Darwinian explanations that operate very slowly through the generations with short-term learned behavior patterns that belong with culture, such as the reading of books. Perhaps he was himself thinking of the Nietzsche of *On the Genealogy of Morals* who summarized economically the whole deception surrounding arguments both for and against situatedness: "Today it is impossible to say for certain *why* people are really punished: all concepts in which an entire process is semiotically concentrated elude definition: only that which has no history is definable." [33] Darrow succeeded in heading off the death penalty: the "boys" were sentenced to life imprisonment. But it seems unlikely that the jurors fully believed all of Darrow's arguments about wealth and reading Nietzsche, or perhaps even those affirming medical evidence about the boys' deficiency in ordinary emotions. In his autobiography Darrow more or less admits that the defendants' lives were saved mostly by precedent: only two persons of their age had ever been sentenced to death in Illinois, and they had been offered life sentences if they would plead guilty; hardly anyone pleading guilty (as Darrow had the boys plead) had received the death penalty.[34] Because Darrow is engaged in a particular case with particular (and I would say admirable) objectives, and arguing in the negative (against the death penalty), he is not compelled to work out the full philosophical or meth-

odological implications of his examples, nor to prove their precise pertinence beyond introducing the shadow of a doubt. He writes as if he were
a novelist, and with the privileges that the novel affords of giving imaginative life to plausible events not to be held up to scientific inspection.
And, indeed, novelist he was: in 1905 he published *An Eye for an Eye*, which
tells the story of a condemned man's last conversation during the long
night before his hanging. The book is nothing less than an extended account of the man's situatedness: "It kind of seems to me that I never had
a very good chance." [35] Poverty, despair, and occupation (the high-risk,
high-tension job of switchman in the railway yards) impel him toward
an inevitable doom, with the death sentence imposed, against the legal
grain, because of a contingent urgency in the public concern about violent crime. Darrow used the same techniques in the Loeb-Leopold plea
that he uses in the novel; as it happened the Loeb-Leopold case would
itself become a novel some thirty years later, and in other hands.[36]

Darrow may be seen as anticipating the recent visible incursion of the
literary mode into legal theory, but his work was also and in its own times
consonant with the legal realism tendency of the 1920s and 1930s.[37] In
the Loeb-Leopold case, and in others like it, the function of the radical
argument from situatedness is, as I have said, compassionate. Because
of the absolute nature of the death penalty, it can only be defended (if it
can be defended) in contexts of complete certainty about both culpability
and use-value. The appeal to situatedness, and to the fuzzy knowledge or
protoknowledge it brings up, forever removes that certainty. But situatedness has no simple or single explanatory power in itself, nor is it liberal in itself or in principle. One could, for example, find oneself arguing
against the release of a possible repeat offender because one is not sure
that the terms of his situatedness have been predictably amended to the
good by the experience of reformatory environments or drug treatments.
But one can say that the higher the stakes, the more careful one should be
with arguments dependent on attributions of situatedness. Thus courts
have been less prone to admit them into adjudications of lesser crimes
where the punishment is not capital or critical. (That they are beginning
to do so now is one of the causes of Dershowitz's concern.) The appeal
to situatedness is polemically useful while remaining philosophically indecisive. This is exactly how extreme arguments from situatedness have

tended to function, both in law and in other social rhetorics. They can and do achieve local persuasion not so much because they can be proved positively but because they cannot be dismissed with absolute conviction as irrelevant. As soon as we move beyond a notion of strict liability for acts regardless of motivation then the way is open for speculation about "life's infinite chances." Nietzsche again: "Only that which has no history is definable." The admission of this "fact" into our deliberations has the result not of specifying any precise degree of determination but of making the whole process of causal ascription fundamentally indeterminate.

Such indeterminacy may well be the long-term consequence of legitimating the society of risk whose emergence Morton Horwitz described in the early nineteenth century, and whose latest incarnations have been made central to late modernity as described by Giddens and Beck: that our most urgent and consequential decisions about personal responsibility are bound to be enacted within a paradigm of ambiguity, skepticism, and provisionality. So it may be that this very indeterminacy, and not any solution of it, is the cultural logic of appeals to situatedness. The apparently desired solutions are not available; they are denied by a "deliberate" social-historical framing, one that has rendered the law unstable to precisely the extent that literature (for example), with its tolerance for ambiguity, has been empowered as a vehicle for our moral self-inquiry and even for our political self-modeling. Our history then develops not as progressive but as repetitive and cyclic, favoring one extreme only to resuscitate the other, and sometimes both at the same time. Michael Sandel has written an important history of Supreme Court decisions in which he traces a tendency after about 1945 toward increasingly treating persons "as free and independent selves, unencumbered by moral ties antecedent to choice." [38] Sandel disagrees with this emphasis and proposes as an alternative what he calls an "encumbered self" conceived in relation to, and perhaps even significantly constituted by, intersubjective, communal factors such as religion or other group affiliations; in other words a version of the situated self, a phrase Sandel himself at times employs (for example, p. 84). In decisions about freedom of speech, the relation of religion to the state, and obscenity laws, Sandel finds the Court increasingly sympathetic to the "rights" of the atomic individual to choose his or her preferred satisfactions. [39] The same tendency appeared in the most fashionable political slogan of the 1980s, "getting government off the backs of the people." But this is only part of the picture. Sandel astutely points out that the modern state consists of "a vast network of dependencies and expectations largely ungoverned by voluntary agreement or acts of consent," where governments and corporations have significantly limited the territory open to individual choice. Thus "the freely choosing, autonomous self has come to prevail in constitutional law just at the time it has faded as a plausible self-image in contract law, and in economic life generally . . . we seek an independence in our personal lives that eludes us in our public life. It is as if the triumph of autonomy in matters of religion, speech and sexual morality were a kind of consolation for the loss of agency in an economic and political order increasingly governed by vast structures of power" (pp. 117–18).

John Dewey, whom Sandel cites in this context (p. 204), had made the same point in 1927 in *The Public and Its Problems*. Individualism as a doctrine in philosophy, political theory, and (eventually) psychology came to the fore at exactly the moment when the individual person was in the "process of complete submergence" in social life itself, which was coming to be governed more and more by "mechanical forces and vast impersonal organizations."[40] This schism guarantees "the enormous ineptitude of the individualistic philosophy to meet the needs and direct the factors of the new age" (p. 96), and it goes to the heart of the syndrome I am investigating—that whereby the antinomies of situatedness are in some way manufactured and controlled. The experience of floundering back and forth between the rhetoric of self-determination and choice and that of passive response to circumstances beyond one's control is not an immanent one but is contrived and historically generated. It is not of course the product of a conspiracy, of a bunch of people sitting in a secret room holding the filaments of culture and politics between their fingers. But it is contrived nonetheless as ideology by and for a set of forces and interests that are not innately human or natural and that should be open to question notwithstanding their profound control of the common language and of the habits it supports. Dewey locates back in the seventeenth century, with Locke and Descartes, the origin of the schism between the language of individualism and the facts of social life, and he sees the American and French revolutionary moments as confirming and extending it.

This evolution, he says, was not inevitable: "There was no logic which rendered necessary the appeal to the individual as an independent and isolated being. In abstract logic, it would have sufficed to assert that some primary groupings had claims which the state could not legitimately encroach upon. In that case, the celebrated modern antithesis between the Individual and Social, and the problem of their reconciliation, would not have arisen. The problem would have taken the form of defining the relationship which non-political groups bear to political union" (pp. 87–88). These insights are profound; they are behind much of the ongoing debate about the First Amendment and they provide a pedigree for much contemporary "communitarian" thinking. Dewey is of course well aware that there must have been powerful forces working to make sure that avoiding antithesis was a road not taken; aware also that such matters are never adjudicated at the level of "abstract logic," and that there were and are just enough institutions that appear to obey the rubric of atomic individualism (private property being one) to ensure that the rhetoric can appear to be just about believable. But his account of the necessary inefficiency of what I have been calling arguments for situatedness and definitive findings about situatedness is crucial and represents at least one possible beginning for thinking through the muddle that we are in.

It will surely seem to many that the consequences of admitting to the aporetic nature of arguments based on specifications or denials of situatedness are, in the legal sphere as elsewhere, threatening to both our intellectual self-confidence (our desire to know and to believe that we know) and to our hopes for clear and justifiable decision making. This need not be the case. Clarence Darrow left his jury with the shadow of a doubt, unsure about whom finally to blame for the Loeb-Leopold murders, or at least sure that the recourse to capital punishment did not fit what could be said about the crime. The system worked: Darrow's plea dissuaded the jury from invoking irrevocable punishment. The fuzziness of the situatedness claim did lead to a clear and reasonable outcome. A significant degree of responsibility was attributed to the "boys," and a lesser but critical degree to society. Responsibility was not denied but disseminated. Charles Horton Cooley, one of the founding fathers of American academic sociology, had previously made the point in his *Human Nature and the Social Order* (first published in 1902) that the origin of "wrong" should be sought not in "individual will" but in the two most familiar forms of situatedness: "heredity and social transmission."

> It tends, I think, not to diminish responsibility but to change its character, to make it an organic whole, including every individual whose will contributes to the wrong in question. It makes more people responsible, and mitigates, without removing, the blame that falls upon the immediate wrong-doer. When a boy is caught stealing brass fixtures from an unfinished house the judge of the Juvenile Court will first of all blame the boy, but, far from stopping there, he will bring into court also the leader of the gang who set him the example, and his parents, who failed to give him suitable care and discipline. The judge may well censure, also, the school authorities for not interesting him in healthy work and recreation, and the city government and influential classes for failing to provide a better environment for him to grow up in. The tendency of any study of indirect causes is to fix more and more responsibility upon those who have wealth, knowledge, and influence, and therefore the power to bring a better state of things to pass.[41]

This habit of thinking was central to, for example, the New Deal generation of policymakers, and it is not extinct even in our current climate of self-making and go-getting. But it is threatening and threatened because its fuzziness does not sit comfortably with the rhetoric of outcomes and clear accountability. If we are all like boys stealing housewares, all embedded in circumstances beyond our control and all thus metaphorically below the age of responsibility, where can that responsibility finally be located? All too often it has been concluded that because attention to one or another form of situatedness does not make criminal behavior disappear, and because the chain of responsibility is now far too complex and confusing to be limited to a patrician conglomerate of "wealth, knowledge, and influence," or at least one that can be identified as such, then we are justified in returning to a model of "individual will," all other options having proved indescribable and inconclusive.

The symptoms of this return to simplicities are not just to be found in the recent discrediting of ameliorative and welfare politics and "government" control but in the new enthusiasm for carrying out the death sentence, one macabre form of seeming to put an end to the problem of responsibility that seeks to militate against the checks and balances also available in the legal system. Yet it can be said that a culture as dependent as ours is on playing both sides of the antinomy of situatedness, affirming and denying it at the same time, should be called to a more critical self-reflection above all at such points where its decisions are nonreversible and absolute. Such is the case with the continued existence and indeed the renewed approval of the death penalty. The befuddled awareness of complex causes leads to or tolerates, it seems, an appetite for crude pseudosolutions. It is the strong conclusion of my account of the rhetoric of situatedness that the death penalty should be held to be completely indefensible on evidentiary grounds. That it is not so held suggests that there is much to be done in understanding and applying that rhetoric, especially if it is the case, as I think it is, that obfuscation rather than understanding is the unavowed goal of our inherited and contemporary historical force field. In the following chapter I look at how the rhetoric of situatedness has fared at the hands of some of the social scientists who are the successors of Dewey and Cooley. More than any other discipline, social science has taken as its very reason for being the elucidation of the nature and consequences of human situatedness.

3. With God on Our Side? The Science of Character

The End of Social Science? A number of specialists are telling us that the social sciences are in trouble, and perhaps in a state of outright crisis. (I became convinced of this myself when the dean of social sciences at my university announced that his disciplines should make up the core of undergraduate education in the new millennium.) Many reasons can be produced to account for this sense of emergency, including the end of the cold war and the apparent triumph of free-market capitalism, which has never had much respect for social planning; the surely related rise of voluntarism and antistatism; and the new acceptability of the rhetoric of self-affiliation whose elucidation is among the major ambitions of this volume. Alain Touraine, we recall, concluded that "there is no longer a recognized model of analysis of social agency. In the strict sense, sociology no longer exists." Immanuel Wallerstein identifies social science as a "child of the Enlightenment" that is now reaching its dotage. It evolved with and within liberalism as a way to "manipulate social relations" according to rational-scientific principles, and it will disappear along with it.[1] Ian Hacking has recently proposed that the "metaphor of social construction" on which so much social science has depended "once had excellent shock value, but now . . . has become rather tired." From the evolutionary psychology camp, John Tooby and Leda Cosmides are loudly negative about the "antinativism" that has dominated what they call the "standard social science model" that now looks to them to be nothing more than "a tired way of defending a stagnated and sterile intellectual status quo." [2] Ernesto Laclau, who has (with Chantal Mouffe) made headlines on the intellectual Left with the idea that (crudely put) society does not exist, insists on the "ultimate impossibility of all 'objectivity.' " [3] One could go on to show at length that the classical social science model has been widely attacked during the period we call the postmodern. Statements from Emile Durkheim are often produced to represent that model: statements proposing, for instance, that because people have no idea of the forces that determine their lives, such forces must be analyzed objectively. Social facts, then, "display . . . all the characteristics of a thing," while their "profound causes" always escape the consciousness of participants. [4]

Now, of course, the social sciences have become visibly reflexive and even literary. Anthropologists, historians, and sociologists find themselves pressured to write as much or more about themselves as about their ostensible objects of study. Some of them, along with some political scientists, are seeking to explain in historical terms how and why this came to be. The disavowal of objectivity has sometimes produced hermeneutically sensitized thick descriptions, where the density of information aspires to outflank or compensate for the insecurities of the observer's positionality, and sometimes the more flamboyant gestures of self-affiliation that govern statements such as "let me tell you where I'm coming from." It is also not uncommon to see some version of the appeal to a renewed personal responsibility, of the sort that Alan Dershowitz called for. In this chapter I am mostly concerned with sociology, but I will make selective excursions into anthropology and other disciplines: sociology, then, in its broadest sense. It is Habermas's contention that it has, indeed, always had this broadest sense; that it was from the start founded in disciplinary crisis, picking up the awkward questions that "politics and economics pushed to one side on their way to becoming specialized sciences," and always above all concerned "with the anomic aspects of the dissolution of traditional social systems and the development of modern ones." Being thus itself "the theory of bourgeois society" it could not fail to register discursive conflicts and epistemological failures. Like its eighteenth-century precursor, political economy, it is committed to looking at "society as a whole" so that it cannot get away with separating out manageable items for the production of easy conclusions.[5] This is the exact sense in which Darrow's defense of Loeb and Leopold, in its omnivorous connection of anything with everything—wealth, Nietzsche, schooling, family, physiology—was sociological. And as we have seen in chapter 2, criminal procedures have been consistently contextualized within sociological paradigms, so that there is a recurring need to establish what is and what is not admissible explanation.

Even in its Enlightenment origins, moreover, proto-social science was only intermittently committed to the sort of objectivism that has so often since been assumed to be the disciplinary standard. Bentham's faith in probability was much more typical of the tradition than any belief in simple objectivism or case-specific predictability. Ian Hacking has convincingly isolated Hume's notorious formulation of the problem of induction, which "doubts that any known facts about past objects or events give any reason for beliefs about future objects or events," along with the related problem of how many observed instances it takes to authorize a generalization, as foundational to an Enlightenment that is thereby rendered distinctly antifoundational.[6] According to Hacking the problem of evidence only appears at the point where its insoluble nature is guaranteed; it emerges, in other words, *as* insoluble (p. 31). Reconfigured by the new interest in gambling, in the statistics governing the incidence of disease, and in the calculation of annuities, epistemological and jurisprudential questions that are not thus specifically constrained pass rapidly to the point of aporia (see pp. 149–50).

The facts, in other words, were never quite facts for many eighteenth-century thinkers; they never were authoritatively and enduringly held separate from theory and opinion, nor were they often held to be easy to ascertain at all. If we take Johann Gottfried von Herder to be our prototypical Enlightenment determinist, then we will find in his writings a highly qualified and skeptical sense of how we might pursue knowledge in a world wherein "not one point on our complicated Globe, not one wave in the current of time, resembles another."[7] Inferences about the role of climate, for example, must always be "in some measure hypothetical" because they "are contradicted almost step by step, by examples from history, or even by physiological principles; because too many powers, partly opposite to each other, act in conjunction" (p. 15). Herder's awareness of multiple powers acting in conjunction to produce an infinitely complexifying whole within which each single determination works rather to "incline" than to "force," and "every one receives all external impressions in his own manner, and modifies them according to his organs" (pp. 20, 23), makes his paradigm sociological in exactly the sense that Habermas specifies. And it leads not to an absolute objectivist model in which every event can be predicted but to a faith in probability as the best that we can manage. The probability standard that informs, for example, Condorcet's "social mathematics," is admitted from the first as "very far from the precision and invariability that a true science requires." [8] Observed facts are never exactly alike, and the same fact observed at different times is likely to produce deviations. So we work by pretending that small differences do not matter in order to "arrive at general results and avoid being lost in the immensity of detail" (p. 188). The "facts" with which we work are thus really to be understood as mean values rather than as objectively simple items.

It is probability and not objectivism, I think, that characterizes the early evolution of social science: we will see this argued in an exemplary way by John Stuart Mill later in this chapter.[9] But at the same time there are visible moments of high confidence in the power of the sociological method to become a "true science." These moments have tended not to endure unchallenged for very long, but they have nevertheless been important. The preface to Montesquieu's The Spirit of the Laws promised to demonstrate a "natural relation" between "first principles" and "particular cases," one so predictable that the dogged listing of all the particulars would lead only to "a most insupportable fatigue." [10] William Robertson, in his History of America, thought that a proper history ought to "contemplate man in all those various situations wherein he has been placed," but he was able to avoid the infinite attention to particulars by a sort of ethnographic reduction: the American Indian tribes "have such a near resemblance, that they may be painted with the same features," so that the same attention to each would be "tiresome." [11] The sheer anachronism of this statement for our present moment indicates how far we have traveled from such sublime ethnocentrism, and it is surely the new awareness of the Other that postwar decolonization processes brought about that has helped to bring the "western" subject to a sense of its own crisis, as Derrida long ago made clear. That crisis, however, has been long nurtured, and it has been one of the tasks of social science to make sense of it and to try to compensate for it even as it cannot but represent it. The end of social science, then, is in fact to end, and it has been on the point of ending, or at least of qualifying itself out of existence, on various occasions. Nonetheless, as we shall see, there have been places and times where the prospects for a scientifically managed society have seemed very good.

Culture and National Security Max Horkheimer and Theodor Adorno published their *Dialectic of Enlightenment* in 1944, at a time when it had become clear that the Allied democracies were going to win the war, and when it was possible to predict that the United States would be established as the world's greatest economic and perhaps also military power. Notoriously they did not like what they saw coming along in the sphere of social life. They refused any absolute distinction between the European totalitarian states (Germany and the Soviet Union) and the liberal democracies, implicating both as symptoms of a "new kind of barbarism" based on the "instrumentalization of science" and the "self-destruction of the Enlightenment." [12] Horkheimer and Adorno saw an inevitable pattern working through modern history whereby a progressive rationalism produced domination over nature and the division of human societies into technocratic rulers and dehumanized masses. In their famous discussion of contemporary culture, they predicted the onset of a totally administered society functioning as powerfully through the control of leisure as through the discipline of work: "Films, radio and magazines make up a system which is uniform as a whole and in every part. Even the aesthetic activities of political opposites are one in their enthusiastic obedience to the rhythm of the iron system" (p. 120). Anticipating Baudrillard, they saw the "whole world" now passing through "the filter of the culture industry," with "real life . . . becoming indistinguishable from the movies" (p. 126). In this not so brave new world, there would be no individuals. Like Dewey before them they recognized that individuality had always been a clumsy or incompetent concept anyway, one "full of contradictions." Henceforth the effort to achieve individuation would be replaced by "the effort to imitate" (pp. 155–56). Within this diagnosis we all share one situation, a bad one, and it determines our lives completely. The hopes that are still held out for a reactivation of the theoretical or critical consciousness and a return to a more positive Enlightenment are in their book only of the faintest kind.

Dialectic of Englightenment is notable for its belief in the possibility of a totally administered society and a single, managed situation. It offers an exemplary statement of the power of what the marxist tradition calls *ideology*, which is in turn an extreme emanation of the social science tradition that had been developing through the previous hundred years or so and that had at times seemed to offer the prospect of an objective analysis (and therefore manipulation) of human situatedness, one made all the more urgent by the disasters of 1914–18 and 1939–45, and (in the West) by the spectacle of state communism after 1917. In Dewey's lectures of 1926, published a year later as *The Public and Its Problems*, he presciently observes that all the rival political systems, communist, fascist, and capitalist, were up to the same game in trying to "bring about a formation of dispositions and ideas that will conduce to a preconceived goal" (p. 200). The only difference between them is that the capitalists do it less consciously than the others. After 1945, if not before, capitalism raised its consciousness level. The gloomy fatalism of *Dialectic of Enlightenment* was not typical of the academic response within the United States to the prospect of military victory and world-economic hegemony. More commonly the conviction derived from the methods of social science was a positive one: we can now institutionalize freedom and democracy in America once and for all and provide the world with a model for its own progress toward the same ideals. Horkheimer himself coedited a series titled "Studies in Prejudice" whose aim was to eliminate just that; even Adorno joined the team whose task it was to educate the world out of anti-Semitism or at least "to help in its eradication." Psychoanalysis and sociology together would work on the two poles of the human experience, the "situational factor" and the "personality factor," and the new expert would achieve the "careful weighing of the role of each." [13] Another emigré from a shattered Europe, Bronislaw Malinowski, saw the task of academic anthropology as the study of social values (democracy, freedom, civilization) and of the ways and means of putting them in place and maintaining them: "The spiritual foundations of public opinion have to be watched with the same eternal vigilance with which we look after the physical foundations of our national defenses." [14] With the tools of social science in hand, the social scientist becomes (or should become) the mastermind behind the politician and planner. The organization of the cultural system toward desirable ends is as important as the governance of the economy and maintaining the defense industry. Culture is part of national security.

The middle decades of the twentieth century, the cold war years, were marked by the publication of a spate of books that addressed the nature and propagation of "freedom": Malinowski's bibliography lists a representative sample (pp. 337–38). The rivalry between the "western" democracies and its antagonists in both communism and fascism made it less possible than ever before to limit the debate about freedom to the specialized (although still very influential) inquiries traditional to ethical philosophy or legal theory. Paradoxically, the contribution of the social sciences was one that promised to organize freedom and to create or maintain individualism. The minimally administered society that was the goal of liberal culture had then itself to be at least to some definite degree administered. The objectivist paradigms of any perfected social science, allowing for the inference of behavior from properly described or established situations, had to be reconciled with the flexibility and openness required of a democratic culture. John Locke had pointed to exactly the same balance of forces in his account of the education of children, which should produce, he thought, a strong habitual discipline working to control behavior, but not to the point of suppressing all the "Vigor and Industry" that can at best produce "Able and Great Men." Reconciling these "seeming Contradictions" is the "true Secret of Education." [15] Postwar and cold war conditions, as we shall see, seem to have brought out both a heightened faith in social science as a tool for the construction of a perfect situation and a desperate fear about the consequences of getting it wrong, as well as of succumbing to the undesirable regime of alternative situations: communism. Too much enforced habit produces inertia and political subservience; too little leads to anarchy and an ungovernable people.

The same beliefs in the power of the forces described by social science governed both of the opposing cold war cultures. They did not of course originate with them. The exemplary philosophical and methodological arguments had been rehearsed much earlier; indeed, they had been a central preoccupation of the anglophone tradition for perhaps two hundred years. What changed most dramatically was the avowed level of confidence in the availability of a solution to the antinomies of situatedness. As we have seen, even this was not new. Some version of Montesquieu's faith in the relation between principles and particulars in the analysis of human society had long subsisted as an alternative to the more self-consciously heuristic paradigms of the probability theorists. The history of the social science disciplines can be written as a narrative of toing and froing between a faith in objectivity and an acceptance of its impossibility. Looking only at the discipline of history, one that sometimes counts itself among the social sciences, Peter Novick finds between the years 1880 and 1960 two periods in which objectivism was in the ascendant and two in which relativism was at its height. For example, he argues that "the aftermath of World War I ushered in a period of negativity and doubt, the climate in which the relativist critique flourished, while the coming of World War II saw American culture turn toward affirmation and the search for certainty." [16] In so doing it echoed an earlier moment of high confidence in the American way, that of the early nationalist period in which Benjamin Rush, for example, thought it "possible to convert men into republican machines" because in America, at last, government could be shown to be of a "progressive nature," unleashing energies hitherto bound up in the "chains" of European practice.[17] The relativist emphasis and the objectivist emphasis have changed places over the long-durational term of modernity; sometimes, for example after 1776 and 1945, a once-and-for-all synthesis is promised, a solution to the obscurities of situatedness. But the rival models are traditional and of continuing relevance, not least because their proposed solutions have never lasted. Wolf Lepenies has argued that the history of social science as an independent discipline has been marked since its beginnings in the early nineteenth century by an oscillation between rational-scientific (objectivist) emphases and hermeneutic attitudes that have come close to identifying it with literature.

These rival inflections roughly correspond to optimistic and skeptical views of the predictability of human behavior. The more emphatically the discipline has declared for one of these extremes, the more effective has been the polemical challenge of the other.[18] A similar oscillation is described by Carl Degler, who sees the history of social thought as veering between two extremes: a Darwinian model of long-term biological adaptation with a minimal role for culture and consciousness, and a reciprocally strong culturalism used by Boas to discredit racialism and used by early feminists to refute biological rationales for sex differences.[19] Biological determinism, he finds, has made a comeback after being discredited in the West during the Hitler years. But a reactively strong cultural determinism is sure to follow. But what is culture, and what is biology? Christopher Herbert has produced a masterful demonstration of the slipperiness of the first, which he finds to be one of those terms that Kenneth Burke called "scene words." That is, it defines not so much a clear concept as a cluster of interchangeable ideas and allusions open to mutual substitution and reciprocal definition (like that of Malinowski's "context" and "situation" discussed in chapter 1). The important uses of *culture* as Herbert describes them have been from the first antinomic: foundational and antifoundational, permissive and restrictive, and prone to self-contradictions. They have led to "inarticulacy and evasiveness" rather than to clear definition, and they have as much embarrassed as empowered their users.[20] To claim to be formed by culture is to claim nothing that can be rendered in precise terms. Perhaps this too is among the frustrations that the contemporary recourse to gestures of self-affiliation is designed to appease.

Character and Environment: Mill, James, and Dewey We have already seen how Bentham's account of the potential for a social science takes account of both problems and possibilities. Causality is always obscure, but outcomes can be proposed on a probabilistic basis. Thus punishment is always an evil because it can never be sure that it responds to exact determinations—it can only be justified according to its effects. The same utilitarian model is taken over by John Stuart Mill, arguably the major theorist of situatedness between Bentham and Sartre, and applied more broadly to the larger project of a social science. Mill's *A System of Logic*, first published in 1843, articulates a basis in probability for the pursuit

95   With God on Our Side?

of social science and social planning. He accepts the doctrine of necessity to the point of claiming that the total knowledge of an individual and his circumstances would allow his behavior to be "unerringly inferred," but he is clear that such complete knowledge will never be available.[21] Mill's model, like Locke's, takes the step required of its commitment to liberalism: it makes room for individual agency. As long as "our habits are not too inveterate," we can employ our own energies toward "self-culture." In this way necessity does not exclude "the power of the mind to co-operate in the formation of its own character" (pp. 426, 428). Philosophical necessitarianism is thus adapted to individual enterprise. But there can never be total knowledge of an individual or a situation. Mill echoes Helvétius in finding that the forces determining human behavior are so "numerous and diversified . . . that in the aggregate they are never in any two cases exactly similar" (p. 433). The study of human nature is thus like the study of the tides: general tendencies can be predicted by working from a sample large enough to minimize the effects of idiosyncrasies, even as no exact prediction of any single event or individual response can be anticipated. Human nature can then be the subject of science within a calculus of probability. And within that calculus, "differences in education and in outward circumstances" afford a large part of any explanation of behavior (p. 447) and thus of any effort at its modification.

Mill responds to the undeniable evidence of difference without giving up on the availability of general patterns. Thus "mankind have not one universal character, but there exist universal laws of the Formation of Character . . . it is on these that every rational attempt to construct the science of human nature in the concrete, and for practical purposes, must proceed" (p. 452). Hence we have "Ethology, or the Science of Character" (p. 457). It is probabilistic, describing "tendencies, not facts" (p. 458), but firm enough to provide a methodology for the administration of nation and empire, as well as for the elaboration of social science. Human behavior, like all phenomena with multiple causes, can never be assessed by pure induction or pure deduction. But the perception of general laws that can then be set into particular circumstances and adjusted accordingly — "the physical, or concrete deductive method" (p. 488) — is enough for "practical politics," the intent of which is "to surround any given society with the greatest number of possible circumstances of which the tendencies are beneficial, and to remove or counteract, as far as practicable, those of which the tendencies are injurious" (p. 492). The search for these general laws is the subsequent task of social science, which, depending on its confidence level, ponders or passes over such phrases as Mill's "as far as practicable." Because the individual case can never be exactly described or predicted, the most exigent instances requiring that the nature of human situatedness be decided (like the determination of levels of criminality) cannot be fully satisfied by social science. But sometimes these qualifications get forgotten.

Mill writes for an entrepreneurial society that places a high value on individualism, but one that is also faced with a complex task of administration, involving the objectification and constraint of other individuals and indeed of other cultures. Hence his ingenious reconciliation of freedom with and within necessity, and his sense of the importance of "remarkable individuals" (p. 540) in carrying out the tendencies of history and progress. In *On Liberty* (1859) he sets out to discover and defend a "limit to the legitimate interference of collective opinion with individual independence." [22] He argues for minimal government (and of course for freedom of trade) as most productive of human happiness. Only with freedom of expression and publication can the ideas regulating social life remain as "fresh and living conviction" rather than becoming "dead beliefs" (p. 50). He anticipates the fear of ideology that will become so obsessive with the heyday of social science in the twentieth century: conformity can proceed to such an extent among the people "until by dint of not following their own nature they have no nature to follow: their human capacities are withered and starved; they become incapable of any strong wishes or native pleasures, and are generally without either opinions or feelings of home growth, or properly their own" (pp. 74–75). To avoid this fate, individuals must be allowed (or encouraged, as is now necessary) to follow their own inclinations, "at their own risk and peril" (p. 67), within only the most general and obvious limits. Only thus can we hope to avoid the reign of "mediocrity" (p. 80). Once again, as for Luther and for Descartes, individual integrity is measured as freedom (although here only relative freedom) from predetermined kinds of situatedness allowing for a fresh choice among new situations. Customs "are made for customary circumstances and customary characters. . . . He who lets the world, or his own portion of it, choose his plan of life for him has no need of any other faculty than the ape-like one of imitation" (p. 71). True "character" emerges as the balance of innate personality with customary presuppositions (p. 73), just as it does in so many nineteenth-century novels. The obligation of the social planners, in the face of a threatened "despotism of custom" (p. 85), is to encourage "freedom and variety of situations" (p. 89). Liberal democracy, again, requires a manipulation of situations that effaces its own constructedness and prescribes the obligation of choice and the experience of permissible self-making, while at the same time seeking to restrain forms of behavior deemed criminal or harmful. Situatedness is affirmed and denied at the same time. Examined as a whole, then, Mill's understanding of the nature and power of situatedness is conflicted or antinomic.[23] He approves its existence as a basis for a probabilistic social science that can produce administrative legitimations and benefits, but he is concerned (as Horkheimer and Adorno will be concerned) with its potential for total determination of belief and behavior. Custom and culture are double-edged swords, admirable and necessary up to a point but repressive and stultifying when allowed full play. To use a Darwinian analogy: if society cannot throw up idiosyncrasies it cannot adapt for survival.[24]

Attention to situatedness is prominent again in the philosophies of William James and John Dewey, although it takes a different inflection from its appearance in Mill and in Bentham before them. James and Dewey in fact share a hostility to the inherited rhetoric of social science in its emphasis on theorization, which they eschew as much as they can in the service of a down-home language of can-do attention to immediacies and practicalities. For James, what I am calling situatedness is the be-all and end-all of every mental task, and itself presents the solution to a whole host of inherited but unnecessary philosophical problems: to situate something is already to be well on the way to demonstrating its workable value. Jamesian pragmatism is consequence oriented and not much interested in causes, aiming instead at "concreteness" and "practical cash-value" within the experience of our individual lives.[25] The importance of an action or event is thus not its absolute philosophical status, if such there be, but its effect on a particular situation. James's faith in instrumentalism and his refusal to abstract philosophical inquiry into a realm of impersonal, desituated operations is a green light for applied and applicable social science to minimize the importance of rational modeling and to measure itself in terms of outcomes.[26] It thereby moves the rhetoric of situatedness toward its modern function as a form of affirmation: to situate something (or someone) is to describe it correctly. Dewey's educational theory has similar priorities. In *Democracy and Education* (1916) Dewey argued that education could not take place by the "direct conveyance" of propositions but could only work "through the intermediary of the environment," physical and social. Practical participation in "some conjoint activity" produces the habit of mind-body experience that is the only lasting education.[27] The mind alone, reached purely by verbal address, cannot retain information as having any value; participatory or "conjoint" activity is required so that students may acquire "a *social* sense of their own powers and of the materials and appliances used" (p. 48). Useful and lasting knowledge is situated knowledge, and situated knowledge is empowering knowledge.

In other words, for Dewey the mental component of the self must be absorbed in and integrated with the physiological component of action and the environmental and social experience of others in a "whole person" or "whole field" situation. In *Human Nature and Conduct* (1922) Dewey makes an extended case for "the establishment of arts of education and social guidance" as a means of helping this along.[28] Recognizing this whole field synthesis would entail a recognition of "social partnership in producing crime" (of the sort that Clarence Darrow proposed) and an effort toward reformist manipulation of the environment: "To change the working character or will of another we have to alter objective conditions which enter into his habits" (pp. 18, 19). Such change cannot happen directly or by selective targeting: the whole situation must be monitored. Hence the need for a social science for the maintenance of civilization, which demands "a congenial, antecedently prepared environment. Without it, civilization would relapse into barbarism in spite of the best of subjective intention and internal good disposition. The eternal dignity of labor and art lies in their effecting that permanent reshaping of environment which is the substantial foundation of future security and progress" (p. 20). Habit, then, is more important than will: "Reason pure of all influence from prior habit is a fiction" (p. 31). Indeed, habit is will (p. 42), and controls consequences (p. 45). Like Mill, Dewey realizes that he can only predict general tendency and not single event, and like Mill he leaves open a space for individual agency in "breaking down old rigidities of habit and preparing the way for acts that re-create an environment" (p. 57).

Dewey and Mill both provide an understanding of situatedness that fits Morton Horwitz's account, discussed in the previous chapter, of the legal profile of an entrepreneurial, corporate culture. They propose indescribably remote and complex causes for behavior (thus blurring doctrines of absolute responsibility) and at the same time maintain a place for critical individual initiative and change. In this way they support and explain a culture of risk. The argument for situatedness, while it could certainly be put to compassionate uses as it was by Darrow and the legal realists in arguing against capital punishment, also makes it much more difficult to assign responsibilities in the day-to-day adjudication of tort cases involving large corporate-industrial interests. The maintenance of a commitment to situational consciousness did then not emanate from any profoundly unitary commitment to moral sympathy, even if it was open to such applications. It speaks, once again, for a deliberately indeterminate or opportunistic component to the vocabulary we have for explaining motives and consequences. As such it can be emphasized one way or the other, toward general tendency or exception, toward exoneration or responsibility. Once again, what appears as a protoscientific finding, the profile of a possible new science of character, is implicitly committed to the maintenance of a culture of contradictions.

The analysis of social conflict that emerges from Dewey's paradigm is an interesting one. Both within the nation-state, where class and ethnic conflicts occur, and between different nation-states (now more conscious of each other than ever before), the subsumption of will and reason into habit means that no merely propositional debate about values and practices can succeed in creating tolerance. The task of mutual accommodation is thus a practical one of social change; a reorganization of sectarian habits as shared habits. In the language of the 1990s it is not enough to recognize or acknowledge another's situation as having some alien integrity, to hear where someone "is coming from." Dewey requires that all must change their (our) habits and routines. The way forward here is pragmatic and local, reformist and utopian. In this respect his advocacy of "specific criticism and specific reconstruction" with an intention to "renew disposition and reorganize habit" (p. 170) is remarkably akin to the agenda of literary criticism as it had evolved between Matthew Arnold and I. A. Richards. But that is another story.

Like Bentham and Mill, Dewey seems to want things both ways in making a claim to science. On the one hand, he applauds the urge to know "exactly the selective and directive force of each social situation, exactly how each tendency is promoted and retarded," as a condition of "effective reform" (p. 148). After all, in this anti-Cartesian ecology where all knowledge and belief is "an acquired result of the workings of natural impulses in connection with environment" (p. 187), situatedness is all-powerful and not to be left to chance. But on the other hand social science must never and can never (Dewey is a key figure in the slippage between *cannot* and *must not*) produce itself to the point of fantasizing an absolute knowledge: a complete anticipatory closure would be the end of liberal democracy. Hence it must eschew theory and "fixed rules" (p. 238) in favor of "continuous, vital readaptation" (p. 240). The case against legal formalism has shown the dangers of following rules "developed under bygone conditions" (p. 239); social science and moral convention must follow a different logic. At the same time the past is not to be simply discarded. Social habit formation is interactive, and so are past and present: old habits remain for revision and adaptation into new ones (pp. 240–41).

I have devoted a good deal of space to an account of Dewey's views on situatedness because they seem to me (along with those of John Stuart Mill) to be foundational for the social sciences that were developing both in Dewey's time and since. In arguing against a merely individualistic psychology he makes a clear case "that substantial bettering of social relations waits upon the growth of a scientific social psychology" (p. 323). But the perceived potential of such science for totalitarian control must be restrained, and moreover restrained administratively because there appears to be little or nothing in human nature that could of itself resist the persuasions of a totally controlled situation. The capacity of human nature for being molded and shaped according to prefigured principles is then both the rationale for social science and also, within a liberal democratic tradition, its nightmare. On the one hand, human plasticity gives hope for the elimination of criminal deviance, the harmony of different social factions, and the final establishment of democracy; on the other hand, as Mill had also recognized, that same human plasticity can be trained to a passive obedience to the tyranny of custom. Fear of absolute conformity from too much control runs alongside an equivalent fear of radical deviance emerging from too much freedom; the same choice of horrors appears every time situatedness is invoked as a manipulable element in human experience. Such instability may be the inevitable corollary of an ideology of risk; it imposes a commitment to interminable adjudications of *how* situatedness can be allowed to count or not toward acceptable explanations of particular behaviors. These adjudications are themselves malleable and open to the reifications of corruption and convenience. They are certainly not to be taken at face value.

In his account of the development of social science as a professional discipline, Thomas Haskell has written about the "recession" of causation that he sees appearing with increasingly complex and interdependent societies, so that "the effective cause of any event or condition in society, from the vantage point of any single component, became more contingent and more difficult to trace." [29] Nietzsche, as we have seen, had made a very similar point in claiming that all processes that are "semiotically concentrated elude definition" and that "only that which has no history is definable" (*Basic Writings*, p. 516). The coming into being of things that have an unignorable history is what Foucault defined as constituting modern life, which he describes as privileging the "sciences of man" governed by an "analytic of finitude." [30] The recession of causation is compounded by the hermeneutic complexities of a human subject that is itself within the history it is trying to understand. The recession of objective causes — in Haskell's words, "never before the watershed of the 1890s did so many thinkers so consistently and so authoritatively locate causation outside conscious mind" (p. 41) — replicates the vertiginous embedding of causal explanation itself within an indecipherable subjectivity. What one sees comes to be in part — an undecidable part — a matter of where one is coming from. This predicament does not seem to favor the emergence or continuous career of an objectivist social science, although it is compatible with a probabilistic one.

Planning Freedom But both kinds of social science did emerge and kept on emerging into and through the cold war years, when Talcott Parsons could look back (in 1966) on a period in which "American sociology has grown faster and gone further than sociology in any other country," although it was almost matched by a comparable process in the Warsaw Pact countries.[31] From the start sociology, although competing with literature in the way that Lepenies has described, also overlapped with anthropology in a kinship that sometimes seemed to reduce or redefine the national culture as just another strange society in need of explanation. Robert and Helen Lynd's pathbreaking *Middletown* announced itself as a serious attempt to study an anonymous midwestern city (Muncie, Indiana) "as an anthropologist does a primitive tribe."[32] They attempted a "total-situation study" (p. 7) of just the sort that Dewey might have imagined as preparatory to useful social reform. The Lynds came up with an account of rigid divisions between business and working classes (pp. 23–24, 505), significant alienation of the workers (pp. 39–40), and a strong tendency toward middle-class conformism prompted by the availablity of credit (p. 47). Reproduction within the teaching class further stimulated standardization (p. 207), as did the increasing claim on children's time made by the schools, which further encouraged "social illiteracy" by "the heavily diffused habit of local solidarity" in which they cooperated (p. 222). An increasing standardization of both work and leisure, enforced by "group sanctions and taboos" (p. 427) in business, law, and journalism, presented a picture of a middle America deteriorating into manufactured consent and apathy: a society that one might think was running down to near inertia.

But this is not where the Lynds leave us, even if they lead us almost to this point. Middletown does not fit the definition of a perfectly controlled situation; it is a place where "small worlds of all sorts are forever forming, shifting, and dissolving" (p. 478). Although this in itself may well be a form of ultimate social control (p. 481) it is enough to allow the Lynds to end with a caution against any lapse into monolithic theory (that is, into the Horkheimer-Adorno paradigm), and with a Deweyan homage to the complexity and "inchoate condition" of this one small city, which presents even in itself an enormous task for social science (p. 496). The weight of the evidence might seem to suggest that the writing is on the wall for the liberal imagination, but the empirical multiplicity of inter-subjective affiliations is such as to leave open a door to a possible better future. Or at least to a culture of invisibly limited self-making.

Insofar as it reflects and maintains the features of the "risk" culture described by Horwitz and subsequently (under the aegis of late moder-nity or postmodernity) by Beck and Giddens, social science is compelled to base its disciplinary claim on being neither fully objectivist nor simply particularist, but something between the two; this is perhaps one way of explaining its competition with literature. To the degree that it describes a society that is itself unstable, as Habermas says it does, then social sci-ence is much more likely than natural science to reflect on its own par-ticipation in the systems that it seeks to account for. Such reflexivity has been characterized as increasingly systematic in modern life, and if this is true then the importance of sociology seems assured, although perhaps more as the articulation of anxieties than of undisputed knowledge.[33] Like Tocqueville before him, Charles Horton Cooley (writing in 1909) saw in the United States a democratic culture encouraging a high rate of geo-graphical and occupational change and producing thereby "a lack of ade-quate group differentiation in its higher mental activities." [34] People are, in other words, very unsure of where they are coming from and where they might be going. But whatever anxiety or confusion this condition might generate is balanced by a positive outcome, which Cooley explains in a manner that seems to replicate the rhetoric of choice (whose adequacy he had already disproved) or at least of affirmative self-development. Be-cause classes and groups are manifold and always in a state of evolution, "several of them may pass through the same individual" without making him or her over in the image of any one "special type" (p. 248). Thus one has "more opportunity to achieve a truly personal individuality by com-bining a variety of class affiliations, each one suited to a particular phase of his character" (p. 249). The anomie of insecure or unclear group affilia-tions — the same group affiliations that are in fact constitutive of identity itself, which is not atomic but a product of group membership — is trans-formed from necessity to virtue. The reifying functions of divided labor as traditionally conceived, where a person's occupation lasts long enough to exercise formative and restrictive influence on the personality, are made over into the opportunity to be all that one can be, as often as one can.

This being so it is not surprising that social science sponsors an emphasis on the I/me relation whose instability I have already (following Sennett and Cobb) specified in chapter 1 as formative of the uneasy oscillation between affirming and disclaiming made by the rhetoric of self-affiliation. In *Human Nature and the Social Order* Cooley emphasized that the I must be understood as a "social sentiment" (p. 192) created by rather than prior to its historical and personal situation, and significantly composed by the desire for approbation, by "the imagination of how we appear to others" (p. 203). Consciousness of others in this way produces a "disturbance of equilibrium" (p. 206) most often resolved into "a just mingling of deference and self-poise" (p. 237). The average person in average circumstances can hope to maintain this balance, although it will always be precarious for "the more sensitive sort" (p. 246). Cooley, according to the optimistic logic I have already described, finds that the social conditions in his own place and time are opening up a prospect of "congenial self-development" to more and more people, because circumstances are "more hospitable to the finer abilities" than before (pp. 257–58). Where Tocqueville found increasing turbulence to be the result of life in a democracy, Cooley finds an increasingly comfortable approximation to the norm for more and more people. He does not predict that identity-panic will be a part of America's future.

George Herbert Mead's *Mind, Self, and Society* (1934) also includes an extended discussion of the I/me relation, one that amends Cooley's model. The self remains socially constructed or assembled, but the taking on of the attitudes of others now fashions a *me* open to self-conscious, third-person inspection by an I. This I is not a transcendental but a "historical figure" generated by the memory of what the self was in the past. It is not directly given in experience but comes from experience; it is the "response of the organism" to all the various *mes* that we collect by memory into identity.[35] But because the I comes to consciousness at a time removed from its past record of *mes* it enters a new predicament, a "certain situation which has a slightly different aspect from what is expected, which is in a certain sense novel": it responds to a "social situation" (p. 177), but it is "always something different from what the situation itself calls for" (p. 178). Looking forward to Sartre, Mead describes our "thinking" as "just such a continual change of a situation by our capacity to take it over into our own action" (p. 181). It is this relation between *I* and *me* that give us what we call the self, to whose "full expression" both are essential (p. 199). But their relation is variable and intrinsically unstable. At times it is the *me* that matters, the taking on of the attitude of others (for example, when we want to defend our property rights in a community), at other times it will be the ego, the *I*, the principle of self-expression or self-fronting. The "great figures in history" (p. 202) are of the second type, the ordinary citizen demonstrates more of the first, which is a principle of "social control" (p. 210). Where the two are fused "there arises the peculiar sense of exaltation which belongs to the religious and patriotic attitudes in which the reaction which one calls out in others is the response which one is making himself" (p. 273).

These moments are "peculiarly precious" (p. 275) in emotional terms because they free us from the unstable relation of the two parts of the self and from the experience of competition: "Everyone is at one with each other" (p. 274). In temporary and noncritical experiences (a game, for instance) they are presumably beneficial and uncomplicated. But what Mead is describing here is also the anatomy of fascism and of its communist alter ego as imagined by the western democracies, and of the totally administered society predicted by Horkheimer and Adorno for the democracies themselves. One can see, once again, that the exploratory, nervous relation of *I* and *me*, remaining open and unstable, is in fact the necessarily prescribed norm for a bourgeois-democratic culture in which the constant attentiveness to and renegotiation of one's position is fundamental to both economic progress (by way of entrepreneurial invention) and social harmony (by way of respect for the positions of others). In other words some measure of uncertainty about one's affiliations must remain part of the rhetoric of such cultures. The question is whether the permitted definitional provisionality provides relative comfort and security, the assurance of always being able to become something else, or generates acute uncertainty about who one is and where one is coming from.

Deciding between these options or resolving the pressure of having to decide between them has everything to do with class and social status. Sennett and Cobb, as we have seen, describe an *I* that holds itself apart from the *me*, and that is extremely wary of any fusion of the two. Their analysis suggests that for the working-class person there is a very tenuous expectation of historically continuous experience and a marked reluctance to assume the participatory consolations of team membership across class boundaries. The openness of the future is here not a source of optimism but of concern. In contemporary culture, wherein the sources of authority and responsibility are increasingly divergent and opaque (this is the "risk culture" that Ulrich Beck delineates) more and more persons come to adopt this hesitation about the linkage of I and me, although of course there remain in place a good many identity forms to appease the anxieties of disaffiliation. However, more and more of these forms are themselves vigorously contested and thereby often sensed as floating between fantasy and reality. (A category such as "race," for example, is at once held to be biologically indefensible and culturally pertinent, although that cultural pertinence is itself disputed and varies according to the nature of the analysis and the moment of its invocation.) The possibility of reward and the fear of accountability are hard to keep apart. It is the antinomic potential of the gesture of self-affiliation (the *azza* sentence) that renders it antithetical to the objectivist component of the social science project; no one fully wishes to be what they say they are, because what is enabling at one moment might become a liability at another. Or, one might say, the objective nature of this gesture itself consists in its structured ambivalence.

As deployed by anthropologists the idea of cultural determination as the primary element of one's situatedness has commonly had as its goal the encouragement of tolerance. Ruth Benedict's massively popular *Patterns of Culture* (1934) played up the power of cultural determination as commanding a neutral, nonpartisan analysis and cosmopolitanism: "There never has been a time when civilization stood more in need of individuals who are genuinely culture-conscious, who can see objectively the socially conditioned behaviour of other peoples without fear and recrimination." [36] Russians and Pueblo Indians alike deserve respect and understanding: doctrines of race are merely mythic in a world where culture is so powerful. Benedict gives us a passionate statement of the value of "the coexisting and equally valid patterns of life which mankind has created for itself" (p. 278). The problems of seeing "objectively" are neither acknowledged nor rehearsed; they are secondary to the moral imperative. The fact of our situatedness is cause for celebration and not despair. Its invocation is, as it is with Clarence Darrow, a polemical one, not designed so much to prove that something specific is or is not the case as to inhibit cruelties and prejudices operating against others who are different.

Benedict's plea for tolerance has, of course, become one of the standard components of the debate about social differences in the 1990s. Its moral ambition may be held to be admirable even as its epistemological or instrumental valency is unclear or unresolvable. Margaret Mead's studies of South Sea island cultures had the same conviction (we have moved full circle from Darwinism here) that "cultural rhythms are stronger and more compelling than the physiological rhythms which they overlay and distort." [37] But Mead's interest is more overtly instrumentalist and ethnocentric than Benedict's. She wants to find in other societies clues about how to better organize our own. She articulates the standard social science dilemma between the route to a "single standard" and that to a "more ordered heterogeneity": anarchy goes unmentioned. The so-called primitive society appeals to her because it presents a manageable object of research. Compared to our own highly complex cultures, a "primitive people without a written language present a much less elaborate problem and a trained student can master the fundamental structure of a primitive society in a few months." [38] Thus a mere nine months in Samoa and a sample of only fifty girls is enough to allow Mead to feel that she can generalize about the conventions governing Samoan adolescence and to provide her with a standard against which to assess the strengths and weaknesses of the more complex American society whose rejuvenation is her ultimate goal (pp. 10–11). In *Growing Up in New Guinea* she is explicit about the absolute instrumentalism of her curiosity about "primitive" cultures. Their destruction is to be regretted not so much on ethical grounds but because we lose the records of an "experiment" from which we can learn; by looking at the educational processes of the Manus, for example, we can "suggest solutions to educational problems which we would never be willing to study by experimentation upon our own children." [39] The conclusion to *Sex and Temperament in Three Primitive Societies* is a plea for a pluralization of sex roles in American society, for an acceptance of the truth that there is "more than one set of possible values," and for a world wherein each person is allowed the pattern "most congenial to his gifts." [40] Like Benedict, Mead ends up with a plurality of differently situated subcultures: "There would be ethical codes and social symbolisms, an art and a way of life, congenial to each endowment" (p. 322). Let a hundred flowers bloom.

As polemical counterstatements aimed at a culture increasingly seen as tending to uniformity or total administration, these appeals to tolerance must have seemed powerful and timely. They were certainly a reminder that the American way, as Dewey and others had articulated it, was a liberal way, quite unlike the roads taken by communists, fascists, and populist conservatives. Cold war social science was largely aimed at legitimating and structuring the culture of liberal democracy, but it was also applied as a corrective to the remaining inequities within liberal democracy. Benedict's case for a sympathetic understanding of Pueblo cultures was imaged in a host of learned essays by sociologists on the "race" question. Much of the 1945 volume *The Science of Man* (there's that phrase again) is an anthropological inquiry into "race" relations, prompted by the shock of the Nazi genocide and by the injustices suffered by minorities inside the United States. If cultural situation is more important than biology in determining human identity, then there is, in the words of *Science of Man* contributor Otto Klineberg, no "racial psychology" and no basis for discrimination on the basis of "hereditary inferiority." Democracy should then properly proceed by attending to and improving our situations, by "making available to the whole community the educational and economic opportunities which pave the way for fuller and richer living." [41] Findings such as this contributed to the later rationalization of the civil rights movement and the War on Poverty; they are examples of solid liberal applications of the argument from situatedness. Like so many in the postwar-cold war period, Ralph Linton, editor of *The Science of Man*, believed in the possibility of the "intelligent planning of the new world order" (p. vii). It is perhaps this moment in the history of the "West," as much as the moment of the high Enlightenment in the eighteenth century, that most doggedly affirms both the power of situatedness and an instrumental optimism about getting it right once and for all. Linton opens his own essay in the volume with the ringing and extraordinary declaration that "the present period is the first in the world's history in which men have turned to science for aid rather than to the supernatural." [42] (He had forgotten Benjamin Rush and others like him.) Now we are in a position to set forth "the basic principles on which all societies and cultures operate," and to discover "the common denominators of human existence" (p. 12). This is indeed one of those moments of "déjà vu all over again," a hyperbolic rediscovery of a wheel already put into service several times before. Beginning with "primitive" societies and "fewer variables," says Linton, we can work up a model of all societies (p. 12). At last, the exact relations between "personality and culture" are within the reach of scientific understanding (pp. 12–13). The coming together of the affiliated special disciplines (ethnology, psychology, linguistics, sociology, archaeology, somatology, physiology) now offers the prospect of a "new Science of Man" (p. 17) with enormous potential benefits in both humanitarian and economic-commercial spheres. In all of this, situatedness is primary. Germans and Japanese can be integrated into a postwar settlement precisely because they are malleable human beings responding not to innate drives but to social conditioning.[43]

John Stuart Mill's model of the probable mean (rather than the absolute determination) of human behavior as the goal of social science remains authoritative throughout the postwar–cold war movement, but the optimism can seem boundless nonetheless, perhaps because it is the job of the criminal justice system and of psychoanalysis (and not of social science) to take up the instances of deviation from the predicted norm. Malinowski, in *Freedom and Civilization*, argued for attention to institutions, each of which is "the organized partial constituent of a community" (p. 153), as the critical bearers of culture and as most conveniently open to control and modification. Attention to the parts produces regulation of the whole. Skeptics such as Edward Sapir continued to insist on the sheer difficulty of assessing the balance of biology and culture in the personality, and the implausibility of the notion of "culture" itself as having any predictive value;[44] but the general tone of the postwar decade is upbeat about the positive powers of controlling situatedness in the cause of strengthening democracy. Empirical studies in symbiotic relation with general paradigms could, it was felt, give us as much as we needed of objective truth. As Henry Murray and Clyde Kluckhohn wrote: "Only recently has a cross-cultural perspective provided some emancipation from those values that are not broadly 'human' but merely local, in both space and time. Only gradually is our culture altering so as to permit social scientists to work and think with something approaching objectivity."[45] There are "universalities" of human life that can be traced behind the confusions of everyday appearances (p. 36). All sorts of relations are now up for investigation and specification: between body shape and the "power motif in Western culture"; between physical illness and parenting patterns; between the "masculine component" and a suitability for military combat.[46] Everything can be potentially connected up to everything else in a movement toward that "total situation" analysis promised in *Middletown*. The ghosts of all who had been tempted by similar ambitions seem to have gone unnoticed.

So, in 1953 Hans Gerth and C. Wright Mills wrote that "the establishment of the reality of the social and plastic nature of man is a major accomplishment of U.S. social psychology."[47] What they proposed was nothing less than an absolute correlation between the general situation and the individual act: "The structural and historical features of modern society must be connected with the most intimate features of man's self. That is what social psychology is all about" (p. xix). With this ambition the inner sanctities of the private life itself, hitherto largely the province of literature (as we will see in chapter 4), seem to become vulnerable to analysis and thus administration. Individualism, which Mill and Dewey so much wanted to preserve, seems to be redefined as a function of the power of situatedness. Ethics and jurisprudence, already under pressure for decades from the case for remote causality and its erosion of notions of individual responsibility, felt the pressure once again in the heyday of social science explanations. In 1957 Sidney Hook organized a conference whose proceedings, published in 1958 and again in 1961, tried to address and assess the threat of a perceived "revolution in moral theory" arising from the sense that "the concept of moral responsibility is completely vacuous."[48] John Hospers, in a contribution titled "What Means This Freedom?" (pp. 126–42), argued that individualist psychoanalysis had already made it impossible to attribute blame, thanks to the relative inefficiency of "conscious control" over human behavior (p. 127). The extended contribution of the social sciences, although they often pronounced themselves hostile to the Freudian tradition precisely because of its individualist emphasis, only added to the case for not assigning responsibility and blame. We do not choose our personalities—

they are made for us. Such firm attributions of the power of determining structures led to equally firm articulations of the other side of the familiar antinomy. The enormous cultural appeal of Heisenberg's "uncertainty principle," which went well beyond its application to quantum physics, must have had much to do with its apparent justification of a nondetermined potential in this onslaught of prefigurations. Heisenberg described a "weaker type of causality" than that associated with Newtonian and Einsteinian mechanics, and suggested its extension beyond quantum physics (where it belongs) to other human phenomena.[49] The argument that the concepts of quantum physics were incommensurable with the old idea of nature as a stable, predictable entity, and that "the very act of observing alters the object being observed when its quantum numbers are small" (p. 24), appealed (as it still appeals) to those anxious to establish a place for idiosyncrasy and unpredictability in human experience, of the sort that social science reasoning when it was most committed to its objectivist (and not its literary) extreme seemed to threaten or deny. Not for nothing did Heisenberg engage with the criticisms of the classic materialists in the Soviet academy (p. 135). But the enemy was also within and was typified in the more extreme claims of the social scientists for a potentially closed culture in which everyone's behavior could be predicted and controlled in every way. Even when such ideas were employed in the service of democracy—so that what was prescribed was precisely a measure of spontaneity rather than merely passive reproduction—there was always the fear that such knowledge might fall into the wrong hands. There was also the Horkheimer-Adorno intuition about the ideological limits of and constraints on spontaneity itself.

The fear of a totalitarian society that contextualizes the extraordinary currency of such books as George Orwell's *Animal Farm* (1946) and Arthur Koestler's *Darkness at Noon* (1940) was not, then, simply and entirely a fear of the Russians or the Germans or the Chinese, but also a fear of a prominent component in the culture of the western democracies, most visibly represented in the social sciences and their clear relation to instrumental goals and political implementations. The social sciences seemed not only to assert the power of situatedness, as philosophers and legal theorists had been doing for some time, but also to offer the prospect of putting it under control and describing it precisely, which were ambitions floated before but only at rare moments of high confidence, usually at critical moments in the articulation of national identities. Finally, it was the unknowability of remote causes that had allowed Clarence Darrow his polemically imaginative speculations about how Loeb and Leopold were driven to their crime. With the coming of a professionalized social science, there seemed to be a way to specify those remote causes, perhaps to define criminality once and for all according to more refined criteria, perhaps to preclude all criminal behavior whatsoever. This prospect was and remains to many of us as frightening as it is appealing. It is this dilemma that still informs our thinking about situatedness, which is at once resisted and embraced by a culture radically unclear about the consequences of admitting or denying it in extended or absolute terms. Hence we tend to situate ourselves when it suits us, and differentiate ourselves (or others) when it doesn't. There is a more or less constant crossing of rhetorical boundaries in response to polemical needs, and a self-perpetuating tradition that subsists by rearranging the family of terms that social science deploys. So, for instance, the quest for "a single organized system of knowledge" has most recently been taken up by evolutionary psychology, which is looking for a "universal human nature" in the psychological mechanisms evolved by our species in its extended existence as hunter-gatherers.[50] Even were this ambition to succeed (which is unlikely enough), its findings are going to remain so general as to be more or less useless in deciding the sorts of questions that the standard social science model has tried to address. Unless, of course, I can avoid a theft conviction by interpellating myself "as a member of a species reproducing a long-term adaptation to hunting and gathering."

For the century that has just ended, the definitive literary treatment of the conjunction between situatedness and social science is George Orwell's *Nineteen Eighty-Four*, first published in 1949. Orwell writes the nightmare of total control. Everything in the situation of the inhabitants of Oceania is monitored and administered, and the drama of the novel is embodied in Winston Smith's efforts to achieve privacy and to preserve an autonomous memory and a choice of alternative situations. Winston's interrogator, O'Brien, speaks the language of social science: "We control life, Winston, at all its levels. You are imagining that there is something called human nature which will be outraged by what we do and will turn against us. But we create human nature. Men are infinitely malleable." [51] Orwell's fear was John Stuart Mill's fear and Dewey's fear, the fear of the complete conformity that came along with the positive project of objectivist social science and monolithic ideology, "three hundred million people all with the same face" (p. 74). It was also the fear that produced Weber's metaphor of the "iron cages" and made it so popular. The project of the Party is "educational," one of "continually molding the consciousness" (p. 209). As articulated by O'Brien, it is also an academic project, having passed beyond the desire for mere efficiency to an obsession with theoretical absolutes: "It is intolerable to us that an erroneous thought should exist anywhere in the world, however secret and powerless it might be" (p. 258).

The maintenance of the nightmare society of Ingsoc (English socialism) is misunderstood by those who see it simply as an allegory of life elsewhere (Russia, for instance), or as a parable of what might happen if "they" conquer "us." Orwell's analysis suggests instead that the disease is within, and not simply a result of others' national traditions. Orwell saw a sinister potential in the social engineering open to us with the new hegemony of social science in the anglophone world. Well before Francis Fukuyama and the postmodern affirmation of an "end" to history, Orwell imaged the Party as putting a stop to any meaningful differentiation of past from present: "History has stopped. Nothing exists except an endless present in which the Party is always right" (p. 156). Personal and public memory are both erased by being continually re-scripted, made over into the present. Winston's job is the rewriting of all records—journalistic, historical, literary—to conform with the party line of the day: books "were recalled and rewritten again and again, and were invariably reissued without any admission that any alteration had been made" (p. 41). Poetry anthologies are modified in the same way (p. 43). There is no record against which the Party's claims can be tested; there is no literature, and nothing of the sense of the past that literature embodies and communicates. Winston wakes from a dream with the word "Shakespeare" on his lips only because of a regression to fading memories (p. 32). Major writers are preserved in place for "considerations of prestige" (p. 314), but only after being translated from Oldspeak to Newspeak, at which point the original writings can be destroyed.

Orwell's book has given us a number of terms now in relatively common circulation—prole, Big Brother, doublethink, Thought Police, as well as Newspeak—and it contains its own dismal theory of exactly such locutions. Newspeak works by popularizing "telescoped words and phrases" and cutting out the "associations" informing language (p. 310); in other words, by destroying the literary potential of language (as C. K. Ogden, whom I take to be Orwell's target here, was quite happy to do in his invention of BASIC).[52] Its aim is to shrink the working vocabulary of its users, and to render its use "as nearly as possible independent of consciousness" (p. 311). As one of Winston's colleagues puts it: "In the end we shall make thoughtcrime literally impossible, because there will be no words in which to express it. Every concept that can ever be needed will be expressed by exactly *one* word, with its meaning rigidly defined and all its subsidiary meanings rubbed out and forgotten" (p. 53). The Party has, it seems, found a demonic-parodic version not just of the BASIC for which Ogden and I. A. Richards worked so hard, but also of the universal grammar which the professional linguists tried to isolate from the plethora of world languages.[53] It is used not in the service of cosmopolitan tolerance but as a tool for thought control. In fact it is so efficient that the state of Oceania does not need to be "centralized" in conventional ways (p. 210): language, purged of literature, does the job.

Nineteen Eighty-Four thus asks to be read as a critique of the objectivist social science tendency so dominant in the western democracies in the mid-twentieth century. The problems of situatedness latent in the very beginnings of modernity, in its philosophical and legal self-projections, can be seen to peak with the postwar–cold war social science project, so full of hope but so close to terror, and prompting thereby a strong individualist reaction. That, as I have said before, is the antinomy of situatedness. It cannot be ignored as constitutive of selves and social meanings, but as soon as it is admitted it becomes a principle of radical instability. Fear of anarchist idiosyncrasy and of completely unfettered selves is balanced by an equivalent fear of total administration. This is an example of the point I have made before: that the "problems" of the arguments from situatedness are not meant to be solved, except with such dramatically negative and therefore visibly unacceptable consequences. And yet their solution remains the avowed goal of much social science and well-intentioned social planning. Clarence Darrow, in arguing against the death penalty for Loeb and Leopold, did not need or mean to prove them innocent, but intended only to establish a shadow of a doubt about their complete guilt according to the principles of rational decision making. The value of the argument from situatedness, for him, was precisely that it *is* insoluble. Social science, in contrast, has tended to have a positive agenda: it must argue that something is the case, if not certainly then at least probably. It does so notwithstanding its own implication in the "wholesale reflexivity" that Giddens describes and that Herbert has found latent in the recourse to spiritualism of the earliest sociological texts, as well as in Adam Smith's prior intuition that the origin of systems is always in the human mind and not in the world it is seeking to account for.[54] The pressures of professionalism and of the culture of expertise, along with a general desire for a benign modification of the social environment, have frequently endorsed a stronger objectivism than the probability-based tradition within social science would seem to permit. The strong persuasions of this model, so dominant in the present century, must be counted as among the reasons why we are now still so involved with the language of situatedness and with the particular confusions it generates. In this chapter I have sought to show why we are likely to be compelled to repeat this past even when we do have a history for it. Sociology, to the extent that it really is committed to wholesale reflexivity, has remained very much what according to Habermas it began by being: the "science" of a bourgeois society whose fluctuations it cannot reduce to order and might even perhaps proliferate by the very terms of its analysis. In this sense the instability of the rhetoric of self-affiliation and of all attributions of situatedness is part and parcel of standard sociology, whose antinomic general features are now increasingly apparent at the level of the single, personal life. Impersonally generated definitions of who and what we are come to be replaced by acts of choice; failure to prosper begins to look like a personal failure, a result of making the wrong choice. When everyone is their own sociologist, then we have reached either the end of social science or (the same thing) its complete naturalization.

4. Literary Situations, Novel Solutions

Literature and Risk Culture In the nightmare world of Orwell's *Nineteen Eighty-Four* literature does not look like the genre we are used to, and there is no need for literary criticism. A totally administered society within which everyone has the same thoughts also gives rise to none of the awkward differences of the sort that the rhetoric of situatedness is deployed to negotiate. History too has disappeared: "Nothing exists except an endless present in which the Party is always right" (p. 156). To return once again to Nietzsche: because there is no history everything becomes definable. The rewriting of all the written records of the past in the language and spirit of the present erases all evidence that things have ever been otherwise. Old spellings, allusions, typefaces, and vocabularies disappear from literature, which thenceforth no longer exists as any kind of record of its time and place of composition and publication. To have a history, to belong to what Foucault in *The Order of Things* called the age of "man" wherein all knowledge has to be figured in temporal-biological terms, is to be indecipherable, or to be open to rendition only by way of plausibility and probability, in the manner of Bentham and Mill. In *Nineteen Eighty-Four*, literature and the human subject whose situatedness it significantly chronicles lose their history and their historicism; situatedness then becomes open to exact specification and determination. The price paid for such clear definition is totalitarianism; the price paid for a world of unpredictable options within a democracy is never being sure where you are coming from or going to.

We have seen that social science has very seldom been the objective discipline that Durkheim, for one, thought that it could become by putting aside "all that too readily lends itself to personal judgments and subjective appreciations." [1] If the argument of Giddens's *Consequences of Modernity* is correct, sociology is indeed becoming more and more fully a part of the world it would describe, and all the more likely to encounter all the hermeneutic problems that the objective science model is designed to preempt. If it reflexively helps constitute the very objects of its own analysis, then its knowledge is no longer objective in the traditional sense. And because it is a human knowledge of a human condition, it stands to appear obscure because it is implicated in the same unfathomable "mystery of man" described by Wordsworth in his great autobiographical poem. [2] It becomes, as Lepenies and Giddens and Herbert have all variously described, something like literature.

But literature, on the other hand, did not always accede willingly to its own hermeneutic instability. Just as social science has entertained the prospect of turning itself into literature, so literature could sometimes imagine itself as a form of social science. There was a strong component in romantic aesthetics recognizing critical self-consciousness and epistemological uncertainty as the defining feature of a modern literature, and it was especially but not by any means exclusively dramatized in the poetry of the time. [3] But there also evolved a clear countermovement that envisaged literature, especially the novel, as itself the most adequate form for a social science aspiring to objective description. Herbert Spencer, for example, was willing to exclude George Eliot's novels from the ban on works of fiction at the London library; [4] Zola and Flaubert (in whom Sartre will take such sustained interest, as we will see in the next chapter) made their reputations as recorders of reality. Lepenies makes much of the secret and not so secret desires of Comte and Beatrice Webb to become poets or novelists, or at least to make peace with them (*Between Literature and Science*, pp. 40, 137–43). There were also novelists who thought of themselves and were thought of as social scientists.

In his *England in 1819*, an important study of historicism in romantic writers and in latterday critics and theorists, James Chandler proposes that the early nineteenth century sees the "invention of the historical situation." [5] Our contemporary preoccupation with historical method is, he suggests, itself to be situated historically, to be understood as taking on exemplary and even original form in the novels of Walter Scott and in other writings of the British romantics. Writers such as Scott not only claim to aspire to represent a historical situation in the past, in something of its own terms, but they also bring up for attention the contrived, present-generated gesture whereby they write it. Along with the invitation to immerse ourselves in the life and times of, for instance, the Scottish Highlands, we encounter also hyperbolic retractions, confessions of anachronism, and flagrant signifiers of fictionality (for instance in the ungainly contributions of Scott's awkwardly named narrators). Scott's novels purport to represent individual situatedness in all its objective complexities (ordinary persons in historically demanding times and places) but at the same time project the ineluctably made-up identity of their own rhetoric. Literature itself, to use Lepenies's terms, is thus between literature and social science.

Chandler makes an important argument for the transformation of traditional casuistry's task of adjudicating individual decisions in relation to moral and theological norms into something very different: a focus on "the case" as part of romantic literature's effort to represent a *historical* situation (see especially pp. 194–264). Putting Chandler's terms together with mine, I would say that the "case" embodies both the normative and the anomalous components of an individual's situatedness. It is thus a site of contradiction and of aporia. It is the place where general determinations of the sort described by history and social science come into precise contact with the idiosyncratic elements of individual situations. As such, it gives evidence for probable or plausible explanations of behavior that are always potentially open to redescription as objective explanations but which most commonly elude precise definition in such terms. The case is often expressed in explicitly legal terms, as it is in many of Scott's novels; and indeed making sense of an individual's role in place and time is very like attempting a legal finding. It is a decision, or a withholding of a decision, about the availability and credibility of choices and compulsions, determinations and results. Walter Scott's readers prefigure Alan Dershowitz's jurors in having to pick their way through a host of arguably mitigating and extenuating circumstances playing on the question of why people do what they do. Both readers and jurors are told that there are powerful impersonal forces working to make us what we are, while at the same time there are possible or arguable moments where we can be expected to exercise personal choice. Telling the difference, if it can be done, happens in and around the "case."

The antinomic potential of this encapsulation of human situatedness appears also in the avowed ambition of Scott's fiction. In *Waverley*, much is made of the power of circumstances to make over the personality along predictable lines. Edward Waverley's early education gives him habits of loose reading and superficial attention and thus trains him to make the errors of judgment he will perpetrate later in life.[6] Fergus MacIvor's character is very much dependent on his "situation" (p. 157), as is that of his sister Flora (p. 214). This is why Scott defends his historical novel as requiring so much "old fashioned politics": the story would make no sense otherwise, given that the behavior of his characters arises from "the feelings, prejudices, and parties of the times" (p. 63). At the same time there is a promise to delineate "those passions common to men in all stages of society, and which have alike agitated the human heart, whether it throbbed under the steel corslet of the fifteenth century, the brocaded coat of the eighteenth, or the blue frock and white dimity waistcoat of the present day" (pp. 35–36). Wordsworth, famously, made a similar attempt in poetry. But how do we tell which is the common, universal passion and which is the characterological culture of the moment? In explaining why he is not about to write another *Don Quixote*, which shows "such total perversion of intellect as misconstrues the objects actually presented to the senses," Scott specifies his own focus on "that more common aberration from sound judgment, which apprehends occurrences indeed in their reality, but communicates to them a tincture of its own romantic tone and colouring" (p. 55). Situatedness, it would seem, is what governs the nature and degree of tincture; it does not quite refigure reality itself. But the tinctures are critical enough to bring about all of the major misunderstandings between the characters as well as the self-deceptions of each of them.

The mitigation of extreme misunderstandings is where Scott's legitimation of the modernization process works its fictional magic. Extreme variations in personal situation are portrayed as belonging to the barbaric past. The rough and brutal feudal habits of the Highland clans are gone for good, and are open to picturesque recovery precisely to the degree that they are no longer to be experienced; Hanoverians and Jacobites have had their day. The closer one comes to the present of 1814, it is implied, the more peaceable and predictable life has become. We have, in other words, come to share an increasingly common situation, and at the same time become more tolerant of the differences that do still obtain. The ascendancy of the new middle class and its polite, commercial customs, comprehensively disseminated after the Act of Union had come to be widely accepted, have softened dispositions and modified manners. What Scott images as a historical transition was theorized by Adam Smith as a natural, human trait. Smith described the way in which the imagination leads us to identify with and enter into the "situations" of others, and to modify our own situations to an ideal normality that makes it easier for others to identify with us. So, if I am feeling extreme pain or pleasure, the desire for approbation leads me to underplay the force of my response in order to permit others to sympathize without feeling threatened.[7] Smith has here found a way to naturalize the dynamics of an emergent democracy within which the interactions between different people must be increasingly self-monitored if they are to remain peaceable; his sketch of the imaginary passage through the situations of others is what we have seen Charles Horton Cooley making literal in his account of the effects of a mature democratic culture on the work habits and the character of its people.

Let me make a bold statement about the place of literature and its criticism in relation to the aporetic or antinomic logic attending questions about situatedness: that the appeal and function of literature has significantly depended on the ingenuity and complexity with which it *represents* situatedness while sidestepping or denying the urge to *solve* or factor it out in exact or limiting terms. This has meant that literature has often given great importance to the power of place and time — that same power of place that Edward Casey's *The Fate of Place* described as incrementally sidelined by mainstream philosophy in its preference for the abstractions of mathematical space. I do not of course mean to suggest that there is or should be some closed category called *literature* whose boundaries can be heroically defended against whatever is not literature, or *good* literature. That commitment has been the energy behind many a battle among literary critics, but it has no place here. In using the term I simply mean to refer to a group of writings that mostly hold in common an exploration or representation of lives and experiences that are not our own or (as in the case of autobiography) that involve seeing ourselves as if from the position of another. Such writings cross the boundaries between fact and fiction and past and present in a fairly uncensored way, and by way of an attempt at aesthetic gratification (or sometimes in refusing this same gratification) they have appealed throughout modernity by offering an imaginative relief from our own immediate situations without for the most part (although there are exceptions) confronting us with what is completely and unnegotiably unfamiliar. The best fit for the job description I have just outlined is probably to be found in some nineteenth-century novels, and it must be said that there has been a strong countercondition argued for high poetry as properly representing types and universals rather than densely situated particulars. It was in just this spirit that Coleridge made his famous case against the "matter-of-factness" of some of Wordsworth's poems, with their "laborious minuteness" of detail and their faithful transcription of "accidental circumstances" that distract the reader from attending to the category of "men in general."[8] Wordsworth, one might say, thus shows himself sensitive to the emergent conventions of the novel and to the concern for matters of situatedness to which it responds. Later literary criticism, in its obsession with dramatic speakers and points of view, would also make poetry over in the style to which Coleridge objected.

On the matter of situatedness, the task of literature has seemed to be one of roving among and between the various options open to us as we try to describe the forms of being in the world: so it is possible for Jerome Bruner, for example, to invoke "the shadowy epistemology of the story" and for Kenneth Burke, in a way quite typical of the modernist critics, to speak of the precision of literary communication as ideally a form of "magic" in which "our assertions (or verbal decrees) as to the nature of the situation come closest to a correct gauging of that situation as it actually is." [9] Both are true to one side of the literary gesture, which is alternatively a way of confusing the issue (novels *are* just stories) or of presenting it as absolutely specific and concrete. Poetry, with the onset of modernism, came to inhabit the extreme of specificity rather than that of general truth, where Coleridge had sought to locate it. But it is the novel above all that can be seen as the appropriate vehicle for representing a "risk culture" in which no one is fully aware of all the determinations that impinge on his or her own situation. Only such awareness seems to promise efficient or satisfied life, but one must function nonetheless without it; its onset would indeed preclude the element of surprise that is unpredictably combined with the satisfaction of expectations as the very fabric of the novel's narrative logic. Providential narratives can confirm or deny one's hunches, or suggest the operation of some other energies beyond those of individual consciousness or agency, and the degree to which these are accessible to readers while being withheld from protagonists provides much of the tension for literary plot. But the uncertainty about causes and effects also carries the plot itself and provides suspense and surprise, whether it vindicates the model of successful social and personal mobility (the happy ending) or shows the protagonist to have been after all doomed by fate or betrayed by unlucky turns of events.

Reading such novels, in other words, is a risk for the reader, a participation by proxy in the uncertainties of risk culture itself. The notorious alternative endings of *Great Expectations* (Pip happy, Pip disappointed) and *Caleb Williams* (Falkland untouched, Falkland repentant) are in their very contingency instances of the unpredictability of what Chandler calls "the case." The same circumstances can, with the tiniest change in the wind, produce completely different resolutions that are thereby always beyond complete explanation. Modernity's notion of literature has usually held at a distance the morality tale or simple predetermination model that limits or immediately interprets our acts and decisions, showing instead a preference for the potentially aporetic spaces of obscure causes and uncertain effects. The popularity of *Robinson Crusoe*, for example, surely had something to do with its format as a counternarrative to the even more popular but all too providential *Pilgrim's Progress*. Defoe images a world that is not clearly if at all charged with spiritual significance and in which emergent allegorical motifs (being saved from the wreck, the building of the boat, being almost swept out to sea, the footprint) remain doggedly at the level of the empirical and are not gathered into a pattern that speaks for the education or salvation of the hero, yet at the same time do not interfere with his well-being.[10] The novel chronicles the career of a man who is willing enough, under the pressure of adverse turns of fortune, to get down on his knees in prayer and to see patterns in his experiences, but who is not punished—who is indeed rewarded—for a life strategy that remains consistent only in its opportunism. Crusoe is a prototype of the early Sartrean individual engaged in a project, taking hold of his situation in response to pragmatic imperatives while remaining ultimately unaffected by the epistemological or ethical puzzles he encounters and meditates on. He temporarily reasons himself out of his instinctive desire to murder the "savages," only to do just that impulsively and under pressure from immediate circumstances. Self-interest is not punished in this novel, even when it is not especially enlightened. For this reason among others, Crusoe has been a hero very few cultivated readers have admired, and with whom fewer still who are beyond adolescence have empathized. But the novel was massively popular and has remained compulsive reading. This must have to do with its efficiency in bringing up for inspection some of the most enduring puzzles arising in the life of a democratic-capitalist society. Among them are the antinomies of situatedness, to which Crusoe gives a good airing without allowing them to distract him from the job of surviving and prospering. Above all he shows that one can survive in a world that may or may not be under the constant surveillance of an all-seeing God, and that if one is indeed so situated then whatever happens must be in some sense justified and can definitely be handled. Crusoe really does manage to be all that he can be. That he does so without needing to cultivate any notable qualities of interiority or moral consistency does not render him less successful.

After Defoe, the novel's dominant concerns about situatedness are almost entirely secular ones. *Robinson Crusoe* has entered literary history as many people's candidate for the first English novel (although this is of course open to dispute), while *Pilgrim's Progress*, the shadow precursor it displaces, has been largely ignored by literary critics and often deemed to be not properly "literature" at all. Throughout most of the eighteenth century the British novel remains dominantly concerned with the lives and adventures of atomic individuals as they move around their worlds and fall in and out of fortune. Some novels of the 1790s, the so-called Jacobin novels, do attempt to make fictional matter out of the necessitarian-materialist arguments of the philosophes, and set out to imagine the careers of protagonists trapped like flies in the webs of that great spider "society." Whereas Defoe has Crusoe imagine the model of total situational determination only to flout it, these novels try to demonstrate that human nature is indeed completely made by circumstances and is describable as such. Godwin's *Caleb Williams* (1794) took up what we would now call something like "ideology" or "cultural determination" in proposing "a general review of the modes of domestic and unrecorded despotism" devolving from the insight "known to philosophers, that the spirit and character of the government intrudes itself into every rank of society."[11] Mary Hays's heroine Emma Courtney was also convinced of the "irresistible power of circumstances" and expressed the desire "to omit no one connecting link in the chain of causes, however minute, that I conceive had any important consequences in the formation of my mind."[12]

At moments like this, novelists begin to sound like social scientists at the high point of their optimism about describing every item in the human personality in relation to social and environmental stimulants. And in *Caleb Williams* Godwin relies heavily on a vocabulary that will feed straight into the social sciences whose disciplinary incarnations are yet to come: the word *situation* occurs on almost every other page of some parts of the novel (a random check provides eight examples in twenty pages). The plot appears as good as providential—accidents always look like contrivances, and almost all random decisions produce narratively critical moments. Caleb himself is an early prototype of Orwell's O'Brien: he aspires to the same total knowledge and total control. Unwilling to rest satisfied with the "shadow of a doubt" (p. 128), he becomes a legalistic scientist of the mind, a "competent adept in the different modes in which the human intellect displays its secret workings" (p. 129). Although prompted to this compulsive surveillance by the very same "passions" (p. 132) that for so many commentators would have preempted any claim to objectivity (for which disinterest was the common prerequisite), Caleb is not portrayed as therefore getting things wrong: his analysis is correct. The symptoms of human behavior and response evinced by Falkland are finally legible and attributable to definite causes and effects. But in his role as social scientist in the making Caleb finds no happiness. First, he is too aware of the effects of a corrupt society on Falkland's otherwise admirable nature (which has been taken to figure that of Edmund Burke) to derive any pleasure from his exposure. And second, the law itself is more or less powerless and visibly inept in the face of the sorts of complexities that life presents. The Hawkinses are hanged (p. 141) after being wrongly convicted by the sort of circumstantial evidence approved by William Paley; in other words from the law's obeying the same kind of probability calculus that social science came to depend on. Circumstances create a real criminal (Falkland) and cause innocent people to be hanged. Despite his innocence Caleb himself cannot outface "circumstances" as evidence against him (p. 175), while his own last appeal to "circumstantial proof" (p. 286) in fact works to his detriment. It is power, finally, and not scientific process, that governs the world; the second can have no effect unless it is supported by the first. Caleb's success as an investigator cannot be effective in a culture that worships rank, fortune, and reputation. It is only the last-minute expression (at least in the published ending) of Falkland's human conscience that saves Caleb from punishment. Godwin seems to vindicate the final force of universal human feelings but shows at the same time that they might just as easily not have appeared in public or even emerged at all. Caleb's expertise is unvalidated by the sort of professional designation that would make people believe in it. He is not yet a social scientist.

The Jacobin novel, with its often formulaic investigation of the power of circumstances over individuals, forms a rather short chapter in the history of British literature, and none of the books written according to its mandates have tended to survive in the familiar canon of "great" novels. Like Pilgrim's Progress, and for similar reasons, they have seldom been recognized as good literature. Situatedness in the nineteenth-century novel, at least for the major characters, tends to appear as a backdrop or constraint against which they must test their strength; even when they fail they often demonstrate some alternative kind of integrity that is not describable in simple situational terms, and is not to be attributed to circumstances. Perhaps because of the increasing sense of the very power of such circumstances, a sense shared as we have seen by John Stuart Mill, the novelists are often in the business of showing something in exemplary human nature that is not manipulable by education or environment. This is in tune with the mission of much social criticism of the times. Mill thought that the major emergency facing British culture was the decline in individuality and the corresponding increase in preformed, situationally regulated personalities of the sort evident in the "warning example" of China where the people are "all alike" and the culture completely "stationary" (*On Liberty*, pp. 87–88). In his 1829 essay "Signs of the Times" Thomas Carlyle had already warned of the influence of the "preestablished apparatus" of a culture governed by mechanical principles and by the notion, attributed to Bentham, that "our happiness depends entirely on external circumstances" to the detriment of any faith in "individual endeavour." [13]

The generally liberal-individualist emphasis of the literary novel thus took up the task of demonstrating the need for and place of what Mill and so many literary writers called "character." In Dickens it is mostly the minor figures who are successfully molded by circumstances, who are mere creatures of their situations, often to the point of physiological as well as mental making over: the central and admirable protagonists are those whose inner values are not manipulable. Fagin says of Oliver Twist that "it was not easy to train him to the business . . . he was not like other boys in the same circumstances." [14] Without these inner qualities no merely circumstantial conditions can improve our lot: families can either be repositories of ideal social interaction or emblems of a claustrophobic and neurotic intimacy, depending on the nature of the personalities involved. The power of situatedness is thus represented as rising the further one goes down the ranked order of admirable literary characters, and decreasing as one goes up it. In Jane Austen's *Persuasion*, for instance, the romance between the minor protagonists Captain Benwick and Louisa Musgrove evolves entirely from a compatibility in "situation"; no profound inner qualities are involved. In contrast Anne and Frederick, as heroine and hero, must overcome "the peculiar disadvantages of their respective situations," which do not determine their personalities but only highlight their integrity by providing opposition to the alliance that properly ends the novel.[15] In the Jacobin novels, the "major" characters who carry the narrative tend to learn that they are "minor" in terms of their susceptibility to passive situatedness; they discover that however hard they try to fashion their own destinies, circumstances always win out. This paradigm is of course completely symmetrical with the definition of authorial genius in the literary marketplace: the task of the writer is to make him or herself recognizable and distinctive and unlike any other writer in both style and subject, in other words a "character" or, as James Chandler might put it, a suitably complicated "case." Those who fail are either ignored or identified as purely generic imaginations.

Celebrating Aporia What I have said so far is admittedly a simplification of the nineteenth-century novel even if it roughly describes a good deal of Dickens. The further the novel goes in its exploration of interior, psychological space—and of course it has gone very far by the end of the century—the more complex its presentation of situatedness tends to become, and the more its minor characters become subject to the same complexities that govern its heroes and heroines. Dickens's characters are famous for their relatively minimal interior life, and they have been famously disliked (by E. M. Forster for instance) for this very reason. The passage into interiority, whether in prose fiction or in the dramatic monologue that becomes so significant in nineteenth-century poetry, is for the reader an escape from his or her own situatedness, but only into that of an imagined other. We move away from the Dickensian commitment to immanent personality toward a refiguring of the aporetic nature of situatedness as we participate in the lives of protagonists who wonder about their own motivations or who act in ways that make us wonder about them. The more empathic the identification, the more difficult it is to make decisive judgments about what is good or bad or avoidable in human behavior. Efforts continue to be made at rendering the novel a form of objectivist social science, but what was in the eighteenth century an ideal narrative posture of disinterest tied up with a belief in the saving powers of economic and political independence—a posture already in itself fragile— becomes in the nineteenth century a more scientistic detachment that is subject to the logical fallacies of all such detachments imagined under the sign of reason. So Sartre deems Flaubert's effort at "de-situating" himself to be an attempt to "tear oneself as pure subject away from the species" that can only lead to "the radical negation of the human." [16]

The human, in these times, has come to be seen as radically bound into time and place, but not in ways that are finally describable. Wordsworth ends the first book of his posthumously published autobiographical poem by claiming to have solved the puzzle of what to write about, seeing in the story of his own life a topic "single and of determined bounds" (*The Prelude*, p. 64). But the solution of the problem of choice only commits him to the insoluble problems of describing where he is coming from, which is a task that is massively overdetermined and not at all single. Hence the governing language of the poem is that of hypothesis or approximation, making heavy use of such terms as "perchance" and "surely" and of locutions such as "if this be error" (p. 88) that withdraw the claim to any absolute epistemological conviction. Wordsworth is of course writing in reaction to an early version of the social science dream, that represented by Jacobin theory, so that the fronting of imprecision is intended as an affirmative gesture, a celebration of the claims of obscurity rather than or as well as (as it sometimes seems) a declaration of limits that are to be regretted. The appeal and power of the "spots of time" is that one goes back to them time and time again without coming anywhere near a sense of understanding or of complete explanation (p. 428). They do give the poet a "knowledge" that "the mind is lord and master" and stand therefore as correctives to any utilitarian privileging of the power of circumstances. But the mind's knowledge is not adequate to its own explanation. Its sources and operations remain in the last instance a mystery. This may indeed be the exemplary paradigm of bourgeois subjectivity, whereby its inability to complete itself *as* a self both reflects a condition of social alienation and stimulates an indefinitely proliferating effort at doing just that. The bad news is the good news. The self that cannot find itself can be happy in the knowledge that it is this precise indefinability that generates an attitude to a speculative future, a commitment to becoming and becoming again that will only end with life itself and—to recall the voice of Tennyson's Ulysses—perhaps not even then.

The Wordsworthian "self as becoming" is rhapsodic and romantic without losing its sense of loss and of the melancholy incompetence of many of its efforts at recollection. It is in this way a self without restrictive situatedness, perhaps too mobile even for the attribution of distinguishable subject positions and responsibilities. But this is a poetic self, a self in poetry. It is an assertion of the self as not being subject to circumstances (just as Wordsworth, in London, is not worn down by all the things that he sees as wearing down others), although oddly enough the avowed reason for this is the power of other circumstances, the ones (lakes and mountains, small human settlements) most powerful in early childhood. Wordsworth thinks that the experiences of physical nature and psychological flexibility in the formative years are what saved him from becoming a mere segment of humanity in a world governed by the culture of divided labor and social class. He records himself as an instance of Locke's argument for the power of early education. To invoke Chandler's terms, in *The Prelude* Wordsworth writes himself as a "case," and he is in control of all the evidence, but he cannot close the case as long as the writer goes on writing. The great autobiographical poem is thus exemplary of one end of the historicist spectrum, the one weighted toward hermeneutically articulated self-consciousness of the sort that features in Scott's prefaces, footnotes, and endings but appears only intermittently (although still visibly enough) in his narratives. Whereas Godwin suggests that the truth of human situations can indeed be apprehended but will not be believed in a corrupted world, Wordsworth projects truth only as something infinitely deferred, always to be sought, and makes it thereby the guarantor of an ongoing life in an unfinished history. Life requires the withholding of truth.

The delineation of the approximate coordinates of place and time —the self moving from here to there and noticing this or that—becomes then the best that can be done in the way of specifying the terms of the self's situatedness. The maximum in circumstantial precision is accompanied by a minimal claim to descriptive completeness. Poetry here engages with the "structure of probable signs." I take this phrase from Douglas Lane Patey's *Probability and Literary Form*, an important study of Augustan and early romantic theory that very much anticipates Chandler's more recent argument about casuistry and "the case." [17] Patey finds in Jane Austen a "precise epistemologist of the probable" who "conducts her novels in the Augustan vocabulary of probable inference, of sagacity in reading signs and circumstances; she builds them as didactic structures of conjecture and expectation, as judged by the event" (p. 218). Austen's most admired characters, that is to say, are shown to be aware of all the normative patterns and probable connections that relate to the circumstances of human situatedness, but they must also and more importantly learn to be flexible and alert at multiple levels, discursive and intuitive, in deciding exactly what governs or follows from a particular person's behavior. The minor characters—Mr. Collins, Mr. Elton, Mrs. Norris, and their kind—are, like Dickens's minor figures, almost always the same and are almost completely predictable. They are no longer if they ever were emblems of an exploratory selfhood capable of change, and they provide a background to the more difficult task of tracing causes and effects carried out by the main protagonists.

Patey has drawn up a very informative list of the vocabulary of "conjecture and expectation" in *Emma*, which Austen provides for the carrying out of that task of speculating about causes (p. 281). Words such as *evidence, circumstance, hope, surprise,* and *doubt* and their many cognates provide the core of the novel's rhetoric. There is, for example, a long discussion at the end of volume 1 (chapter 18) between Emma and Knightley about the power of what I have been calling (although they never would) situatedness. Everyone has been awaiting the arrival of Mr. Frank Churchill, but Mr. Frank Churchill does not come. Emma does not much care at this point whether he comes or not, but to keep up appearances and to appease his father and mother-in-law she proposes that Frank's uncle and aunt are to be blamed for keeping him away. Knightley disagrees. The Churchills (the aunt and uncle) may be at fault, but Frank could come if he cared to and the final responsibility for not doing so lies with him. Not so, says Emma; yes indeed, rejoins Knightley, who launches into a long speech proving that Frank is a bad sort because he has been badly raised. Emma, whose own situation makes her very sensitive to the constraints of circumstances, makes reference to the "difficulties of dependency" of which the independent Knightley can have no experience.[18] Knightley parries with empirical (and circumstantial) evidence: Frank Churchill is known to travel widely. And then Emma makes a strong pitch for the importance of situatedness: "It is very unfair to judge of any body's conduct, without an intimate knowledge of their situation. Nobody, who has not been in the interior of a family, can say what the difficulties of any individual of that family may be. We ought to be acquainted with Enscombe, and with Mrs. Churchill's temper, before we pretend to decide upon what her nephew can do. He may, at times, be able to do a great deal more than he can at others" pp. 121–22). Knightley comes back with a counterargument in defense of universal duties that are beyond situatedness (thus going against his own earlier situational explanation about bad upbringing), defending not just their intrinsic integrity but their instrumental usefulness: "Respect for right conduct is felt by everybody" (p. 122).

The debate goes on, in topsy-turvy fashion. Knightley sounds variously like a Lockean, a Jacobin, and a Kantian (he is properly none of these), while Emma comes close to proposing a position of *tout comprendre tout pardonner*. Both parties pursue the argument much further than it needs to go because it is a way for them to engage in intense exchange without speaking of or perhaps even recognizing their own mutual affection. Knightley may be jealous in advance of a new bachelor who is about to enter the neighborhood; Emma may be flirtatiously curious about the same thing and willing to claim more than she can know in order to provoke Knightley into expressing his insecurity. She herself is an individual in a difficult family, one in which her father's heavy hand effectively discourages her from any comfortable thoughts about marriage. The content of the argument is a debate about the deciding power of situatedness as applied to a relatively trivial case, the case of Frank Churchill's nonappearance. But Austen also entices and entraps her reader into setting about a "finding" of Emma and Knightley themselves, as they are *having* the discussion. We are encouraged to surmise that this is a lover's tiff, or a testing out of the consequences of disagreement between people who are getting close to one another, so that the triviality of the Churchill "case" is its very point—it does not in itself much matter. Then we are inclined to wonder whether they know that it does not matter, whether they are being self-conscious or unconscious. And at this point we have as active but compliant readers been ourselves thoroughly involved in the inquiry about situatedness that is the manifest content of the literal debate between the characters, like willing flies in a very attractive spider web.

The manner of this book is not, in other words, that of objective social science, but of "literature" as Lepenies describes it—that which calls attention to itself as partial and incomplete. The probability standard that is becoming the core of the social-scientific method is indeed at work here, but it is explored rather than expounded, within the dramatic contexts in which characters find themselves. Emma is not like Caleb Williams whose passage through Godwin's novel is not marked by critical self-deceptions and whose command of the truth of circumstances is not itself in question even though the fate of that truth is not to be publicly vindicated. Emma maintains to be sure a belief in her own transparency as she complains about Jane Fairfax being reserved: "There was no getting at her real opinion" (p. 140). But here Austen's readers enjoy their overview of Emma's limits and self-deceptions, and they rest in that enjoyment at their cost if they fail to go on to realize that they too are constructing explanations of why Emma and Knightley do what they do, explanations that go beyond any evidence that the novel actually hands over. This is one of the delights of reading Jane Austen, and it is also what marks her as very much a writer of the early nineteenth century. Emma is a social scientist manqué, and Austen makes her so. The author is fully aware both of the commonplace availability of arguments from situatedness and of their insufficiency; and she requires that her readers extend that knowledge not only to the characters in her books but also to themselves. Like the characters in the novel we cannot be sure where we are coming from.

Often the element of mystery or obscurity is dramatically played up in order to force us into the experience of not knowing when we most urgently want to know, so that we are encouraged to be aware that we are expecting fiction to provide us with reality: Emma says nothing about love or desire in accepting Knightley, and every reader wonders whether she feels any. The moment of Knightley's proposal has Austen breaking into the spellbound reader's empathic absorption with a startling alienation effect: "What did she say?—Just what she ought, of course. A lady always does" (p. 354). At the end of *Mansfield Park* Austen coyly administers a similar rebuke to any of us (that is, most of us) who are still trapped in the mode of realist expectation: "I purposely abstain from dates on this occasion, that every one may be at liberty to fix their own, aware that the cure of unconquerable passions, and the transfer of unchanging attachments, must vary much as to time in different people. — I only intreat every body to believe that exactly at the time when it was quite natural that it should be so, and not a week earlier, Edmund did cease to care about Miss Crawford, and became as anxious to marry Fanny, as Fanny herself could desire." [19] Here we are at once whisked out of the fantasy of being in a real world and reminded that we have been reading fiction—a fiction that is, despite its uncanny verisimilitude, sparsely furnished indeed with the dates, times, and places that seek to represent our place in the world.

George Eliot also takes up questions of situatedness, and in a much more expository and sustained manner than Austen: Eliot is much more aware of and interested in the pressures and preoccupations of the emerging social sciences, and the questions that are implicit in Austen's narratives are fully thematized and expounded at some length in Eliot's. Chapter 16 of *Adam Bede*, for example, is titled "Links" and it is significantly given over to proposing that "the human soul is a very complex thing" and a medium wherein "a great deal of hard work is done by agents who are not acknowledged." [20] At the beginning of *Middlemarch* Eliot opines in her own narrative voice that as we contemplate the "mysterious mixture" of human personality behaving "under the varying experiments of time," we can trace general conditions that enable some personal developments and prohibit others. Thus many potential Saint Theresas have gone unnoticed for want of a "coherent social faith and order which could perform the function of knowledge for the ardently willing soul." [21] But this does not mean that every ardent soul would be a Saint Theresa under the same conditions, just that conditions place a set of limits on what any individual can do. Eliot's habit is to point out how much more there is to any situation than meets the eye, and to emphasize the variety of partial perspectives that are brought to bear on its explanation and public reception. The more interested persons there are who interpret an event, the more interpretations there are. Sometimes, as in Jane Austen, information is withheld from the reader, who then becomes dramatically involved in the search for critical knowledge. The death of Raffles in *Middlemarch* offers an instance of this strategy (3: 260–78). We are never told the exact degree of Bulstrode's crime and Lydgate's compliance. We do know more about the situation than most of the characters in the book; for example, we know that Bulstrode allows the patient alcohol and omits to tell the servant about limiting the opium dose, and we read of Lydgate's moment of unease at this knowledge, which is suppressed when money is mentioned. But Eliot does not provide definitive comment on the evidence, whose implications tend to emerge in dramatic dialogue without authorial summary (for example, 3: 353–54). The full motivations for Will's taking Rosamund's hand (3: 371) are never convincingly elaborated even when they are explained (3: 406). Eliot includes her readers in the circle of the potentially deceived, even when they are told more about things than the protagonists can know.

The novel gives full play to the persuasive power of circumstantial evidence, which Alexander Welsh has identified as central to literature's investigative method between the Enlightenment and modernism.[22] But when we try to infer exact motivations or degrees of blame simply from circumstances, they turn out to be not what they seem, or simply what they seem, and they seem different to different people. The art of the novel is to show that the "fragment of a life, however typical, is not the sample of an even web" (3: 455). And the forces at play even on the fragment are obscure enough. Eliot's feminism does require and is vindicated by the conviction that "there is no creature whose inward being is so strong that it is not greatly determined by what lies outside it" (3: 464). Dorothea cannot become a Theresa or an Antigone, and she is condemned to the minimal recognition that comes from a "hidden life" and its "unhistoric acts" (3: 464). But these are general constraints that explain what is impossible or unlikely; they do not prescribe every single incident or motivation. Eliot can preserve a convincing polemical case against the consequences of "an imperfect social state" (3: 464) and its effects on talented and imaginative women without suggesting that a perfect social state is either imaginable or necessarily preemptive of further tragedies and inhibitions. In this sense she creates a novelist's version of Bentham's understanding about what social science can and cannot do. It can persuade us, after a review of the statistics, to try to modify the general social condition in some or other desired direction. It cannot however fully analyze the individual event and any one person's situatedness in any thoroughly scientific way, even when it knows that the same general conditions are vitally important to both. Eliot's creation of the fictional narrative of a limited locality—a middle-sized English country town some decades before the time of writing—seems to promise an exactness of description and perhaps a prospect of complete explanation of its significant internal dynamics. But Middlemarch is affected by national and nonlocal tendencies, just as Hardy's Wessex and Austen's country houses are impacted (respectively) by the railways, by the metropolis, and by the fortunes of war and commerce. Locality is never just local. The tasks of describing it and of accounting for the doings of its inhabitants become indefinite and perhaps infinite.[23]

Lessons from Literature What then are the lessons of literature for the task of coping with or finding alternatives to the aporias of situatedness? This question is important to us now in view of the recent popularity of the literary turn in the legal and social sciences. The realist (or roughly realist) novel can provide highly detailed accounts of human situatedness, but it mostly stops short of the claim to complete explanation in just the way that George Eliot stops short. Some novels have claimed to present the case for the comprehensive and scientific determination of character by situation, as Godwin did, but most of those that have flourished in the canon of "great books" enact a significant hesitation about their capacities to fathom all the depths and complexities of human situatedness. Even Thomas Hardy, who comes close to proposing the total inadequacy of human choice and effort in overcoming its allotted situation, resorts not to a biological or social-historical but to a pastiche metaphysical vocabulary to explain the doomed careers of his protagonists. The terms of their existence are not in other words social-scientific, but still are mysterious and unfathomable in advance. What is the use or value of this hesitation about completely specifying situatedness?

At times such hesitation has been made the bearer of our best social hope, as it was by Matthew Arnold, I. A. Richards, and F. R. Leavis in their various ways.[24] Martha Nussbaum has made a recent and eloquent case in her book *Poetic Justice* for the revivifying effect of literature (and particularly the novel of social realism) on critical thinking about legal decision making. Literature and the literary imagination are "subversive" and "disturbing" because they present and encourage participation in "powerful emotions" that call into question both the "conventional pieties" and "one's own thoughts and intentions."[25] They cannot provide the whole of what is needed for "public rationality" (p. xvi) but they are an essential component of any adequate response to and judgment about human behavior. Sounding rather like a reborn F. R. Leavis, Nussbaum finds that a novel such as *Hard Times* engages us with the "full world of human effort" and the " 'real substance' of life" (p. 72), providing a knowledge that should be essential to, for example, a judge presiding over criminal trials (p. 118). Novels "make readers participants in the lives of people very different from themselves and also critics of the class distinctions that give people similarly constructed an unequal access to flourishing" (pp. 45–46). They can also, it is claimed, make us "free from personal bias and favor" (p. 83) without our having to be free from the historicality that we all share, and promote "habits of mind that lead toward social equality in that they contribute to the dismantling of the stereotypes that support group hatred" (p. 92). A similar commitment to the literary informs her 1990 collection of essays, *Love's Knowledge*, which seeks to complicate the perceived scientific bias of normative ethics by fresh attention to the "complex particularity" that literature portrays. General rules and categories are not to be given up (as some radical theorists might argue that they should be), but we must learn through the example of literature to cultivate "a much finer responsiveness to the concrete." [26]

The Wordsworthian "matter-of-factness" and "undue predilection for the *dramatic* form" so disliked by Coleridge (*Biographia Literaria*, 2:126, 135) has here become something of a virtue: it is the refusal to speak of men in general and of universal human traits that renders literature so valuable as a corrective to the potentially impersonal application of abstract paradigms. Cleanth Brooks wrote powerfully and influentially about the capacity of poetry to present a "total situation" that has nothing to do with our "personal beliefs"; because at best it can delineate "concrete experience, many-sided, three-dimensional" it renders our beliefs irrelevant.[27] Kenneth Burke, we recall, said much the same thing. The force of these arguments is surely important to any subculture as wedded to general, rational-scientific models as Nussbaum claims law and ethics to be, although this finding might itself be disputed. One test case might be that of Britain, traditionally administered by a relatively uncodified common law and a society wherein for a variety of reasons academic sociology was a late development. Lepenies has attributed this partly to an enthusiasm for applied statistics that made professional social science somewhat redundant and partly to the sociological functions already enacted in British literary criticism; Perry Anderson, in a famous essay of 1968, found in the hegemony of that same literary criticism one major reason why British culture was able to resist or ignore continental theory and thereby theory in general.[28] According to Anderson, this constituted a limitation and not a virtue in the national imagination. In other words, it is not clear that the compulsive suspicion of rational paradigms is intrinsically any more humane than their proliferation. Some might wish to argue that, for example, the abolition of the death penalty in British criminal law might have something to do with a cultural predisposition to pay attention to what Nussbaum calls the "complex particularity" of the "concrete," and that this in turn has something to do with the traditionally high status of literature and its criticism.[29] But others would surely respond with a critique of the perceived sloppiness and justificatory exceptionalism that have inhibited any move to a bill of rights and permitted (or at least not prevented) all sorts of notorious abuses and politically motivated false convictions.

The case for and against the socially beneficial consequences of privileging the literary education has been made over and over again, so that a historical account suggests its participation in the same series of antinomies and aporias that we have seen throughout this study as typifying the articulation of (modern bourgeois) subjectivity. The professional lament of the literary critic has mostly been about the hostility of the broader culture to the findings of the literary imagination. Sir Henry Newbolt in 1928 could pass for Martha Nussbaum in 1995 in hoping for a world in which, thanks to literature, "it shall be possible for every one to forget the existence of classes and to find a personal interest in each other's circumstances and events."[30] I. A. Richards similarly believed that our impulses were disordered by social and historical forces and that the skilled reading of poetry could put them right. This case goes back at least to Schiller and to his analysis of the nature and prospects of the aesthetic education. Can literature succeed where so many other disciplines have failed, and where literature itself has been trying for so long? Can it create the state of mind and taste by which it is to be enjoyed and understood, as Wordsworth once thought that it must and Nussbaum thinks that it can, or is that state of mind and heart the precondition for and not the result of its successful reception?

These are empirical rather than or as much as theoretical questions, and it must seem churlish to dispute Nussbaum's conviction that judges and juries would be assisted in their decision making by a good reading habit. Clarence Darrow, as we have seen, certainly made good use of this principle both in his own novel and in his defense of Loeb and Leopold. Moreover, writers such as Stowe, Lawrence, and Solzhenitsyn among many others have effected powerful conjunctions between works of fiction and the events of national cultures, and we might do well to remember such moments in the context of our generally more negative current estimate of the power of the written word. More intimately and routinely, the reading of literature can indeed help us to imagine ourselves in the position of the other and thereby expand our sense of what Roy Harvey Pearce, writing about the first new historicism, called "the realm of human possibility." In fiction, he says, we are told not of what did happen but of what might have happened; accepting the form of literature means accepting also the life and culture that created it, and it introduces us to "an infinite series of exemplars of what we would possibly have been, were we not what we are." [31] Paul Ricoeur has made the same case in describing how narrative actually engenders variation, making of literature a "vast laboratory for thought experiments" for "exposing selfhood by taking away the support of selfhood." [32]

But Ricoeur is also well aware of the fact that it is a "very thorny problem to reconnect literature to life by means of reading" (p. 159). So indeed it is. First, our sense of the power of situatedness is such that no author is assumed to be disinterested, so that no fictional world can be taken in complete good faith. According to Sartre, the posture of detachment in the case of the postromantic author is impossible to maintain because he must "exhaust himself trying not to see the social conditionings that allowed him to become what he is" (The Family Idiot, 5: 139). Preromantic authors are commonly more comfortable in accepting their affiliations. Only the Enlightenment moment permitted the fantasy of complete disinterest, which could even then be held credible only because it was the polemical, universalist doctrine of a bourgeoisie that was still in the ascendant and in opposition, and was therefore supported by enormous cultural pressures. In her fine study of the nine-teenth century, Regenia Gagnier has found the "modern literary subject" to be specifically generated in that period as "a mixture of introspec-tive self-reflexivity, middle-class familialism and genderization, and lib-eral autonomy." For working-class writers, in contrast, subjectivity was "not a given" and "often meant something different from emplotted self-sufficiency." [33] Viewed in this light the openness of the realist novel to acts of empathic imagining is to be attributed to a false universalism that emanates from an aesthetic analogue to the economy of laissez-faire.

Second, and for the same reasons, no reader can be assumed or as-sume herself or himself to be in a position of disinterest and complete openness, or to be fully aware of the terms of such differences as fiction is able to represent. This is an absolutist objection and does not com-pletely disable Nussbaum's argument, which indeed recognizes the in-evitability of a shared historicality as one of its basic admissions; but it does suggest that the tendency of acts of empathic reading might well be the confirmation of such alliances and differences as are already rec-ognizable and in place, rather than or as much as any education into the mind of another. Alternatively, the immersion in the place of the other may be so complete as to deprive the reading subject of all critical pur-chase on its own place and time. Schopenhauer, repeating Keats and a number of others, declared that "great poets transform themselves en-tirely into each of the persons to be presented, and speak out of each of them like ventriloquists." [34] But readers who imitate this self-effacement risk the loss of exactly the "character" that Mill and liberalism value so highly. This is, of course, the Platonic case against the theater whose ex-emplary reincarnation in the modern period is in the voice of Rousseau. In the first book of the *Confessions* the author gives a comic account of the power of his youthful reading of the classics: "I believed myself to be Greek or Roman; I became the character whose life I read." [35] Inso-far as the books read are the "right" books, and as long as the reader is not already rightly formed, then the power of books can be positive. But in an efficiently constituted republican culture, the effect of artistic rep-resentation can only be harmful. In the "Letter to D'Alembert" on the topic of theaters in Geneva, Rousseau asks the deeper and more trou-bling question about empathy: does it really open the minds and hearts of those who experience it, or does it do the opposite by providing a substitute experience that takes us away from the real situations analogous to those represented? Rousseau makes the second claim: "In shedding tears at fictitious misfortunes, we discharge all the duties humanity requires of us on such occasions, without any farther inconvenience to ourselves: whereas, when persons are under real miseries, humanity requires something more: it requires us to offer them assistance . . . from which our natural indolence would willingly exempt us."[36] If this were an average response then art would not encourage but work *against* moral action. Furthermore, the spectacle of events on the stage (and one could include fictional events in general) has the potential to arouse a "sensibility" that has nowhere to go and is "afterwards gratified at the expence of virtue" (p. 74). In other words, being aroused by mere representations sends us back into the world in a state of unrealized attention that we seek to satisfy as soon as possible: we are out of control. In at least two ways, then, Rousseau offers a proleptic response to the question of culture during and after Auschwitz, a clue to the possibility that the experience of fictional identification may actually harden us to real suffering, or lead us to mistake it for real suffering.

Literature, then, may not necessarily make us more sympathetic to the situated lives of others, and given that it must now compete with the more immediate photographic and televisual media in their provision of the data of otherness, its capacity to do so may be more contextually inhibited than ever before.[37] It does at least, however, mostly not claim to fully solve the terms of human situatedness: its purpose, consciously or otherwise, has been the cultivation of aporia rather than its simplification or resolution (which was at least until recently the declared task of various philosophers and social scientists). Literature is not then significantly in the business of providing false solutions or false confidences, unless they be the confidences of *not* knowing. Roy Harvey Pearce suggests that the humanistic disciplines exist precisely to focus on the antinomic qualities of situatedness: "We know ourselves to be . . . neither conditioned nor contingent. But at the perimeter of that awareness, we know ourselves as in all things conditioned and contingent. On the one hand we are vital existences . . . never deprived of our individual vitality. On the other hand we are acculturated creatures whose least gesture can always be accounted for in someone's encyclopedic register of the life-style which obtains at our particular moment in history. We are both of these at once; so it has always been, so it must always be" (*Historicism Once More*, p. 31). Always, one must add, only as long as the question is put in this particular way and framed within these particular disciplinary and more generally historical circumstances. Pearce's statement reads very well until the end, where what can only be a finite and culture-bound condition of the sort that is negotiated by the rhetoric of self-affiliation as well as by the more comforting experience of reading literature is phrased as a permanent condition of life. Here the function of literature as presenting the *not known* becomes a comfort instead of a challenge; an avoidance of science instead of a harbinger of better science. In this mode of reception, literary insight becomes an end in itself ("so it must always be"), an acceptance of the antinomy of situatedness that becomes almost triumphalist and certainly preemptive of further reflection.

What can be made, then, of the literary turn represented by Martha Nussbaum, and of its hopes for critical redefinition of our priorities as intellectual and social beings? Richard Rorty has expressed similar hopes, but his latest word on this matter is, depending on your viewpoint, either refreshingly explicit or bewilderingly slapdash: a polemic against an enemy variously defined as "cultural studies," "Jameson and his admirers," and "the Foucauldian academic left," all gathered under the banner of a preoccupation with "knowingness," and all of them opposed to the cultivation of "shudders of awe" that is so necessary and best left to "unprofessional prophets and demiurges."[38] Rorty's reliance on a simplified model of awe, or wonder, as the keystone of a "cooperative commonwealth" (p. 17) is even more undefended than Nussbaum's hope that because the realist novel may expand some people's minds and hearts it can therefore be offered as a regenerative principle that can do work in empirically positive ways: this despite the efforts of a hundred years or so of academic literary criticism failing to bring about just this. What we may be seeing here in both Nussbaum and Rorty is an instance of the import-export trade between the disciplines, as they reproduce material that appears new only to those who have been unaware of what has been going on on the other sides of various (never very efficient) fences.[39] The issue for my present inquiry, though, is this: why should it be felt useful to reemphasize the aporetic quality of all efforts at analyzing situatedness, which is what literature does so well? Could it be that the appeal of the literary turn represents a terminal exhaustion with the rational and social-scientific ambition, repeatedly expressed and repeatedly frustrated over two or three hundred years, to delineate in absolute terms the science of character and thus of social control? Has the social science aspiration really exhausted itself, as Immanuel Wallerstein says it has? Or is this just one more instance of a compensatory swing of the pendulum, a reactive restatement of one-half of the antinomy of situatedness, protesting that humankind is not a conditioned animal but a fount of novel and self-transforming sympathies, new metaphors and renovating imaginations? And this at a time when one part of the academic community is claiming the possibility of a new synthesis of culture and biology that sees us all as residual hunter-gatherers, while the global economy threatens to consign all cultural creations to the status of inauthenticity and pastiche? It may not be possible to answer the question. But it is worth wondering, given its persistence, whether there is any point in going back and forth about situatedness, or floundering within its aporetic sublimities. Or, because there clearly has been a point for so many for so long, perhaps we should try to find out what it was, and why it persists. Locke, so important to the development of modern educational theory, saw (in a passage from which I have already quoted) the matter of mind control, control of situatedness, not as a philosophical problem but as a pedagogic response to the demands created by the need to maintain the operations of a liberal society:

> A Compliance, and Suppleness of their Wills, being by a steady Hand introduced by Parents, before Children have Memories, to retain the Beginnings of it, will seem natural to them, and work afterwards in them, as if it were so; preventing all Occasions, of Strugling, or Repining. . . . On the other side, if the *Mind* be curbed, and *humbled* too much in Children . . . they lose all their Vigor and Industry, and are in a worse State than the former. For extravagant young Fellows, that have Liveliness and Spirit, come sometimes to be set right, and so make Able and Great Men: But *dejected Minds*, timorous and tame, and *low Spirits*, are hardly ever to be raised, and very seldom attain to any thing. To

avoid the Danger, that is on either hand, is the great Art; and he . . .
that knows how to reconcile these seeming Contradictions, has, in
my Opinion, got the true Secret of Education. (*Educational Writings*, pp.
147–48)

No one has proved that they *know* how to achieve this reconciliation. I have
suggested that the goal may be illusory, and should perhaps be understood as the ongoing monitoring, through time, of the agreed excesses
in either direction, with the aim of maintaining a working norm whose
identity is only imaginary and to be imagined by way of the negative, by
way of a sequence of perceived infractions.

This would suggest, once again, that modernity's vocation has only
pretended to be the solution of the questions arising from situatedness.
Its real goal, which it has achieved very well in the liberal-democratic
nation-states, has been the management of extremes, the setting of limits
to the more dangerous energies of a risk culture that is fundamentally
committed to the positive evaluation of those same risks for its own purposes. Literature, in this light, becomes an experience in the virtual management of extremes, and as such may have no more or less to teach us
than other forms of inquiry. Such is indeed the remarkable conclusion
of William Empson's *Seven Types of Ambiguity*, first published in 1930 just
as the definitive modern arguments for the socially positive powers of
literature were gaining some acceptance. The symptom of "journalistic
flatness" and apparent vagueness in language that other critics saw as
antithetical to good poetry was precisely what interested Empson, who
found there the necessary lineaments of democracy. The experience of
the "last few generations" has been one of increasing social mobility
and thus of more and more unpredictable encounters in which one's responses are always hesitant and insecure.[40] Words are thus most efficient when they do not specify exact meanings, when they leave a margin
for negotiation and redefinition. (Tocqueville had made the same point
about American English in the nineteenth century.) This state of "indecision" is what poetic ambiguity stages, and it makes people "less sure of
their own minds" than they might otherwise be: "doubt becomes a permanent background of the mind" (pp. 243, 255). The task of the critic
is then to provide "reassurance" by offering a "machinery for analysis"

that cycles the willing reader through a sequence of poetic ambiguities that give a sense "not so much of what is really there, as of what is necessary to carry a particular situation 'off' " (pp. 255, 245). What counts here is having the experience, not analyzing it or making it precise. In this way we are trained not to lapse into dogmatic states of mind through the apprehension of somewhat vague rather than concretely precise sets of feelings and perceptions: aporia with pleasure, and with the confidence that allows us to pass between unreconciled alternatives.

After reading Rousseau and Empson and pondering the question of culture during and after Auschwitz, it is no longer possible to be sure that the reading of Hard Times (for example) must make us more compassionate rather than simply more comfortable. At the same time, a case can be made (as it is by Nussbaum) for the pertinence of literature's presentation of situatedness to the elaboration of specific decisions involving judgments about blame or responsibility. But it might take a very good lawyer to make that case: a lawyer like Clarence Darrow. Or a very good novelist in the right place at the right time. Or a moral philosopher, who can make primary a subdiscipline (ethics) whose very existence has largely depended on the categories of subjectivity that problems about situatedness themselves put into question (a topic I will discuss in chapter 6). The outcome of a literary turn in the legal, ethical, and social scientific spheres is therefore not to be predicted as necessarily positive because the conditions of its reception cannot be known in advance. And the same is true of objectivist aspirations in the same spheres. The contest between the two is a traditional and prescribed contest, and the invocation of each as the alternative to the other replays a long-durational antinomic logic governing decisions about the nature and knowledge of situatedness. To be aware of this is to withhold approval in advance of either priority, to refuse to take sides in an all too often prescribed "war" between science and literature, reason and imagination, theory and practice. A new understanding of the contrived and constructed nature of the antinomies of situatedness, which have themselves been significant polemicists in persuading us to such approvals, can only assist in this withholding and encourage us to think about new ways of imagining a description of social life.

5. Reasonable Situations: Philosophy, Biography, & Private Life

Philosophizing Situatedness The commitment of social science to dealing with and at its most ambitious moments "solving" the antinomies of situatedness has encouraged and still encourages national governments to look to its practitioners to provide recipes for social control and social development, models of general description with apparent predictive value for managing complex human relations. This ambition has not always been felt to embody the sinister, repressive consequences detailed by some of those who believe in the omnipotence and oppressiveness of an administered world; it has in the western democracies often emerged as an Enlightenment ideal, as the last best hope for the progress of the species. The prestige of social science has been significant enough to put pressure on other disciplines to conform or respond to its paradigms, but the response has sometimes been critical. And according to Wolf Lepenies, as we have seen, the critique has also been internal: social science's own objectivist aspirations have often been countered by an alternative movement toward literature. Literature and social science together may thus be taken to compose a composite and dialectical metadiscipline, each part of which offers to correct the excesses of the other. In recent years, under the aegis of an announced postmodernity, the literary and reflexive component of the social sciences has achieved relatively high prestige, although this has by no means inhibited a thriving parallel continuation of the rational-objectivist segment of the discipline as it provides expertise and data for social planning. And as the reading of novels is felt to matter in ways that go beyond a private aesthetic education, so literature is made into something that offers more than just a private experience limited to leisure time: it becomes once again what it had been for the first generations of university-based literary critics, an urgent response to a critical omission in public and administrative life. So the question must continue to be raised (as it was by Rousseau) about the degree to which this resource is indeed an empirically benevolent one, whatever it might in the best of worlds ideally perform. We cannot afford to ignore its possible compliance, in the hands of its new apologists, with a refigured disciplinary network whose function is the general management and prearrangement of the rhetoric of situatedness and the preservation of what used to be called, in the age of confident critique, *mystification.* Here one might see literature arrayed along with psychology and ethics (which I will discuss later) and with the refigured social sciences as part of a general shift toward emphasizing social control as a self-administered function whose not so occasional failures are picked up by the legal system.

The existence of social science as a discipline (or set of disciplines) has, as I have suggested, had much to do with the efforts of Bentham and his successors to find some way to address incipiently aporetic questions about situatedness without giving up completely on the prospect of predictability and probability. These pressures come not simply from disciplinary formations themselves but from the larger world conditions that make the disciplines what they are. Situatedness is the peculiar sort of thing that it is because it is seen and felt to be a significant site for the presentation (which is not, I have been insisting, a resolution) of the antinomies of the self as they are created and experienced in liberal-democratic capitalist cultures that simultaneously value entrepreneurial individualism and a manageable citizenry, and that must therefore make possible a fairly constant shifting of the boundary between the one and the other. For these reasons the encounter with situatedness is not just limited to social science and to its loyal antagonist and fellow spirit, literature, but shows up in other disciplines, some of which (anthropology, psychology, and history, for example) are not treated in any detail in this book. But I do want in this penultimate chapter to address the field of philosophy, which itself includes a wide range of intellectual practices and affiliations that do not always mutually cohere, but which has always been marked by a strong incentive toward identifying rational or plausible conditions for the assumption of real and objective components of self and world, and to relating them in some way toward decisions about how we might best live our lives. At least since Descartes, philosophy has been intensely engaged with the project of subjectivity, which it has been visibly anxious to explain or assure. The questions raised by the Cartesian cogito, by the arguments about personal identity in Locke and Hume, and by Kant's distinction between phenomena and noumena, to mention only three prominent examples, are questions about situatedness and the attempt to think beyond it. To some they seemed like breakthroughs and foundational insights; by others they have been taken as nothing more than pseudoconcepts or rhetorical do-it-yourself kits for the performance of identity and the attribution of responsibility.

The generally secular disposition of modern philosophy is symptomatized by its preoccupation with what I have been calling situatedness. Christian doctrine has commonly sought to transcend this same situatedness by positing the state of being within it as a state of sin. Augustine proved to himself that only by giving up the local and temporal coordinates of locatedness in the world could he hope for access to God and to an experience in which the soul is "bathed in light that is not bound by space." [1] To be preoccupied with the terms of one's place in the world is the sign of sin: the goal is to get out of being thus situated. So Luther and Calvin proved able to tolerate the world order and the civil law pretty much as it was because they did not consider it to have anything critically to do with spiritual truth; the world may be full of signs, and so must be the object of constant scrutiny, but the ones that matter point beyond the world, or through it. What Niklas Luhmann has called the "devotional moment" is staged to establish desituatedness as the desired condition.[2] The equivalent of this among the secular (or secularizing) philosophers is the transcendental or disinterested subject ontologically secure from and prior to experience. But its most commonly designated inventor—

148

Descartes—described himself as coming to such knowledge from a very distinct position in place and time, "all day shut up alone in a stove-heated room."[3] Indeed, the melodramatic narrative that recounts the origins of the cogito, as well as the cogito itself, have been controversial from the very start: Descartes published the objections along with the argument of his *Meditations*. Since this same moment, says Susan Bordo, it has been impossible *not* to worry about "locatedness" and the question of where one might be coming from.[4] Much recent work on Descartes has been busy reconsidering the objectivity claims of the cogito and finding them either wanting or calling for serious redescription and limitation.[5] And with the cogito thus resituated in place and time, the figure of Descartes moves that much closer to parity with the figure of Montaigne, whose famously indecisive if compulsive self-scrutinies have made him so amenable to being produced as the harbinger of the postmodern subject.[6]

John Locke's intellectual career was as much or more than Descartes's explicitly responsive to place and time, and to the legitimation of the political settlement of the late 1600s. In his important study of possessive individualism C. B. Macpherson has argued for the appearance in Locke and his contemporaries of a new formulation of the relation between *I* and *me*, one governed by the model of property relations in a developing capitalist economy. According to Macpherson the Lockean individual comes to be "essentially the proprietor of his own person or capacities, owing nothing to society for them."[7] Here the *I* claims ownership of the *me*, and can dispose of it as it pleases in a free market. *I* also becomes *me*'s protector, posting signs to prevent others from trespassing on its personal territory. The isolation (and obscurity) of the essential self is thus preserved in a world marked by scarcity and within which the empirical self must compete for limited resources. Macpherson cites the Leveller Richard Overton's conviction that to write or speak for others is to become "an encroacher & invader upon another Mans Right, to which I have no Right" (p. 140). We may see in this position a prefiguring of our own contemporary nervousness about speaking for others, and thereby also of an indefinitely extending series of self-affiliation sentences. If the self cannot be spoken for it must be constantly announcing and defending itself in its own voice. And if the *I* is always prior and other to the *me* as the guarantor of some sort of connectedness between past, present, and future subject positions, then the self can never be declared or identified other than provisionally or metaphysically. Humean naturalism emphasizes the first option, and Kantian theory the second one. Adam Smith, in *The Theory of Moral Sentiments*, makes up for the epistemological aporias by describing acts of imagination. We can never fully know the terms of another person's situatedness, but we are programmed to respond to others by imagining how we might feel if we were in the situation we think that they are in. Because of our desire for approval, we fashion our response in accordance with an imagined norm or standard which by being imagined becomes exactly that. Divergent situations are in this way rewritten and moved toward some sort of socially sanctioned average, as if in anticipation of Oliver Wendell Holmes's "ideal average prudent man" (*The Common Law*, p. 89).

One might say then that the philosophers of the postmodern or late modern are the heirs of Descartes and Montaigne as they attempt to formulate and resolve the operations and implications of situatedness. There is a continuum of concern about its importance stretching from Descartes's admission (neither negligible nor fully trustworthy) that his topic is nothing more than the reconstruction of his own thoughts, through Friedrich Schlegel's determination (part excuse and part imperative) to greet the dawn in his own way and from his own "point of view," to Wittgenstein's claim that appropriate descriptions are only appropriate for a "narrowly circumscribed region" and not available as general truths.[8] But the methodological weight of these remarks is not in all cases the same. Descartes clearly intends to outmaneuver the threat of relativism or solipsism, while Schlegel means to flaunt it and Wittgenstein means to take very seriously indeed the nonavailability of universals. For Descartes (although not for Montaigne), philosophical inquiry may begin in the biographical condition but does not remain there. For many coming later, thinking beyond the constraints of personal situatedness becomes harder and harder to do. After Kant, the major philosophical endeavors either eschew altogether the effort to describe or argue for a transcendental subjectivity, a desituated self, or struggle to maintain a place for it against odds that often seem insurmountable, even as they have sometimes been felt to provide the last guarantee for philosophy itself as an independent discipline. Thus, for Hegel, the metaphysical dimension has to enfold within it the whole of human history, which can only of course be represented as radically edited, almost to the point of pastiche. Schopenhauer works hard at the abolition of disinterest only to produce it like a rabbit from a hat in the uniquely confined spheres of the aesthetic and the ascetic. Sartre and Heidegger, so influential for a wide range of academic and other writers in the later twentieth century, labor at maintaining the credibility of an ontological language, and thus at still being thought to "do" philosophy, while making massive commitments to the seriousness of ordinary life—a life already flaunted as absolute and primary by Nietzsche, Freud, and Marx, all in their different ways. Nietzsche is uncompromising in his claim that all rational thought is only "interpretation according to a scheme that we cannot throw off." [9] It is easy to read this as confirmation of the now-postmodern nostrum according to which there is no disinterest, no metalanguage, no self that is not a self in place and time; but it is important also to read it as a suggestion, which Hume for one had taken to be true, that we *cannot* throw off the interpretation that requires deploying rational thought and all of its attributes even after we have lost faith in their epistemological credibility and durability.

The modern philosophical engagement with situatedness has in part taken form by way of a rereading of the rationalist tradition, but more often it begins in an engagement with the likes of Schopenhauer and Nietzsche, who answer the perceived dominance of mind in the western tradition with a dogged insistence on the powers of body. They thus argue against the efforts of Kant and Descartes to desituate the intellect from its locality in corporeal time and space. For Schopenhauer the world of representation is given only through a body whose desires and urges are the starting point for all that goes by the name of knowledge. Knowledge does not then guide the will but is guided by it, often quite unconsciously. The "will" itself is not the vehicle of rationally chosen acts but of compulsive and irresistable drives expressing the most fundamental biological needs. What we call "mind," then, is irreversibly situated in body: the fundamental Cartesian move is countered and dismissed.[10] Human interaction and human history are thus driven not by rational and predictable decisions but by arbitrary conflicts between individual wills; and "willing as a whole has no end in view" (1: 165). On the personal level there is no such thing as satisfaction because the principle of all behavior is itself a drive, or series of drives. On the social level there is no experienced or achievable stability because the sum of individual wills is simply a mechanical aggregate rather than an organic system: *homo homini lupus* (1: 147). With these arguments Schopenhauer seeks to eviscerate the methodology of the social sciences and of narrative history writing, which can have no significance beyond "accidental configuration."[11] He thus appears to negate completely the claims made for the social-situational determination of human behavior (arguments about where we're coming from) by means of a maximum claim for the absolute (biophysical) situatedness of mind in body. Because this is a relation not open to either recognition or control by the conscious mind, jurisprudence cannot base its principles on judgments about intention or motivation; acts alone are decisive, and only to be judged according to the dictates of deterrence rather than according to notions of retribution or moral adequacy.[12]

The only experience of disinterest and desituatedness open to the human spirit as described by Schopenhauer comes in the aesthetic and ascetic states, which offer our only chance to savor, for the moment, a life without conflict. Set beside the later arguments of Nietzsche, this appears as a touchingly rearguard or residual remnant of an increasingly vulnerable idealism, a last cry for desituated humanity. Nietzsche too values art, but not as a resting point outside the world of will; rather it is an enhanced distillation of the energies that Schopenhauer himself called "will," an "excess and overflow of blooming physicality into the world of images and desires," a heightening and not a negation of "animal vigor." Instead of negating desire, art inflames it; instead of freeing us from sensuality, it returns us to the senses we have forgotten.[13] Nietzsche, then, would solve the problem of situatedness not by seeking to stand outside it, which he deems impossible, but by cheerful immersion within it, in what he imagined to be the manner of the ancients. We can know neither the causes of actions nor their consequences: the utilitarian emphasis is thus as false as the rational psychology whose deficiencies it sought to displace. The vocabulary of "thinking" is itself no more than an "arbitrary fiction" (*The Will to Power*, pp. 164, 264). The otherwise unbearable presentness of everything is relieved by the power of forgetting; to search for historical and contextual (that is, situational) explanations of events, to seek for reasons for what has already happened, is the mark of the old age of mankind.[14] Nietzsche is ruthlessly cynical about the currency of situational excuses: "To let oneself be determined by one's environment is decadent" (The Will to Power, p. 31). And the supposition of such determination is in itself false: "Much that looks like external influence is merely its adaptation from within. The very same milieus can be interpreted and exploited in opposite ways: there are no facts" (p. 47). All kinds of arguments from situatedness, social and religious, arise to spread the blame for our sufferings and to disguise from us the autonomy of an irrational selfhood, libidinal, somatic, and unconscious. After Nietzsche, there seems to be nothing for philosophers to do except give up and go home.

Husserl, Heidegger, Wittgenstein That philosophers have not given up is not least because they have continued to grapple with the problems of situatedness that Nietzsche declares off-limits, or at least pointless. The effort of much twentieth-century philosophy is directed simultaneously at the acknowledgment and containment or making positive of a perceived condition of situatedness. Husserl felt that he was witnessing the threatened collapse of philosophy into literature and biography, a radical falling off from the pursuit of disinterested, desituated truth: "More and more a skeptical mood spread which crippled from the inside the philosophical energy even of those who held fast to the idea of a scientific philosophy. The history of philosophy is substituted for philosophy, or philosophy becomes a personal world-view, and finally some even try to make out of necessity a virtue: philosophy can exercise no other function at all for humanity than that of outlining a world-picture appropriate to one's individuality, as the summation of one's personal education."[15] In other words, as we now say, it is all a matter of where you're coming from, of lifestyle, and of rounding up a few like-minded persons who believe or can be persuaded to believe that they are coming from the same or a similar place. Husserl blamed this predicament on our collective and frustrated reaction to the false gods of mathematical realism introduced by Descartes and Galileo and deployed as the rationalization for scientific method and technological change. Mathematical models were substituted for the "everyday life-world" and proposed as its inner, essential identity (p. 49). But because our "actually experienced" and "actually intuited nature" does not accord with such models, frustration and confusion are the inevitable results of seeking to apply them beyond their limits, and rampant relativism takes over.

Hans-Georg Gadamer has, however, made very clear the degree to which Husserl's own concept of the life-world (Lebenswelt) embodies "a revolutionary power that explodes the framework" of his "transcendental thinking." [16] Life-world is not lifestyle, but one can sense the immanence of the slippage between them within a culture for which what Gadamer calls life-world's "variable wealth of modes of givenness" (p. 191) must always tend to be made over into a rhetoric of options and opportunities. There is a "situational cognition involved in the direct form of life-interests," which made "historical investigations" incumbent on a method that sought to remain transcendental (pp. 194, 192). And when historical investigation itself can no longer rely on transcendental narratives, which is hard to do in the face of the "great wealth of subjective-relative life-worlds" (p. 192), then its findings become more and more occasional and nontransferable. Husserl himself saw all the pitfalls toward which rational ontology was headed: his effort at avoiding them involves the restoration of a bodily space-time experience that is nonmathematical but at the same time still intersubjective. There is no given self to be isolated from its body and from other selves. Sounding very like Charles Horton Cooley, Husserl's The Crisis of European Sciences argues that even "what is straightforwardly perceptual is communalized," producing a world made up not of inert, objective things with which we make desperate attempts at explaining our solitary epistemological interactions, but an "openly endless horizon" of persons and things wherein we all recombine and reinterpret everything all the time in a process of "incessantly mobile relativity" (pp. 163, 164). What philosophy is given to work with is thus an "interhuman present" in historical time and space (p. 253). Individual life-worlds are the starting point for its descriptions, but out of this "multiplicity of separated souls" (p. 255) philosophy's task is to account for a transcendental (interpersonal) subjectivity that is the true grounding of our objective life. Our life with and among others in the world of things is carried on by exercising the "intentional complex" in a process of "reciprocal correction" through historical time (p. 254).

If it is situatedness that characterizes our true being in the world, a situatedness that remains ultimately indescribable except by guesswork or by a calculus of probability, do we then give up on philosophy or redirect it to other more manageable tasks? Not yet, according to Husserl. An understanding of ontological (rather than merely individual) situatedness can still lead to a recapturing of "self-reflective clarity" (p. 153), albeit a clarity reduced now to general rather than singular description, and one thus unavailable for ethical or jurisprudential decisions seeking to resolve the questions raised by the most exigent kinds and consequences of human situatedness. We could not, in other words, look to Husserl to solve questions about criminal justice or social planning. Indeed, the act of transcendental *epochē* required for an understanding of the world is an act of standing outside and above the world, although not with the emptiness of content Husserl found in Descartes's model. As with Kant's moral and aesthetic and Schopenhauer's aesthetic and ascetic judgement, "all natural interests are put out of play" (p. 152). The world does not disappear but is held in suspension; the coordinates of our ontological situatedness (place and time) are defined in a moment of holding them at a distance. Disinterest, the classic gesture of objectivist philosophy, is reinvented as the act of mind necessary for a recognition and acceptance of interest and motivation as the mechanism of human life. We learn to live with situatedness by seeing it, momentarily, as if from the outside.

Husserl's effort is an ingenious rescue of a transcendental dimension made constitutive of situatedness itself; once again, all conflict becomes harmony not understood. There is also a visible effort to apply these philosophical findings about subjectivity and situatedness to the "European crisis" of the mid-1930s. Husserl projects a cosmopolitan ideal founded in but not limited to a European humanity (p. 269), one evolving through time and one that is infinitely inclusive and not to be confused with nation-states or with pseudobiological categories of race. The Greek project of *theoria* in which it has its beginnings is not "bound to the soil" of a "national tradition" (p. 286). Husserl takes pains (pp. 289–95) to distinguish what he is defending from the naïve objectivism of an overextended scientific method. The overcoming of this last is, indeed, precisely the task of transcendental phenomenology, which seeks to project "an inward being-for-one-another and mutual interpenetration" and to displace the "serious mutual exteriority of ego-persons" that is the legacy of a misunderstood modernity (p. 298). Against Hitler's model of an essentialist Europe, Husserl offers a deliberately internationalist and nonempirical alternative. But by its very foundation within the European mind, and not in, for example, the Indian mind or the minds of Eskimos and Gypsies, who can only aspire "to Europeanize themselves" from the outside (p. 275) (the Jews are dramatically unmentioned and thus momentously invoked) Husserl's own model assumes a priority that would by today's standards be deemed incorrigibly sectarian. Perhaps a nonaggressive and benevolent Eurocentrism was what was most powerfully available in Vienna in 1935, one whose self-imposed imperative was to think its own dissolution as a way beyond the dangerously ideologized situatedness of "national" politics and culture, of "blood and soil." [17]

The questions raised by Husserl's efforts at transforming situatedness from a problem into a positive conceptual advantage occur again in the much more controversial work of Heidegger, who shares with Husserl a refusal of Cartesian dualism and a rejection of the extreme consequences of technological culture, which tended to present a world of objects manipulated by a disembodied and desituated human subject choosing whether or not to come back into the world in order to act and to discover. Heidegger argued for a life in which everything is already interdependent, interactive, and under way: situatedness is everything. The familiar divisions of western philosophy (mind-body, self-other, real-ideal) were only imposed in the first place because something went wrong, putting us at odds with the unconscious, happy functioning that now becomes so hard to think and to restore. The going wrong, which is embodied in metaphysics and perhaps in philosophy itself, began with the Greeks. Ordinariness, the innocent immersion in activity, becomes the goal that is only now held out as a loss. All of our ideas about "being" or *Sein* (sometimes *Seyn*) are posited only under the condition of *Dasein*, or "being there," awareness of which is disclosed in the state of anxiety, the state of "being-not-at-home." [18] (Being-not-at-home, being anxious, is the precondition of the self-affiliation sentence in its near-epidemic contemporary incidences.) Similarly, all seeing is seeing *as*, the result of preinterpretations that are not in everyday consciousness brought to the surface (pp. 189–93, 202). In the 1951 lecture "Bauen Wohnen Denken" Heidegger took up the matter of the postwar housing crisis to argue that mankind's metaphysical legacy is a "homelessness" far more profound and enduring than anything brought about by recent history, or anything that could be put right by a positive application of the findings of social science or by mere government spending. There is nothing here of the positive endorsement of mobility and flexible subject positionality that was endorsed by Cooley and that has become the upbeat side of the rhetoric of postmodernity. Our basic project in life, Heidegger proposed, is not to climb every mountain but to learn to "dwell." [19] In a second lecture that same year, "Dichterisch Wohnet der Mensch," poetry is specified as that which "first causes dwelling to be dwelling," that which "first brings man onto the earth, making him belong to it," bringing him thus "into dwelling" (pp. 215, 218). Heidegger thinks of "poetry" in its extended, Shelleyan sense, as the fount and origin of all purposive creation. Thus poetry is not about putting up houses, but it is the "primal form" of all building and the "original admission of dwelling" (p. 227). It provides what philosophy cannot provide; it fills the space that philosophy evacuates. Or perhaps philosophy, not for the first or the last time, becomes poetry.

The Heidegger of *Being and Time* had been less committed to the provision of even this kind of limited solution. Not-being-at-home registers the existential pathos latent in the language of respectable bourgeois self-positioning: anxiety is a "basic state of mind" and discloses the truth of *Dasein*'s existence (p. 233). The facticity of *Situation* (Heidegger's term) is that it is never to be predicted or anticipated but is only ever "disclosed"; when it is known as such it is already there (p. 355). The invocation of the *Situation* in the early lectures (which comes at the same time as Karl Jaspers was refining his own use of the term) has something of the pragmatic affirmation of Nietzsche's and Sartre's sense of being in the world: one is involved in something, directed toward something, happily purposive.[20] It is part of what Charles Taylor describes as Heidegger's argument for "engaged agency" and "concerned involvement," recognizing "incomplete articulation" as insurmountable but accepting it as the outcome of bringing one's situatedness to consciousness in the first place.[21] Awareness of *Dasein* itself is thus as process and in process, an embedded life experience rather than a moment of detached contemplation. The will does not figure as a priority in Heidegger's argument. *Dasein* can (and should) deploy will and volition, but its state of mind or mood (*Stimmung*, a word with a purposively large range of applications and cognates) is prior, and ensures that the experienced event will always appear an "enigma" (p. 175). *Cogito ergo sum* can only take the sense that "I am in a world" already (p. 254).

But this relatively happy sense of life as being all about going out and doing and performing, hoping for the satisfactions of practical achievement even as those of conventional (detached) knowledge are withheld, is not the last or most important word. The Heideggerian emphasis on human situatedness seems to be at once abstract and tragic. It is abstract in the sense that, as philosophy, it does not pronounce on the empirical particulars of specific situations of the sort that must form the basis of social planning and legal judgment. It has no predictive authority and does not allow for the generation of theory or method. In this sense Heidegger's deflection (or, some might say, deconstruction) of the housing crisis in 1951 is entirely typical. It is also tragic insofar as it is individuated, in that the most powerful terms in which situatedness is represented are those of fear and death. Once one has accepted that man is a bodily being and not a spirit that has the misfortune to be temporarily lodged in corporeal form, then humankind can no longer conceive of itself as already radically (spiritually) desituated and beyond (physical) harm. Fear (*Furcht*) is thus critically prominent among Heideggerian states of mind, and *Dasein*'s "ownmost possibility" is death (p. 307). It is in the complex state of "freedom towards death" (p. 311) that *Dasein* is most fully itself, most completely individuated from the collective, most cognizant of its specific reality. Death, then, is the most intransigent of all situations, as the one beyond which one cannot think, the one putting an end to all others, to the Husserlian "endless horizon" of mobile relativities. Death is the ultimate confirmation of individuality in its existence within and for history and temporality. In this denial of modernization as progress, the Heidegger of *Being and Time* is, like Nietzsche before him, profoundly Greek. As long as our situatedness is thus ontological, and the very condition of our being, then it is not to be struggled against, dismissed in gestures of fake transcendence, or argued away as a product of imperfect social conditions. Heidegger seems to have no time or space for the trivial and evasive convenience of the rhetoric of self-affiliation. Situatedness takes on an existential seriousness that cannot be approached by declarations of merely contingent positionality. This is perhaps one explanation for the complexity of his appeal to a postmodern generation visibly anxious about a rhetoric of homelessness that it is seemingly committed both to celebrate and to critique as it oscillates between antithetical endorsements of migration and localization, performing and identifying. Sartre, Jaspers, Merleau-Ponty, and Gadamer among others will seek to make something more positive and pragmatically redeeming out of situatedness, but its materialist incarnation as a body bound through time toward death is never for long forgotten.

Many who have no appetite for Heidegger have been willing to read Wittgenstein.[22] The famous "duck-rabbit" figure from the *Philosophical Investigations* is almost as well known to the layperson as Newton's apple. It is usually taken as a conclusive example of the relativity of perception, and produced as evidence that it is quite acceptable to see things differently from the way others see them. This is the inevitable spin supplied by a democratic culture that approves itself by granting one person permission to see a duck where another sees a rabbit, explaining the difference by reference to where we are respectively coming from. Wittgenstein was after different game; he was after the game itself. If I understand his point, it is to argue for the impossibility of going behind the duck-rabbit conundrum to establish why one sees it now as one thing and now as another; he suggests that we have no means of knowing or saying a distinction between seeing and seeing-as, or between seeing as a visual response and seeing as an act of knowing.[23] To be in the game is to be in the game, and to imagine oneself outside it, or to speak as if one were outside it (the classical role of disinterest in western philosophy), is simply a mistake. The ordinary is all that we have, and as itself it provides enough of the mysterious to keep us fully absorbed. Situatedness is the place of life, and not a limited condition *within* life that we can inspect; it is integral to what we see with, and therefore cannot be seen.

Wittgenstein thus shares with Heidegger a commitment to reminding us constantly that all questions about being in the world are posed only while being in the world. Language functions do not make up a single system containable by metaphysical description; they share the same things as the tools in a toolbox (*Philosophical Investigations*, p. 6), always to hand at the service of particular needs. Language does not so much "make" a human subject as dispense with the need for one. There are countless sentences (p. 11); they are indeed governed by rules (the "game"), but the rules are simply rule-giving, not metaphysically ordained, at least not so in any way that we can hope to describe. Being in a situation is not then a closed or completely determined condition. Or if it is we do not know it as such because it contains and permits indefinite responses to new experiences. The job of philosophy is no longer to go behind appearances and to reveal what makes them work, or to discover secrets: "Since everything lies open to view there is nothing to explain." Philosophy simply describes what is open to view, "puts everything before us, and neither explains nor deduces anything" (p. 50).

There is a strong pragmatist component to Wittgenstein's thinking. There is no single philosophical method but rather different methods, "like different therapies"; confusions arise when "language is like an engine idling, not when it is doing work" (p. 51); all descriptions are "instruments for particular uses" (p. 99). The address to our concern with the paradigm of situatedness would then seem to be as follows: simply accept it. To be situated is indeed the condition of us all, but none of us can know the terms of our situatedness nor the degree to which those terms make possible or preclude understanding others or seeing things differently. That we do understand and misunderstand, or agree and fail to agree, is simply a fact of life. There is available to us no position from which to inspect this condition. A strict Wittgensteinian response to the uses made of arguments from situatedness, which I have argued to be fundamental to our way of talking about ourselves, would seem to be the recognition that the whole question is a false or hopeless one, the result of trying to go behind or within appearances instead of recognizing and accepting the given disposition of appearances. Wittgenstein brings us close to the prospect of life without cause-and-effect explanations and perhaps without metaphysics, and he offers us a philosophy whose job it is to lead us away from these "problems" (and hence from the image of solutions), leaving us with the mostly inexplicable but nonetheless commonly functioning rituals of ordinary life. Philosophy's job is not to support or underwrite but to question the language-moves we make to claim knowledge of definitive kinds of situatedness.

Wittgenstein thus seems to tell us either to give up on the sorts of questions we ask ourselves by way of the argument from situatedness (such questions being insoluble) or to find quite other ways of addressing those questions. My own view is that we do not yet have much of an idea how to stop asking the questions, and that we are probably destined to go on asking them for a while longer, so that the best hope for fresh ideas and "other ways" will come from a playing out of the aporetic logic within the rules of the game as we currently have them. Only then might a full sense of the aporia itself become more familiar, perhaps to the point that a new consensus might begin to build. This is utopian thinking, and it may well require the "integrated theory of reality" that Thomas Nagel wrote about in *The View from Nowhere* (p. 51) and that we are nowhere near achieving. Because there is no evidence that we have yet given up on our efforts at making use of situatedness as an analytical or justificatory concept, or that we are ready to dismiss this most central and heavily worked paradigm (now indeed so heavily worked that it has become almost meaningless), it is still worth trying to understand the work that we have tried to do with it, and to think further about why it has been given to us to work with. Here there looms the unignorable figure of Jean Paul Sartre, whose work exemplifies the destined passage of philosophical efforts at understanding situatedness into the morass of biography even as it also looks to imagine a world in which the biography, and the obsession with situatedness for which it speaks, might become less critical.

The *Situation* in Jaspers and Sartre The first appearance of the *Situation* as a philosophically freighted term whose fuzziness Sartre will exploit as a positive principle may not have been in Heidegger but in the writings of Karl Jaspers, who anticipates Sartre in some detail. The term is not conceptualized in Jaspers's first major publication, the *Allgemeine Psychopathologie* of 1913, which adopts a conventional sociological relation between *Anlage* (disposition) and *milieu* for its explanation of human behavior and potential. *Situation*, when it appears here, has a merely commonplace meaning.[24] By 1919, in his *Psychologie der Weltanschauungen*, it has taken on philosophical weight and specificity within an analysis of the antinomic structure of experience bounded by limit situations (*Grenz-situationen*), such as death, struggle, and guilt, that cannot be negotiated away.[25] In the completely rewritten 1942 version of the *Allgemeine Psycho-pathologie* the *Situation* is the fundamental condition of human life in a world where practical activity matters but only within limits: "In real life, the situation releases activity, and gives birth to performance and experience. . . . Situations have urgency, their sequence is changeable and unfixed, and mankind can contrive them."[26] But the contriving goes only so far. There are limit or boundary situations (*Grenzsituationen*), such as death and guilt, that cannot be transformed but only encountered. (Death is biologically determined; guilt is unavoidable because having choice means that we could always have chosen differently.)[27] And our encounter with nonlimited, alterable situations is unconscious: "Both the situation and its demands and the meaning of our own attitude are hidden from conscious scrutiny" (p. 330). In *Man in the Modern Age* (a translation of *Die geistige Situation der Zeit*, published in 1931) Jaspers allows for conscious access to situations in the form of "purposive behavior," but he maintains that there is no "generalisable situation, but only the absolute historicity of those who encounter one another, the intimacy of their contact, the fidelity and irreplaceability of personal ties. Amid the general social dissolution, man is thrust back into dependence on these most primitive bonds out of which alone a new and trustworthy objectivity can be constructed."[28]

Jaspers here offers a telling adumbration of the late-twentieth-century predilection for situating oneself. His existentialism familiarizes what to so many of us remains an obscurity or strangeness—that we cannot share a common situation, or cannot know for sure that we do. Or perhaps it is us who are making familiar, by claiming to say where we are coming from, that which Jaspers can, precisely by virtue of his existentialism, preserve as unknowable terrain. For even as we desire and work toward a trustworthy experience of the "primitive bonds" of personal contact (whose contemporary form is in various endorsements of civil society), all such "concrete situations" will be lacking in epistemological conviction (*Man in the Modern Age*, p. 34). This is because "I cannot possibly survey from without that entity which in no circumstances whatever I can leave" (p. 32), and because all of what is experienced as authentic and anxiety-dispelling is itself caught up in time. Jaspers here undermines the rhetoric of the "concrete situation" that has recently once again become popular as a licensed alternative to the general or theoretical knowledge that we think we can no longer achieve. Because of the insecurity of even the concrete situation, wherein "we do not know what is," we should understand it not as confirming us in what we are but in spurring us to pursue "what can be" (p. 35). Situatedness then becomes not the mark of a self that knows where it is coming from but of "selfhood trying to achieve orientation" (p. 34).

There is a more systematic exposition of these same insights in Jaspers's summational *Philosophy*, which appeared in 1932. Again, consciousness of situatedness is part of the reflexivity of all situations, making them emphatically unavailable to any inspection as if by a third person: "I never come to be entirely aware of these rules because my *consciousness* of them is a *new factor* that goes into the making of the situation. It will change the situation, and thus the rules." [29] Being situated is thus itself a limit or boundary situation: it cannot be changed and is a precondition of existence. Situations are "neither psychological nor physical, but both in one." They are thus the object "not of one special science but of many," each of which (biology, economics, history, and so on) affords us some purchase on some element of our own or others' situations (2: 177). The whole, with "all its possibilities," is "never surveyable" (2: 178). And the boundary situations that place limits on all other situations are not at all negotiable; all one can do is to meet them and become one with them. Because they are without content, because they are themselves the condition of existence, recognizing them can lead to a sensed possibility for transcendence, a glimpsing of "*my own existence as if it were a stranger's*" (2: 179). From this point on one lives with a duality of being in the world, at once within situations and, in the awareness of boundary situations, *aware* of being within situations and situations that have limits. Because boundary (limit) situations show life to be "inherently dubious and brittle," existence has from this point an inevitable "antinomic structure" (p. 218).[30] Knowing or experiencing a situation is simultaneously recognizing the possibilities one cannot know or experience. Jaspers finds the aporia at the heart of the antinomy, which is different from contradiction or antithesis: "An antinomy . . . is what we call an incompatibility that cannot be overcome, a contradiction that will not be resolved but exacerbated by clear thinking, an antithesis that does not round itself into a whole but remains an irreducible fraction at the bounds of thinking" (p. 218). Surplus becomes unmanageable and undescribable: "Everywhere we have something unwanted to take in the bargain." Freedom and dependence, historicality and universality, and communication and loneliness each call up the image of the other. Life outside of *Existenz* (the principle of infinity and freedom that is always unique and indescribable but comes from making boundary situations clear to oneself) encourages only "restating the antinomies and their endless variations in every situation" or a contemplative detachment that tries to hold itself back from all commitment to experience. Or one can pretend that the antinomies are not there by "making generally valid choices favoring one side" (p. 219), which might for us include, for example, preferring one disciplinary account of situatedness over others and effecting thereby certain decisions and priorities.

Perhaps Jaspers could afford to see the antinomies of situatedness for what they are because he wished, or was able to use them after all, for a metaphysical and ontological purpose, the apprehension of *Existenz*, and not the elucidation of the epistemological problems facing social scientists and legal theorists. Historicity, being situated in time and place, is all-governing for everything except thought itself in its intuition of transcendence through the acceptance of boundary situations as such.[31] Sartre, who replicates a good deal of Jaspers's thinking about the *Situation* as well as the term itself, is not interested in transcendence, and his work builds incrementally toward positing history as the sphere of all critical thought and engagement. Whereas Wittgenstein's understanding of the indescribable givenness of human situatedness inclined him to a fetishization of brevity and a minimizing of philosophy's allowable tasks, Sartre's response to the same syndrome was a massive overwriting, a production of big or unfinished books. In *Being and Nothingness* (1943) he follows Heidegger (and anticipates Lacan) in interpreting the cogito as a "lack" rather than a fullness of being. Human reality does not precede the world, on which it can then focus its desires; human reality *is* desire for the totality that it can never be.[32] Being is already situated in the world, already in search of the ultimately satisfying situation that it can never

164

achieve. There are only evolving and successive situations. The outcome of this is an inevitably "unhappy consciousness" (p. 90): Sartre makes normative what Hegel had rendered as historical and subsumable. But this predicament is also foundational for human freedom. By dismantling the distinction between (voluntary) acts of will and (involuntary) actions or instincts, Sartre makes all acts free, and freedom the essence of existence (pp. 441–44). That the freedom is generated by nothingness makes it melancholy in its psychological projections even as it is affirmative in its existential identity.

Human life is then a constant passage between situations, and never an escape from situatedness or a reposing in absolute situatedness.³³ Nothingness is the mode of passage: "Freedom is the human being putting his past out of play by secreting his own nothingness" (p. 28). The human being is not a consciousness entering the world but finds itself already there, at the heart of ongoing "projects" (p. 39). Sartre's "situation" (like Merleau-Ponty's) is analogous to Heidegger's being-in-the-world and Wittgenstein's language-game: we cannot think ourselves outside it. There are no boundary situations leading us to metaphysics, as there were for Jaspers. But we can and do generate new situations. Situations are neither objective nor subjective, understanding those terms in the traditional sense according to which they produce an anxiety or indeterminacy driving us to try to compute the exact degree of each that is at work *within* situatedness. The situation cannot be "considered from the outside; it is fixed in a *form in itself*" (p. 548). Philosophically speaking no situation is freer than another. But there is change. The human being can choose (in Sartre's circumscribed sense of the word) what is not yet existing, even as such choice does "not constitute a *knowledge* nor even an affective comprehension of the state of the world by a subject" (p. 549). So one cannot think of oneself as "*being* in a situation" because the situation is a given of one's being that does not allow for "positional consciousness" (p. 260). It is thus impossible for "the for-itself to distinguish the contribution of freedom from that of the brute existent" (p. 488). Experience simply does not provide disaggregated information about either the for-itself (the classical "subject") or the in-itself (the classical "world"). Like Wittgenstein, Sartre insists that there is no disinterested position from which to survey the (one's) human condition: "It is not possible for me not to have a place" (p. 490). There is nothing like Jaspers's *Existenz* to allow us to shift gears into a compensatory vocabulary.

So the place in which we always have to be is never known as a place that can provide a confident declaration of situatedness. Sartre's redefinition of choice as an act that is *not* knowledge based speaks volumes to (and against) our contemporary rhetoric of self-affiliation as it purports to tell where we are coming from. It is in the "look" of the Other, Sartre says, that "the 'situation' escapes me," that one becomes no longer *"master of the situation"* (p. 265). The sense of the Other as occupying the position of inspection creates "a *fear* which lives all my possibilities as ambivalent" (p. 264). Again: "To be looked at is to apprehend oneself as the unknown object of unknowable appraisals" (p. 267). In this way there is "danger" in the "permanent structure of my being-for-others" (p. 268); hence perhaps the uneasy hyperbole and preemptive aggression of so many of our self-positionings. Every sense of mastery is simultaneously a sense of slavery—if one is not being looked at, then one fears being about to be looked at. As Jeremy Bentham knew well enough, if one cannot hold others under constant inspection then it is almost as efficient to have them thinking that they are.[34] The confirmation of place in the look of the Other is also a sense of being placed, of being looked over. The sensation Sartre attributes to this complex precursor of the Althusserian interpellation is a mixed one, a "strange freedom" and an "uneasiness" that sometimes upgrades to fear and danger (p. 275). The forward-looking prognosis adumbrates "an infinite and inexhaustible series of unrevealed properties" (p. 268); but as they occur they too will be unknowable because located in the "appraisals" of others: "I can not truly define myself as *being* in a situation" (p. 260). This concern with *the look* in Sartre's 1943 classic is of course prophetic of an enormous outpouring of responses to Lacan and to Foucault's rediscovery of Bentham's panopticon writings. But the early Foucault's panoptical society is one in which there is minimal opportunity to look back at the Other looking at you: the freedom that comes from recognizing the Other as similarly positioned with regard to others (and potentially oneself) is unavailable or unemphasized in carceral circumstances. Sartre wants to retain a sense of freedom along with the fear and uneasiness. In so doing he offers yet another account of why self-affiliation is at once compulsive—"it is not possible for me not to have a place"—and epistemologically redundant—"I can never know the coordinates of that place." He also suggests that the unignorable awareness of the Other has moved the discourse about subjectivity once and for all beyond the imagining of a self contemplating itself as a series of aspects more or less open to detached (and unobserved) private inspection.

Sartre has then argued away the provisions of Kantian ontology, aesthetics, and moral judgment. The world is a series of "instrumental complexes" (p. 323) in which we are from the very beginning already involved: there is no unmarked point of entry and no moment of innocent respite thereafter. But he preserves the loneliness that is at the heart of Kantian disinterest, even as he disputes disinterest itself. Kant guaranteed consensus only as a projection, as an assumption made by the single subject about the responses of other subjects. He realized that any effort to institute such consensus as an empirical condition would either founder or, if successful, negate its own transcendental potential. Sartre puts us back into the world from which the transcendental maneuver was designed to remove us and plays up the loneliness and anxiety of being there, now figured as existential isolation. No two situations are alike, or can be known to be so. Sartre here reaffirms the findings of Helvétius and Holbach, the radical materialists of the eighteenth century: "There is no absolute point of view which one can adopt so as to compare different situations, each person realizes only one situation—his own" (p. 550). And he does not realize (understand) what he realizes (makes real).

In other words, there is here no apparent way forward for a theory of justice or a method for the social sciences. Nor, having been thus put back into the world by philosophy (and only in fantasy were we not always there already) in order to justify human freedom, are we offered the consolations of either a struggle-free situation or a lasting bond with others in the world. Temporality itself and alone precludes such satisfactions. Sartre turns situatedness into an a priori condition in order to displace the questions that had always arisen when it was viewed as a contingent condition that a subject could choose or not to inhabit. But no descriptive or analytical paradigms for the conduct of life or the description of the social sphere can come from a priori conditions. It is as if we have learned once again, as with Wittgenstein, what questions not to ask. If philosophy has returned us wholly to the world we have, to ordinary life, then it has not provided us with anything beyond a formal solution to the antinomies of that subjectivity in whose terms the social and judicial sciences still conduct their business.

From Philosophy to Biography: Sartre on Stalin and Flaubert Sartre's *Being and Nothingness* is principally a contribution to existential philosophy and as such imagines its reader as one concerned with establishing his or her presence in the moment. There is only a hint that the condition of lonely existential freedom there posited as the normal human condition might itself be historical. It comes at the point where Sartre describes how the bourgeoisie is unable to imagine itself as belonging to a class: "Although it has at its disposal precise and rigorous means for coercion, it is within itself profoundly anarchistic" and unable to recognize its "community of being" by any means short of revolutionary threat (pp. 428, 429). Sartre's later work devotes itself to trying (by way of marxism) to discover the history of and in the existential moment. This effort to go beyond formalism necessarily brings him back to the classic problems and the classic pseudosolutions of the inherited debates about situatedness. What makes individuals do what they do? Where are they coming from when they do it? What are the situational limits on what they can do? And if there are such limits, are they responsible for their actions? In the face of such questions Sartre's arguments remain visibly formal even as they are illustrated with historical and empirical examples, ordinary life situations. The two volumes of his *Critique of Dialectical Reason*, published twenty-five years apart (in 1960 and 1985), and the related *Search for a Method* (1960) represent his major project of totalization, his effort at "finding the intelligible foundations for a structural anthropology" and at showing that "there is *one* human history, with *one* truth and *one* intelligibility" revealing itself through the totalizing trajectories of multiplicities.[35] Sartre recognizes these multiplicities as differently situated and as composed of individuals irreducible to an essence of "man," while still insisting on the emergence of a single history (p. 39). The model of dialectical reason attempts to hang on to the notion of order in the world while factoring in its emergence through actually located persons involved in a seemingly disorderly " 'situated' *praxis*" (pp. 20, 29). So "the dialectic as the living logic of action is invisible to a contemplative reason: it appears in the course of *praxis* as a necessary moment of it; in other words, it is created anew in each action" (p. 38).

Sartre's solution to the problem of reconciling the truth of the individual with the truth of history is elegant enough as far as it goes, but because it does not have comfortably available to it the earlier Lukácsian specification of the emergent proletariat as the truth of history, it still has to rely on a conventional "critical investigation" (p. 52) whereby the individual can understand, by regressive analysis (that is, beginning in the present and looking back), his or her own particular place among the social-historical energies that combine and clash with one another in the process of totalization. Clearly some experiences will matter more in this respect than others; there will be redundancy and repetition in the individual's experience of and contribution to history. Hegel had been absolutely frank about this in paring down what mattered about history to a few exemplary moments and building his narrative of historical progress on them. Sartre, already sensitive to the move away from grand narrative (and of course from Hegel himself, its great communicator), is necessarily more circumspect about what the single history might be and where it is leading. The priority of human freedom in his thinking indeed makes it desirable and possible for him to pose this as an open question. But his analysis thus wanders between formalism and utopianism. He wants to answer the classic questions about situatedness, to adjudicate "the respective role of relations of interiority and exteriority." But he can avoid the correspondingly classic problems about all answers to such questions only by proposing a pragmatist way out: that we will "find ourselves situated, through the investigation itself, at the heart of a developing totalisation" (p. 57). We will only know where we are when we are there, and we will only know where we have been coming from when we have left where we were. The history that we thus create is only open to being known to us as it is performed and is retrospectively intelligible to the degree that one defines knowledge itself—as Sartre eventually and polemically does— as a category inclusive of the unconscious (things not recognized at the time of performance). Correspondingly the effort at relating interiority to exteriority is always mounted within a present that guarantees one's place in the developing totalization of history to exactly the degree that it displaces the traditional desire for seeing oneself and one's past as if from a third-person position. It is implicit that critical investigation can produce some knowledge of the not-self that is historically true—for instance, knowledge of the pivotal role of scarcity—despite its departure from the model of the self as a disinterested and out-of-time contemplator of a passively accessible experience. Sartre is reversing what he sees as the marxist analytical habit whereby individuals are deduced from prior productive forces, proposing instead that the knowledge of history starts with the present of the individual. But he retains the knowledge claim that marxist analysis also made; that our knowledge of history can be true as well as subjectively located. We come to knowledge as we live through our various situations.[36]

These situations always evolve by dramatizing our placement in groups and our actions as group actions (p. 505). Sartre's model is not as general as a class-based analysis, but it does seek to head off the priority of any single-subject consciousness of the sort that had dominated *Being and Nothingness*, where it was more important to him (in his early effort at an articulation of freedom) to stress that no one person could know the situation of another. In this way his goal of establishing the availability of "an intelligible totalisation from which there is no appeal" (p. 817) seeks to preempt the accusation that whatever is produced as knowledge is always and only a strictly subjective knowledge. The appeal of the "group" is presumably that it is loose and informal enough to preserve a place for assumptions of choice while retaining also a place for preformed constraints. Fredric Jameson sees the term as symptomatic of the historical condition of Sartre's time of writing, one where "there is no longer any national or social unit, only a jumble of various groups and ruins of groups, serial collectivities, and groups of all kinds coming into being simultaneously."[37] For him the group works to summon up the residue of Sartre's earlier pessimism about collective or any other identity: it is "a set of individuals trying in vain to become a substance, straining toward some ultimate hyperorganic status which they can never attain" (p. 268). If the group is indeed thus disabled, then we must question the more favorable spin put on what remains essentially group membership in the later culture of the postmodern as it celebrates the mobile subject positionalities and dialogic associations that are open to us once we have given up on "substance." Thus Jameson himself rounds forcefully on the postmodern sentimentalization of groups, whereby they are taken to provide all "the gratifications of psychic identity" while maintaining a "horror of consensus" so that "everything in our social reality is a badge of group membership and connotes a specific bunch of people." [38]

Examples of group behavior—soccer matches, boxing tournaments, the Resistance—are important to Sartre's argument, but he does not give up on his interest in what used to be called the world-historical individual, and to the project of biography it requires, which Jameson, once again, has attributed to his "lifelong ideological attachment to the framework of the individual consciousness." [39] The second volume of the *Critique of Dialectical Reason* offers the case of Stalin as active and passive agent of history. With this effort at making critical sense of the individual life, Sartre replicates the commitment to case studies identified by James Chandler (who himself makes much use of Sartre) in romanticism's "invention of the historical situation" (*England in 1819*, p. 305). He must thus engage also with the contradictions that the biographical investigation cannot but produce. David Hume, early in his career, had expressed his hopes for a "science of MAN" to be had by marching up "directly to the capital or center of these sciences, to human nature itself; which being once masters of, we may every where else hope for an easy victory." [40] The mastery famously never came, but it remained an enduring fantasy for many later would-be scientists of man; and in a culture imagining itself as made up of individuals it required a biographical application. Here is Dilthey's exemplary articulation, in 1883, of the human science alternative to dead systems: "Thus biography represents the most fundamental historical fact clearly, fully, and in its reality. Only the historian who, so to speak, builds history from these life-units, who seeks, through the concepts of type and representation, to interpret social classes, associations, and historical periods, and who links together individual lives through the concept of generations, only he will be able to apprehend the reality of a historical whole in contrast to the lifeless abstractions which are usually drawn from the archives." [41] A similar ambition appeared as we have seen in the synchronic mode of the social sciences: Ralph Linton's (1945) *The Science of Man* hoped for a "pure science" leading to the "planning and direction of cultural change" founded in an understanding of the interrelations of "personality and culture" (pp. 12, 14). So too did C. Wright Mills. Impossible tasks, but ones that we seem to have been regularly compelled to undertake. Sartre's own choice of a particular individual was of course not arbitrary. Stalin had been the test case for a number of left-wing intellectuals concerned to justify the positive potential of state-enforced communism without appearing to sanction the excesses of Stalinism—the trials, the executions, the labor camps, and the invasions of neighboring countries. In the face of Stalinism, many in Europe and America had broken with communism itself and turned to democratic socialism or liberalism; others looked to China for an alternative incarnation of political hope. A few (mostly in Europe) kept to the party line and were faced with the task of excusing one perceived atrocity after another on the part of the world's most powerful communist state. It was into this debate that Sartre entered his thoughts on Stalin, although very much as a latecomer; and it is this context that renders any discussion of Stalin also a process of putting on trial, of finding for and against, very much in the manner of a criminal prosecution. So the question of situatedness is particularly urgent here. Did Stalin have choices about what he did? Could he have done otherwise? Can he be justified by the power of situational pressures, imagined as mitigating or extenuating circumstances? These questions arise within a very traditional crux for marxist theory, inherited from Hegel but unignorable anyway, which we may call the "great man" syndrome. Crudely put, the issue is this: would history have developed in the way that it did, given the power of economic and social determinations, without the contribution of significant individuals, or were those individuals critical to the making of history? The question is especially significant for western marxism because its materialist priorities engage with a well-established liberal tradition privileging individual freedom and agency. Plekhanov had decided that general history always develops "under the impact of what may be called the fortuities of private life," even as those fortuities cannot radically redirect more general social energies.[42] Sartre offers a more thoroughly dialectical relation between self and society. The Russian "organs of sovereignty" required embodiment in a single man and not just any single man, but Stalin specifically: "The individual required by the system will be determined, and will determine praxis by his very determination." This is the "*overdetermi-*

nation of History" whereby "praxis is obliged to receive more and less than it has asked for." The individual *must* cause history to deviate as long as history cannot do without the individual.[43]

Every incarnation of praxis is thus a deviation (p. 225): "The men History makes are never entirely those needed to make History, be they even as unrivalled as Stalin or Napoleon" (p. 223). It is the scarcity of men as well as of the means for subsistence that marks the course of historical events. Russia, in other words, could not have had anyone but Stalin; at the same time Stalin was not and could not have been entirely adequate to or congruent with the historical moment. History, therefore, is "not rigorous"; it does not unfold according to inflexible laws but by "*chance* incarnation" and "mistakes and corrections" (p. 227). Sartre does not exonerate Stalin, as if he were the lawyer for the defense, but neither does he simply blame him, as if he were the prosecutor. The question at issue here is in fact not one of justice but of understanding. At the same time it is not quite enough to fall back on the notion that the world-historical individual is simply innocent of his functions: there were too many dead bodies in Stalin's record to allow that move. History does not entirely make the "great man," but rather it requires his existence and in so requiring has to offer him a space in which to interfere with history's own abstract trajectories. He will inevitably do so. Sartre faces up to what I have been describing as the antinomy of knowledge claims about situatedness, wherein we struggle to decide how much of an act is inevitable and how much a matter of options and choices. We have seen how this plays out in the formal-ontological framework of *Being and Nothingness*, where it affords the self in action a sense of both freedom and anxiety—the psychological constitutents of the rhetoric of self-affiliation. Being in a situation, Sartre there showed, does not provide *being*. Knowing about situatedness in ourselves happens largely retrospectively and feeds memory. But in his effort in *Search for a Method* to explore "just what is this *situating?*" Sartre also again played up the future-directed role of the situation as the starting point for the "project" that will supercede it through "work and action."[44] Looking to the career of a person in the historical past—Stalin for instance—makes clear that determination and deviation (which may be choice, or look like it) are both always in play: we cannot choose to have one without the other. Without Stalin, no Soviet state:

without the Soviet state, no Stalin. If there is a message here it is that only by getting outside of this particular antinomy can we expect to resolve it. And the way outside calls for a state situation in which there is no longer a reliance on the individual as the principle of sovereignty, so that the matter of individual behavior will be a lot less critical. It calls, in other words, for a true democracy, to the imagining of which Sartre's account of a disordered history may be said to contribute. In a world without scarcity, or with different or less critical kinds of scarcities, both Stalin figures and *azza* sentences might become rarities.

Much of Sartre's career was devoted to the articulation of the "great man" syndrome in relation to the besetting questions of how individuals incarnate or deviate history. Baudelaire, Genet, and Flaubert all are noted as representative men. Echoing Dilthey's complaint about the historians, Sartre found "Marxist formalism" deficient in its ignorance of "real men in depth" and of the "concrete determinations of human life," and he set himself the task of finding "mediations that allow the individual concrete—the particular life, the real and dated conflict, the person— to emerge from the background of the *general* contradictions of productive forces and relations of production" (*Search for a Method*, pp. 48, 43, 82, 57). In pursuit of just this articulation, Sartre wrote a few thousand pages about Flaubert and still left the task unfinished, still short of the major reading of *Madame Bovary* that had been promised as the conclusion of *The Family Idiot*.[45] The Flaubert project is an effort at totalization, at showing that "irreducibility is only apparent, and that each piece of data set in its place becomes a portion of the whole, which is constantly being created, and by the same token reveals its profound homogeneity with all the other parts that make up the whole" (*The Family Idiot*, 1: ix). But this homogeneity is a triumph for method only because it is a failure for life history. Flaubert's life shows how "a poor insertion into the world of language" (1: 223) made him a writer, and what it meant to grow up with a mother who wanted a daughter. The process of "personalization" that is the activity of life is an effort at unification, "endlessly returning to the original determinations on the occasion of more recent ones in order to integrate what cannot be integrated" (2: 6). For Flaubert this meant writing, and a constant return to the scenes of childhood in which the writing compulsion took shape and form. His history is repetition, and so too is that of the mid-nineteenth century of which his individuality is exemplary.

Sartre admits quite frankly that much of his account of Flaubert's childhood is speculative and hypothetical (for example, 1: 46, 132), even as it is the primary moment in his narrative. He admits also that "Gustave does not react to the *objective* aggressions explained by his real situation but to the coded interpretations he gives them, which originate in the prefabricated schemes of his subjectivity" (5: 5). But those schemes were, Sartre proposes, themselves the form of objective history in its own "neurotic determination" around the year 1850 (5: 32, 35). Because the public experienced various and general kinds of disappointment and collapse it found itself attending sympathetically to writers "whose subjective neurosis consists *precisely* of an intention to fail" (5: 390). Flaubert and Baudelaire were the first to meet this need because their own early histories "disposed them to become neurotic" (5: 619). Sartre argues that Flaubert has already embraced his situation and has taken his place in the world as one constituted by the synthesis of subjective neurosis with objective historical process: Flaubert is to the bourgeoisie what Stalin was to the Soviet state, and vice versa. There is no point in worrying over what might have seemed to another to be the case—did Gustave really experience this or that in this or that way?—because what matters is what he thought he experienced, and what he thought he experienced was generic. We can gain retrospective access to that thought by the recognition of compulsion, the syndrome that made all experience essentially the same. Situatedness becomes describable because it has already been packaged for description by Gustave-in-history, by Gustave "himself."

The length of Sartre's biography of Flaubert is itself an issue. Endlessly detailed and yet governed by the same few details, selected out of a childhood whose events are themselves imagined or deduced from later events, *The Family Idiot* might easily be taken as a symptom of methodological paranoia, as if sheer persistence might make the case more convincing, or even complete—for Sartre does sometimes speak as if we could know everything if only we had enough documents.[46] The sheer size of the project—some twenty-six hundred pages in the English translation—suggests an effort at completion, at saying everything there is to say about Flaubert. At the same time the repetition of a few key concepts and events suggests that the critical moments in even the most representative life are relatively few. Like Hegel, Sartre is writing a highly selected "history," a narrative dependent on a small number of events, one that Douglas Collins has called "a structural representation or summational fiction." [47]

Questions then arise: Is this an adequate history? Adequate to what? Could one write a similar history for other writers in other times and places, and if so, what would be revealed? Sartre on Stalin is, as I have said, not so much resolving the antinomies of situatedness as standing outside them by proposing the inevitable misfit of idiosyncratic and general-historical determinations in an unsatisfactory world. The Flaubert project, with its strong emphasis on the formative experiences of a (hypothetical) childhood, does read as a closed and coherent narrative, one in which there is not much freedom for deviation. But the price of such methodological tidiness is (was) existential misery. The coming together of objective and subjective neuroses as here described does not seem to allow Flaubert much room for acting on his situation except by way of bringing into being what is already latent. Sartre does not speak here, as he does in the case of Stalin, of the deviation of history brought about by its reliance on singularity. The point here, Douglas Collins supposes, is not the articulation of freedom but that of sameness. Flaubert's complete representativeness makes him an everyman figure whose reality is communicated almost brutally by the sheer length of the book. As we read on and on and "become" Flaubert, the grimness of his moment is "lived as well as thought" (*Sartre as Biographer*, pp. 175–76). The other becomes the same, as Flaubert is the "same" to the mid-nineteenth-century culture that produced and was reproduced by him. And as the other becomes the same, there disappears the need for laws, "or for exterior precepts that arrive from the outside" (p. 175). Judgment itself is then suspended, so that we have no need here for a Clarence Darrow. Biography, Collins argues, solves for Sartre the problem of how one person can be other, and others: it is at once "paranoia and unanimist rapture" (p. 201). It does away with the need for representation, according to which one person stands for or speaks for others. It does away also, then, with the compulsion to speak one's group affiliation or one's right to speech itself, a compulsion founded on the acceptance of divided societies. The grim determinations of Flaubert's life, as narrated, function as utopian pointers, as instances of what life will *not* be when it is made subject to quite other versions of the "objective spirit" and of the subjective spirits that can conjoin with it. As he does in the account of Stalin, Sartre is here hinting at a socialist democracy, one not driven by the conditions of scarcity. He does not here speak of justice and human rights because he is looking toward a world in which those concepts either would not exist or would be transformed beyond recognition. We do not have to judge the other when we have become the other. To be in the situation of the other is to be temporarily unaware of the obscurities of situatedness as the signature of a divided society. Literature performs this suspension of disbelief for the moment: its permanent or longstanding experience can so far subsist only in the utopian imaginary, where no one, so long as she or he is addressing our own species, would need to be introduced "as a human being."

Lucien Sève, whose *Man in Marxist Theory* (1974) again takes up the project of theorizing personality, also proposes that the failure of existing theories is inevitable given that a true flowering of personality can only occur after the end of capitalism. What is currently to be theorized, in other words, is itself a site of incompletion and contradiction, and not a coherent entity. Both humanism and antihumanism are falsifications, two sides of a compulsive antagonism to be understood not as choices but as symptoms of another antinomy whose dissolution is the task (and therefore not yet the achievement) of Marx's project. Historical materialism cannot then be a coherent and closed achievement but must remain a "pilot science in relation to the science of personality."[48] Its method should be that of "scientific humanism"—neither humanism nor scientism but something of both. Although Sartre's and Sève's ideas are not completely congruent they do both project a future for which the models we now have to describe our world will no longer suffice. The strong determinations of Flaubert's world point by negation to a world in which other freedoms might obtain, so that the emphases of *Being and Nothingness* are not completely abandoned in the later work. When all is said and done, the method of *The Family Idiot* remains historical, specific to place and time and thus open to change. Indeed it is Flaubert's effort at disinterestedness, at being beyond place and time, at "de-situation" in the service of some sort of "*panoramic consciousness*" (3: 454) that renders him most thoroughly a situated mind, a mind in place and time. Sartre elegantly describes the way in which the Enlightenment ideal of disinterest could be maintained only insofar as the writer remained "suffused with bourgeois ideology" (5: 92) and thus by class interest. In the eighteenth century the ethic of disinterest had had a critical function: it was aimed against the restrictions of the status quo. In the nineteenth century, with the bourgoisie in the ascendant, that same ethic could only turn against itself, so that the dominant trope of romanticism becomes that of failure (5: 101–7, 138–43). Humanism began as a protest against inequality on behalf of a rising class; it could therefore (like many of the French revolutionaries) afford the rhetoric of universals as long as it remained in opposition. In the nineteenth century—Sartre says after 1830—"the task of the professionals is to restore humanism and base it on private property" (5: 195). Thence arise contradictions and hypocrisies that are sustainable only because the proletariat is "embryonic" (5: 195) and that become increasingly untenable or conflicted as it emerges. The world of Flaubert, in other words, is a world of the past. In its completely determined character it shows us the need for a different world. If in the exhaustive following through of the biographical narrative we do indeed become Flaubert, become the other, then it is only in order to realize, at last, the radical need for a new self.

It is the form of biography, and not its specific content, that bears the hope for a different world. The form shows how to become the other; the content reminds us that this particular other, Flaubert, is not one we ought to become. The play between idiosyncratic and general determinations and the difficulty of knowing the difference that makes up so much of the narrative energy of a George Eliot novel is in Sartre's Flaubert flattened into undifferentiated repetition. Biography, the genre that might be expected to privilege idiosyncrasy, does not here do so. We may agree with Collins that Sartre here combines the recovery of a compulsively repeated history with the projection of an uncompelled future. But that he does this so haltingly, obscurely, and obsessively—to the point that it takes much good will and ingenuity to decide that he is doing it at all—may be attributed to the residual power of the very antimonies of situatedness that he is trying to displace, and to the difficulty of giving shape and form to a world in which they are not any longer to be the governing terms of analysis. If Sartre is our own Flaubert, our representative neurosis, our exemplary subject, then his writings suggest, precisely in their obsession with the past of Flaubert himself, that we are a long way from bypassing those antinomies in an alternative present or imagined future. *Being and Nothingness* sought to prove that freedom is not just possible but fundamental, even within the shadow of unhappiness. *The Family Idiot* shows how that freedom could, in place and time, be restricted entirely to the task of reproduction. The case of Stalin makes the uncomfortable argument that we deserve what we get even as what we get is not exactly what we need.

Sartre is our most determined and committed philosophical analyst of situatedness. The limitations of his efforts suggest that the issues raised by a full acceptance of situatedness as a life condition exceed what "philosophy" can expect to cope with. The same is true of the other disciplines that have made the same effort, so that we can begin to sense that there is a necessary misfit between the questions we want to answer and the methods we have come up with to try to answer them: a sort of disciplinary sublime. Sartre's problems with situatedness are less his own than those of our generation and all modern generations, which cannot yet imagine a world that is neither Flaubert's nor that of the liberal individualists against whom Sartre's Flaubert is itself reconstructed. We are not beyond the antinomies and aporias of situatedness, except insofar as we can imagine a world we cannot yet describe. But Sartre has shown that these antinomies and aporias are historically variable and therefore not immanent: the case of Flaubert is not the same as the case of Stalin. And neither is the case of modern human nature. In 1956 Georges Burdeau is once again adumbrating a version of Tocqueville's and Cooley's anomic democracies, finding in "situated man" a constitutive "lack of stability": "The situated man is thus a man without roots. He camps out in life: spiritually he cannot place himself."[49] The situated man is, that is to say, precisely *not* situated in the way that is so often claimed. He is "constantly looking for a physical milieu or a system of ideas that could allow him the appearance of personality," so that he finds consolation only in his "perpetual mobility" of mind and body (p. 43). He thus puts into question the very social order that makes him what he is, but not to the point of revolutionary transformation (p. 46). The western democracies govern, according to Burdeau, by the "institutionalisation of ambiguities" (p. 16). Prominent among them may well be the antinomies of situatedness I have been describing throughout this book. According to Sartre, Flaubert's response to and embodiment of his social-historical pathology was the desire to fail and the syndrome of compulsive repetition. Our own representative men seem more invested in the rhetoric of compulsive innovation and the imagining of repeated success. The unstable rhetoric of situatedness, however, shows these options to be at heart the same, two sides of the same coin.

Psychoanalysis and Private Life   There are times and places where we have traditionally been and are still encouraged to imagine ourselves as beyond situatedness and also outside history in all the ways that Sartre critiques. The traditional spheres for such imagination, religion and the aesthetic, continue to be available and may even be proliferating and diversifying (for instance in the new popularity of ethical philosophy). The notion of a self that can be detached from its worldly situatedness was critical to the description of Protestant interiority and to the Cartesian epistemology that came after it; and the aesthetic moment as Kant described it was similarly premised on an indifference to empirical confirmations and contingencies. It is also commonly accepted that these psychologically internal experiences have been substituted for or matched by an increased commitment to the private life as a nourishing alternative to the demands of occupational and political identification. The nuclear family, for example, has been for some time imaged as a site wherein situatedness is either manageable or clearly defined, a place where one can relax from the demands of self-declaration, where one is "at home." But true privacy has also been conceived as threatened by the structured intimacies of the family itself, or theorized as strictly unavailable, so that it becomes that imaginary place where there is no situatedness, always to be wished for but never to be occupied. Habermas's famous account of the eighteenth-century public sphere proposes that we once had authentic privacy but have since lost it: solitary time within the patriarchal household once provided for the cultivation (through reading) of a critical reason that created the basis for a genuine *public* sphere:

"The experience of privacy made possible literary experimentation with the psychology of the humanity common to all, with the abstract individuality of the natural person." This could be deployed in "the public sphere of the world of letters" and thence in the wider cultural-political world.[50] But now interiority has been colonized by the mass media, and no one is trained in the skills required for a properly democratic public sphere. Consumer culture has ensured that our sense of ourselves as "critically reflecting private people" can be nothing more than "false consciousness" (p. 194). Richard Sennett's *The Fall of Public Man* offers a different but compatible version of the collapse of the public sphere, which has now become simply the stage for the expression of (manufactured) personality within an "ideology of intimacy" (p. 259).

Habermas writes with the self-confidence of a certain kind of social scientist: he knows what goes on in the places he cannot see. And he reminds us that the analysis and even restructuring of the private life was itself the goal of much social science. Hans Gerth and C. Wright Mills, in a passage I have already cited in chapter 3, looked forward to a perfected method by which the "most intimate features of man's self" would be connected with "the structural and historical features of modern society" (*Character and Social Structure*, p. xix); Orwell's *Nineteen Eighty-Four* imagined the nightmare version of this dream of reason. This brings us to psychoanalysis, whose business has been the articulation of intimacy, and to its role in the address to that knowledge about situatedness that I have defined as compulsively aporetic. Sartre's *The Family Idiot* makes relentless use of the language and methods of psychoanalysis. It argues that Flaubert's subjective neurosis was confirmed in childhood in relation to the dynamics of the family; henceforth its congruence with the objective neurosis of mid-nineteenth-century culture meant that Flaubert's freedom was only ever exercised in the service of reproduction. Flaubert's situatedness thus seems more or less complete in its explanatory power and in its practical constraints. The kind of freedom about which Sartre wrote so much elsewhere, whereby the individual lives his or her situation by transforming it and carrying forward a history that is at once personal and collective, seems only formally available to Flaubert. As we have seen, his history is the history of repetition.

Flaubert, in other words, essentially remained always a child, and thus his personal profile invites maximum application of the language of psychoanalysis, itself established as "a method which is primarily concerned with establishing the way in which the child lives his family relations inside a given society" (*Search for a Method*, p. 61). The specification of "a given society" indicates that Sartre does not regard psychoanalysis as foundational and universal but historical.[51] It is a critical methodological tool in overcoming the preoccupation with adult life traditional to a marxism that behaves as if "we are born at the age when we earn our first wages" (p. 62), but its particular importance for understanding Flaubert comes as much from the historical syndrome as from the formal method. Psychoanalysis tells us how the individual is initiated into history. Sartre is quite comfortable with flagrantly reconstructing the events that he thinks must have occurred in the life of the young Flaubert, without any hard evidence that they actually happened. Because Flaubert's place in history is one of repetition, a construction of that history is just a reconstruction of the early psychoanalytic experience.

Sartre's solution of the question of psychoanalysis in history is thus not the same in Flaubert's case as it was in Stalin's, where he made no explicit use of psychoanalysis at all. Simply, they are different individuals in different histories. The psychoanalytic emphasis in the case of Flaubert does not then necessarily negate Sartre's early and emphatic refutations of the institutional functions and general-theoretical claims of psychoanalysis itself. In *Being and Nothingness* he had argued against Freud's rejection of "the conscious unity of the psyche" and against his modeling of an unknown, unconscious driving behavior in directions different from those consciously intended (p. 53). For the early Sartre, consciousness produces the unconscious as part of its projects; he seeks to head off the assumption of political-historical passivity that he sees in conventional psychoanalysis by stressing the coherence of the individual's being-in-the-world as embodied in the history of its projects. So the environment does not act "mechanically on the subject under consideration. The environment can act on the subject only to the exact extent that he comprehends it; that is, transforms it into a situation" (p. 572).[52] Investigation discovers a "*choice* and not a *state*" (p. 573). There is no necessary or theoretical continuity between the predicaments of different subjects, nor between the same subject at different times. Existential psychoanalysis is "a method destined to bring to light, in a strictly objective form, the subjective choice by which each living person makes himself a person; that is, makes known to himself what he is" (p. 574).

The psyche, in other words, is always potentially available to itself and to others. Sartre has thus "turned" (or tried to turn) the threat that psychoanalysis presents to philosophy's search for general truths and visible principles and to political activism's desire for authentic human agency. He shows that it can, in specific cases such as that of Flaubert, describe childhood as the primary conditioning experience, but that it need not always do so. Its historicity itself allows for the imagining of other histories. Sartre's reading of psychoanalysis is less critical than some other marxist accounts, such as those of Sève and Timpanaro, who fault Freud for his blindness to the formative energies of social labor and class.[53] But it is consistent with them in its insistence on the visible, public functions of analysis, and in its rejection of a hidden, secret, and uncontrollable origin for human behavior.

Husserl claimed that no psychology could be modeled on natural science or ever become "exact" (*The Crisis of European Science*, p. 222). Freud's work is at the very least ambivalent (too much so for Sartre) on the question of what can be revealed and what scientific status such revelations have. The cure is a process that takes the patient out of a private hell and into a public sphere where positive sociability becomes possible once again. As such it is judged by its effectiveness as much as by reference to any definitive scientific account of the objective effects of the suffering subject's formative situatedness. Freud's (early) placement of critical events so firmly within childhood and the unconscious privileges spheres of experience that are never open to direct observation by patient or analyst. Thus to set about a reading of Freud himself from the perspective of the problem of situatedness is to encounter a baffling range of actual and potential theorizations, varying along a spectrum between outright occasionalism (if the analysis achieves a cure, then why worry about how?) and grand theory. Freud was often quite modest and skeptical about the status of psychoanalysis as general theory, but he was also a scientist who sought a transportable method latent in individual case histories. His rhetoric is thus often of the "both-and" rather than "either-or" variety. Symptomatic acts are not always available to inspection, because individual resistances and expressive capacities must vary;[54] mental life may indeed be completely determined, but the terms of that determination are not always accessible. Psychic events may well be ultimately explicable as organic events, but their psychic status is not thereby negated, nor can the balance of each component in the dreamwork of particular individuals be predicted.[55] Dreams almost always have multiple meanings (p. 312), and interpretation can be true without being complete. Indeed, it is not just individual resistances that preclude complete interpretation (p. 339): every dream has at least one point beyond which we cannot go, "a navel, as it were, that is its point of contact with the unknown" (p. 186). Reading Freud, one comes away not so much with *a* Freudian method clearly argued and refined from one book to the next but more a series of meditations and hypotheses on and around the question of method itself, producing what Paul Ricoeur has described as "a mixed or even ambiguous discourse." [56] Most dramatically in his shift of emphasis from neurological to psychological determinations, but also within the psychological model itself, Freud projects ideas that are as much symptoms as resolutions of the antinomies of situatedness. A combination of the idiosyncratic and the general is proposed as the typical operation of the dreamwork, so that each has to be set against the other (*Interpretation of Dreams*, pp. 470, 477). Thus Freud looked to examples of "unconscious ideation" (p. 467) such as folklore for assistance in selecting out what might be arguably generic. But by this point he is on the edge of anthropology.

Indeed, in his effort at incremental simplification and prioritization the later Freud moved away from the tentative and eclectic approach of the early work toward nonlocalized and general models of human behavior. The work that seems to make the definitive break with neurological materialism, *The Interpretation of Dreams* (1900), also looks forward to the later, culturalist phase in its suggestion that the dreamwork might be the place where phylogeny enters ontogeny as some "archaic heritage," allowing psychoanalysis to claim "a high place among the sciences which are concerned with the reconstruction of the earliest and most obscure periods of the beginnings of the human race" (p. 700). By the time of *Beyond the Pleasure Principle* (1920), and after a devasting European war, Freud's model of the psyche has become much more fixed in its inscription of a controlling, immanent situatedness from which there seems to be no escape. The instincts are now described as innately conservative, tending always toward "the restoration of an earlier state of things" (as they happened to do for Sartre's Flaubert).[57] The pleasure principle is now less powerful than "the compulsion to repeat" (pp. 16–17). As the repository of everything in a person's history, the unconscious always provides more material for assimilation than can be efficiently processed, so that the mind is always under stress. There is less emphasis on the cure and more on the unavoidability of pain and the difficulty of happiness. In *Civilization and Its Discontents* (1930) it seems that there can be only brief respite from the pain inflicted by the body's materiality and by social conditions: situatedness has become negative situatedness, beyond repair or restoration.[58]

Freud here joins a number of other thinkers for whom civilization is, if not outright barbarism, at least an enervating or painful predicament. The early work, while it was undoubtedly intended and received as a critique of bourgeois inhibitions and hypocrisies, had proposed a therapeutic and socially beneficial function for the dreamwork in normal cases, as it allowed for the passage of indestructible unconscious material into the preconscious by way of a "safety valve." [59] Without the dreamwork, the weight of the unconscious threatens to prevent normal functioning, as it does when "the watchman is overpowered" in the state of psychosis (p. 722). Dreaming is self-regulation, as efficient as the faculty of reason described by Kant and Hegel, and perhaps more so. Its function is healthy and curative. In *Civilization and Its Discontents* the mood has changed. Dreamwork helped to preserve sanity by working efficiently in solitude; Freud later comes to believe that solitude is not enough. The work of culture now becomes that of repressing the sexual instincts in a process only neurotics refuse to accept, so that they become, in a perverse way, normal (pp. 52, 55). Human relations are marked by a "primary mutual hostility" (p. 59) that makes repression necessary even as it imposes unbearable strains on the individual. Dreamwork can no longer contain the aggressive and self-destructive instincts whose restraint requires vigilant, external, cultural controls. Freud does not go so far as to recommend the world that Orwell represented in *Nineteen Eighty-Four*, a world where there is no privacy and no place for dangerous deviations: the totally administered society. But neither does he preserve the private as a refuge from the public, any more than he had done in his earliest studies of the dysfunctional effects of the family. We cannot look to private life to repair the damage done by participation in social experience; or, if we do, the gratifications of privacy threaten subsequent social participation and perhaps even the social order itself.

Freud's reaction against the liberal tradition's defense of the private sphere from outside interference is but one turn in the longstanding engagement with privacy conducted throughout western modernity. One emphasis constructs privacy as an escape from situatedness, a withdrawal from the pressures working to make us over into something or other, a locus for authentic as opposed to socially determined selfhood. Another perspective sees the private sphere as an imaginary space that presents obstacles to a clear understanding of the social foundation of life. Sartre, as we have seen, took the second position, as did Dewey, Sapir, and Sève, all of whom regarded the private life as a historical fiction to be dissipated by the proper application of the social sciences.[60] The more commonly held of these attitudes to privacy has been the first. Montaigne declared that person miserable who "has not in his own home a place to be all by himself, to pay his court privately to himself, to hide" and he pitied those so famous and public that "even their privy is not private."[61] John Stuart Mill argued for a strong domain of individual independence in On Liberty; and G. E. Moore proposed that "personal affections and aesthetic enjoyments include all the greatest, and by far the greatest, goods we can imagine."[62] Legal debates have made positive use of privacy as a bulwark against all sorts of social and political pressures; and when they have failed to do so, individuals have arguably been harmed. At the same time, the private-public boundary has never been stable or consensual, but has always had to be made again or reimagined. This is one consequence of the aporetic quality of all proposed knowledge about our situatedness. What is the private self before it is engaged with its world, and how can it be known?

Privacy itself is of course a historical condition. No one has yet been able to decide between the various theses proposing a definitive origin for a recognizably modern notion of private life, but many (and many distinguished) historians, philosophers, and social scientists have contributed their ideas. Charles Taylor, in a chronology that seems generally convincing, has noted the anticipatory appearance of an "affirmation of ordinary life" (of which privacy is a part) in Augustine's "inwardness of radical reflexivity" and "intimacy of self-presence," which emerges in early modernity as a notion of the dignity of the person and of the simplest and most habitual contexts for personhood—the private sphere. The philosophical analogue of this process is a "strong localization" producing the modern "subject."[63] Norbert Elias has proposed a critical connection between modernization and internalized self-regulation, which he sees as a response to the increasing division of labor and social function and an increasing insecurity (or hypersecurity) about one's position in a bewilderingly diversified system.[64] This process has been particularly characteristic of "the West," where the "division of functions" has attained levels unmatched elsewhere (p. 457). It first took exemplary form in court society "because it is here that vigilant self-control and perpetual observation of others are among the elementary prerequisites for the preservation of one's social position" (p. 478). And it was enhanced by the development of "bourgeois professional and commercial functions" that required the same behavior at a more intense level among more people (p. 504). An acute anxiety about the terms of one's situatedness (of the sort that Sartre discovered in his remarks on the "look") is thus for Elias a fundamental component of the "civilizing" project of modernity, even if it does not (as I am suggesting) emerge as rhetorically compulsive in the common language until quite recently.

Variously refined chronologies within the general category of modernity have been offered as explaining the emergence of the private life as a fundamental element of subjectivity. Richard Sennett's *The Fall of Public Man* finds that the full development of privacy does not come until the nineteenth century, at which point it had become clear that "the public was a human creation: the private was the human condition" (p. 98). For Sennett, the "behavioral and ideological confusions" between public and private are, in their critical forms, about two hundred years old (p. 25). Lawrence Stone's *The Family, Sex, and Marriage* takes the period from 1500 to 1800 as that in which individual autonomy and privacy in their modern senses appeared along with the growth of "affective individualism."[65] The imposing, multivolume *History of Private Life* published under the general editorship of Philippe Ariès and George Duby locates a critical shift in *mentalité* at the end of the seventeenth century.[66] Macpherson's thesis about "possessive individualism" makes the same point.

Proposed origins cannot be rendered exact, and will vary (as they have varied) according to the national and disciplinary focus of individual scholars. But although it seems to be true that the condition of privacy in something of its modern form was articulated as early as the fifth century by Augustine, it also seems clear that there have been moments of intensified concern during this long-durational history. One of them was the Puritan revolution; another was the genesis of philosophical liberalism culminating in the writings of John Stuart Mill. It is Mill (with Rousseau before him) who seems most visibly our contemporary in that he is no longer interested in the private sphere as a place to encounter God (although this is a feature of the academic subculture within which and for which I am now writing, there are many around us who still employ privacy in just this way, and their gods are many). More definitively, perhaps, Mill is interested in the social functions of privacy: he takes as his first principle the highly diversified society whose emergence was described by Elias, as it had been by Adam Smith and a great many others.

But once again Mill reproduces the antinomy of situatedness to exactly the degree that he attempts to resolve it. His argument depends on a workable distinction between the public and the private that close analysis cannot sustain, or sustains only approximately. As I have said before, his principal intention is to preserve the private sphere as a repository of and birthplace for the kinds of individual imagination on which the future of society is seen to depend, and without which society must become more and more tyrannized by uncritical worship of mere custom. Mill's *On Liberty* fears the power of habit as "enslaving the soul itself," not just by direct and overt coercion but by a subtle control of the interior life, compelling "all characters to fashion themselves upon the model of its own" (p. 7). He projects the image of the world that Orwell and Foucault, among others, will reinvent: the totally administered society. England lacks individuals; it is falling under the "despotism of custom" (p. 85). Against this tendency it becomes crucial that the private sphere be protected as a place where "personal impulses and preferences" (p. 74) can develop. These are the same impulses that the later Freud sought to

188

control by a reassertion of the power of culture. And Mill too acknowledges that the private sphere must be subject to outside control at such moments as its preservation threatens harm to others, and their right to protect themselves (pp. 13, 92). He is fully aware of the difficulty of establishing any model of privacy that is categorically exempt from someone's definition of harm (p. 97). The way one lives one's life can be called harmful by the example it sets; nonparticipation in public life (that is, privacy itself) can be deemed harmful in both act and example, as it has been by various communalistic mandates in various cultures. But it is precisely because the tendency of public life is to impose such definitions that some strict effort at protecting privacy must be maintained. Mill offers a working category of "distinct and assignable obligation" to others (p. 99) as marking the point at which corrective interference becomes warranted. He relies, as had Bentham, on a judgment about consequences. And he is aware that the terms "distinct" and "assignable" are open to endless dispute. It is the same dispute that has haunted arguments about intention (for example, in judgments about diminished responsibility or insanity) and it is an inevitable function of the antinomy of situatedness whereby it is as difficult to prove conclusively just how one person's behavior affects another as it is to define exactly the forces determining one's behavior in the first place. Mill relies, as everyone else has had to rely, on the perspicuity of extreme cases and the achieved, local consensus about the more difficult ones.

The argument of On Liberty also prefigures the contemporary localization of public life that takes for granted that our world is a world of subcultures or Sartrean groups: "The world, to each individual, means the part of it with which he comes in contact: his party, his sect, his church, his class in society" (p. 22). We all identify ourselves "as a" member of some or other subculture, but the normalizing effect of such pressures on individuals is always toward a relative and impermanent standard that we will risk taking for something more absolute unless we are continually exposed to the challenge of dissenting individuals. Such errors of parochialism are "corrigible" by "discussion and experience" (pp. 24–25) provided that our social sphere offer up the maximum possible numbers of opinions and models for discussion and experience. The constant discussion of and choosing among them can be imagined to produce all that we need of progress (p. 56). It is at this point that Mill looks most like one of our contemporaries. His faith in truth and progress might at first look a bit dated, but his confidence in the power of "discussion and experience" prefigures a whole host of more recent, optimistic prescriptions based on dialogic, conversational, and discourse models for the solution of social conflicts. Many of these, however, presuppose that the critical social need of the present is the enticement of selves out of an overabsorptive privacy so that they may make up for the breakdown of or loss of faith in bureaucractized state formations by creating interactive and responsive small units: consciously chosen conditions of situatedness, or groups. It seems that there is either too much privacy or not enough, so that once again the rhetoric describing our predicament is confusing, even antinomic. Sennett has pointed out a series of "behavioral and ideological confusions" governing accounts of public and private over the last two hundred years (*The Fall of Public Man*, p. 25). Some say that there is too much value given to private life, that we are too obsessed with cultivating its satisfactions, while others lament that there is no longer anything authentically private (or original) to be experienced. There are endless debates about whether the private sphere is already and completely public, and about whether it should be. The notion of privacy is so contested not least because it so often functions (as it does in the legal system) as the last best place wherein we can hope for unaccountability and an immunity from the Sartrean "look" of the "other." A defensible private sphere promises to underwrite nothing less than selfhood itself—the I that is prior to and different from all deployments of the *me*. In such a sphere one imagines that one could manage. Notions of manufactured intimacy and consent, and the postulation of microscopic invasions of self and psyche by the agents of a pervasive risk culture, threaten or destroy this dream of managing (coping or controlling) by proposing that the available space is already managed by someone or something else. This prospect undermines the enabling mystery of the "self" because it is precisely the sense of not being able to fully delineate the terms and limits of the I that guarantees (as it did in the Wordsworthian sublime) an excess of meaning (imaged as absence) and a continued identity. As soon as there is shape and form there is situatedness and its attendant antinomies and aporias, which are at once objects of concern and incentives to subsumption. The form of the self that is given to us, in other words, requires the experience of indecision because a strategic suspension of sentence is what is called for by the historical formation we have inherited. One could call this formation capitalism, or late capitalism, or liberal democracy, or modernity—it is something of each of these. Is there any prospect of a shift into a new register and a new rhetoric? Have we exhausted the old one? Does the reiterated and overreaching incidence of the claims to and for *situatedness* promise to bring this term and its attendant informational conventions into crisis, or are we stuck with them as the only approvable language for self-declaration and justification? What happens when what used to be the "militant praxis" of "situation analysis" becomes a "defensive praxis," in Lyotard's words?[67] Or when it becomes impossible to tell one from the other?

Lyotard's remembrance of a time when situation analysis was attached to "militant praxis" should remind us that the apparently dry and technical efforts of the philosophers to make theoretical sense of the vocabulary of situatedness should not be assumed to be absolutely detached from political debate and from the events of history itself. Although the movement was predictably accused of a disabling theoreticism, the motivations of the Situationist International (1957–72) visibly included doing away with theory, as well as with the credibility of Jean Paul Sartre and the Soviet state. The term *situation* appealed because it could not be reduced to theory or prised out of its implication in the here and now of time and place, in the "concrete construction of momentary ambiances of life."[68] The situation, wrote Guy Debord, is "made to be lived by its constructors."[69] We have mostly lost, in English, if we ever properly had them, the terms *situationism* and *situationist*, and the subsequent invention of *situatedness*, with its opportunistic passivity, is very far from suggesting that we are where the situationists thought they might be, at "the moment of the qualitative leap, of all or nothing" (p. 84). Can we manage without it, and should we be trying to? What might be gained and what lost by such imagining?

6. Lost for Words: Can We Stop Situating Ourselves?

History on the Brink of What? In this concluding chapter I shall try to show that admitting to and reflecting on the confusions in the rhetoric of situatedness can actually benefit some of the causes that have traditionally been defended by pretending that those confusions can provide clear kinds of knowledge. In so reflecting, we may have some chance of inhibiting the radical swings of the pendulum whereby, for example, frustrations with or attacks on rational social planning have been followed by equally or even more extreme assertions of the priority of free will and individual opportunity. Exposing the problems in the rhetoric of situatedness does not mean that it is going to disappear, banished forever by the force of critical analysis. Nor is it clear that it should disappear if it can be shown that its difficulties, once understood as such, can have positive implications. But there is surely a need for some serious clarifications. In the next section I will show in some detail the problems that arise from misconceived certainties or assurances about specifying situatedness, where people think they know where they or others are coming from; but I will also show that an awareness of the fuzziness of situatedness arguments can be just as disabling and just as open to opportunist exploitation. First, however, I would like to recapitulate some of the points made already and to raise some questions about the very possibility for critique.

"So who are you?" Adorno's question stands as an epigraph to this study, and I hope I have by now made clear why it has remained unanswered or poorly answered, and why at the present moment especially it has been so often answered provisionally, with a sort of retraction clause appended to it. Adorno of course does not quite mean his question as a question. It comes up as belonging historically to the "shadow side of personality," the price one pays for entrance into the recognition system of bourgeois individuality. The point of that system is not to have us answer the question once and for all but to make us go on asking it. The confusions, obscurities, and opportunities attending arguments about situatedness are, as we have seen, quite purposive for a liberal-democratic culture whose governing rhetoric must preserve both the entrepreneurial incentive to change oneself and one's given conditions for a self-selecting or designated few and a language for discouraging access to ideas about radical self-determination for the many. The awareness of situatedness is for some people an opportunity for acting on the world; for others it is the reason why they have passively become what they are. For many of us much of the time it is both, or one after the other in a sequence whose instability we can indeed exploit but that also holds us prisoner in its mysteries and confusions. Whenever we have hoped or pretended that we can achieve an accurate description of our own or others' situatedness we have apparently been compelled to repeat the rehearsal of antinomies and the encounter with aporia. It seems obvious that no merely academic effort at demystification, even if the effort is a convincing one, can expect to banish from use a confusing or incompetent terminology when that terminology visibly performs the functions of purposive obfuscation. Such may well be the case with *situatedness*, or with the family of ideas called up by this term that is after all not yet quite commonplace, a family whose function I have argued to be exactly the preservation of certain confusions and undecidabilities in the description and attribution of our various subject positions in the world. For this reason the exposure of contradiction does not produce resolution but rather a more contested debate between the terms of the contradiction, so that the antinomies do not yield to the sublimation or subsumption that in ideally progressive systems ought to follow their exposure *as* antinomies. If they are to remain compulsively repeated, worked through again and again in a desperate attempt to resolve themselves from the inside, then each encounter with aporia will send us back to the beginning, as if we feel that we might in a purely formal sense have missed some critical step along the way, the one that when put properly into place will revolutionize the system into clear and distinct conclusions. That is not likely to happen until the time is ripe for an interruption of mere repetition.

Might we now be at that point? The sheer ubiquity, awkward visibility, and visible incompetence of arguments from situatedness, not just in specialized dictions but in the common language with its "as a" and "let me tell you where I am coming from" sentences, suggest that the paradigm may be on the point of exhaustion from sheer overuse. Imagine a language community in which everyone who is about to situate himself or herself were to stop short and struggle to find words. Imagine the disappearance from the language of American teenagers of the overuse of the word *like*. It seems, like, impossible, totally. *Like* will persist as long as there is a need for an unsubordinated and always only approximate blurring of causality and analogy whereby speakers can suggest the relation of one thing to other things without specifying exactly what that relation might be; as long as such specification is held to be either bad manners (an affront to the linguistic opportunities of others) or impossible (because everything connects to everything and to nothing), we will have the word *like* doing its work in the language. The functions of the rhetoric of situatedness are not so different, they allow us to fill the place of specification without making any very definitive statement. Any change would be momentous indeed. Because we are dealing with nothing less than the constraints of the rhetorical apparatus of late first-world anglophone capitalism in its intimate alliance with liberal democracy, it is worth pondering what would be changing also in that larger historical figuration, "our" world, the world that has sustained and employed the rhetoric of situatedness all along. If we are butting against the limits of our given language and therefore facing the prospect of wanting another language, another set of terms, are we then also about to enter a differently deployed set of worldly constraints and opportunities? If so it is likely that these terms cannot yet be spoken, can only come good when there is another world in which to use them; this was the utopian element in Sartre's work. It is intimated also at the end of Jameson's great essay "The Antinomies of Postmodernity," which warns against the tendency to give up altogether on a theoretical thinking that has hitherto experienced only the "static reversal and repetition" of "identity and difference" at the threshold of a history "whose dynamics representationally escape us" (The Seeds of Time, pp. 68, 69). The task is then to sustain a utopian thinking without a clear sense of the "imaginable change" it will bring about, and to listen hard for "the missing next tick of the clock, the absent first step of renewed praxis" (pp. 70, 71). Meanwhile, one fumbles around with ungainly neologisms (whose ungainliness is paraded as their virtue, their critical power) or retreats into silence (one of Wittgenstein's complicated mandates) or takes up again the task of critique. Above all, if one is a literary academic, one pays attention to what Derrida memorably called "the historical sedimentation of the language which we use," one of the principal tasks of his own "deconstruction."[1] *Situatedness*, I have been suggesting, is one of the currently fashionable neologisms that claims to indicate if not a breakthrough then at least a temporary accommodation with the intractable demands placed on the self toward justifiable self-description. To announce one's situatedness appears to preempt the accusation that one is not being adequately self-aware, and at the same time to provide a limited authority to speak from a designated position. It is at once defensive and aggressive, and in this way it fits the needs of a world-condition that requires the subject's self-descriptions to be at once abject, made by others, merged into prior formations, and at the same time to bear all the marks of a recognizable *agency* and *responsibility*. Let us remember the early anglophone response to Althusser and to the associated idea of the death of the subject, which was both to pontificate and desperately to methodologize some place for agency, for praxis, for a traditional version of the *struggle*. Alternative attributions of agency and passivity have been switching roles ever since, leading to an indecisive consensus according to which the subject is always both made and self-making, reproductive as well as reformatory or revolutionary.

Situatedness is one of the terms that speaks to the aspirations of that consensus. The work it is doing in managing distinctions and identifications that are impossible to simplify into coherent order might perhaps tell us that it is time to imagine a world that would not need such management. The conditions affecting contemporary life are or have been made to seem so confusing and manifold as to be open to infinite analysis; they are embedded in patterns of cause and effect that are reflexive, recursive, and beyond confident representation. Some of this is surely tinfoil working to jam the radar systems of cultural critique, so that we must constantly suspect ourselves (and indeed this is the burden of reflexivity and recursivity) of mystification in the very description of life in these terms; we must be constantly anxious that we might be missing something, that we are reproducing what we most wish to dispute. The mandate is toward complexity and increasing complexification in so many of the technological and conventional systems for life maintenance that apparent simplicities can never be trusted as such: it is only the more brutal determinations such as death, sickness, and unemployment that can occasionally register as challenges to the radical second-guessing that goes with almost every life decision among the affluent or would-be affluent persons who are for the most part the designated speakers for our culture at large. For such persons at least, declarations of situatedness, always tending toward aporia, are perhaps more desperate and fraught than ever before.

The job of critique can thus hardly expect to get very far if it assures itself of a place to come from by embracing the hyperbolic rhetoric of situating itself. On the contrary it must take up once again or perhaps for the first time Sartre's question "what is this *situating*?" Sartre's aim in philosophizing the "situation" as he did was clearly egalitarian: a world in which each of us could indeed purposively modify our situations or apprehend them clearly enough to work for change would be a better world than the one we have. In the meantime those of us who make the claim to situate ourselves risk the reproduction of a purely pastiche democracy, an assertion of legibility and accountability that has mostly been neither earned nor deserved and that closes off rather than opening up any further analysis. Situating oneself then becomes not so much an imperative to what used to be called praxis as a way of avoiding it—it becomes the goal of enunciation while pretending to be its originating permission— while we situate others mostly in order to dismiss them or identify with them. Or we expect them to situate themselves. Less and less, outside of the best efforts within social science, do we make the attempt at any complex understanding of the positions of others. The confession of one's own situatedness is, even at its most apparently abject, always also a gesture of exaltation; and the gesture of exaltation is but a protest against an overwhelming sense of impotence. A pretty paradox, and a point at which speculation about subjectivity in the world can tend to stop, either by way of an embrace of a now legitimate inertia or by the imperative to take a position anyway and damn the torpedoes (both are common enough responses). Some have even made the articulation of limits into a form of empowerment, as if one becomes better, stronger, and wiser by this particular epistemological adversity. And some continue to speak as if they really do know where they are coming from and so are off the hook as soon as they have told us. What opportunities, if any, are there for responding to the antinomies and aporias of questions about situatedness without reducing them to parodic resolution? Is there a place for a patient and seriously applied ignorance or skepticism that is usefully rather than noncommitally evasive, that can contribute to social policy thinking by the effort of its very negations? An ignorance or skepticism that does not set out to destroy or discredit the objectivist component of the social science effort (for example, in the name of *literature*) but that insists on stringent constraints on its truth claims? An ignorance or skepticism that is also kept free from being made metaphysical, mystical, and itself the mark of some superior form of knowing? Can we catch ourselves at that moment of counter-Althusserian interpellation that I described in chapter 1; the moment where I have not decided who is being called, and where I have also not yet passed over into regretting getting caught in the act or celebrating either my undecidability or my good luck in getting away with something? Where I have not yet given way to the urge (which is a pressure) to justify myself? Above all, how can there be an ignorance or skepticism that is not itself simply and entirely a symptom of the aporias of situatedness it hopes to hold at a distance, that is not itself the product of the late capitalist management system it seeks to expose?

Here I can only once again offer a faith in history: a faith not in standing aside from but being fully implicated in a history whose terms I cannot fully understand but that nonetheless prompts a specific concern.

The synchronic component of critique has often seemed to rely on standing outside or above. But things do change and make possible insights that were not possible before. There has been a tendency to validate such insights as ahead or in the vanguard of historical change, making them prophetic, and thus to place the analyst in a position of privilege. One could as easily suppose that a particular set of circumstances, a form of situatedness that we can recognize only partly if at all, simply makes it possible for some people to see some things differently or at a sharper angle, and in a way that may or may not emerge as a significant consensus. I do think that the pressure currently being put on the rhetoric of situatedness is greater than it has been in the past, even though the terms of the contradictions and forms of ignorance within that rhetoric have been around for a long time. The rhetoric might then be coming to the point of crisis, the point when it can be exposed for what it is and when one can hope to be just far enough from the center of its force field — always historical — to avoid being completely trapped by its given terms and assumptions. Something about the way we can convincingly account for ourselves may be on the point of shifting or changing.

We can speculate about this without claiming a conventional or un-contested understanding (and what would that be if it could be claimed?). Lauren Berlant has recently described our condition as one in which the "simultaneous contraction of the state and expansion of the nation produces an incoherent set of boundary-drawing panics" whereby persons are made into "kinds of people who are both attached to and under-described by the identities that organize them." [2] One response to this condition is panic, and we can surely see plenty of that. Hyperaffirmative instances of self-affiliation are one of its indicators. Another response is agnosticism and detachment, or a zestful embrace of every opportunity to try on identities without being committed to any of them: this is one dimension of the culture of performance, which may well have clear critical functions in the sphere of gender politics even as it cannot escape its conditioning by a late capitalist economy of short-term contracts and enforced vocational flexibility in which the taking up of opportunities is far from simply volitional. Closer to the response I am aiming toward, however, is Niklas Luhmann's prospectus for an "ecology of ignorance." Luhmann too notices the "deliberate exaggeration of rhetorical devices" of which I would say the vocabulary of situatedness is a leading instance; he too finds that "society is irritated" and "disquieted by the futility of attempts to achieve clarity on the relationship between social systems and the environment." [3] The dominant response to the irritation, he finds, is a culture of admonition and a recourse to ethics (a topic that I will address later). The complexity of threats and risks is such as almost to excuse the "lack of reflection on admonitory activity" according to which "those not for us are against us" (pp. 77, 83), but not quite. Luhmann's own preferred reaction is to promote a "shared culture of ignorance" (p. 100). If we are to use this word, however, it is not easy to imagine how it can be freed of its own history and its own consolatory metaphysics, to the point that Luhmann's own very specific usage can establish itself as the primary terminological norm by displacing the received celebration of ignorance as some sort of enhanced spirituality or fastidious unworldliness. Only with regular reminders of these problems and constraints can it prove useful as a critical rather than a merely reproductive item.

Staying within the Limits The first and continuing task in the promotion of a shared culture of *critical* ignorance is, I think, to bring to light the limitations and illusions of the emancipatory and affirmative declarations of situatedness that are all around us. Situating oneself is popular because it is a contemporary form of politeness, a way of establishing one's modesty. Like many kinds of politeness it can also be self-justificatory and even aggressive. Clifford Geertz finds the acknowledgment of the limits of situatedness — "this observer, in this time, at that place" — to be "attractive" and "empowering." [4] It makes its exponent socially conversible and nonthreatening but does not inhibit him or her from getting on with the business at hand. Donna Haraway's hope for situated knowledge, as discussed in chapter 1, is that it can offer a working degree of objectivity without making the now widely discredited claim toward rational universality; it is neither absolutist nor relativist, but it intimates an available consensus. Here the purpose of invoking situatedness is more pointedly epistemological: it is a new version of "standpoint epistemology," seeking to accept and privilege "radical historical contingency" without giving up on the prospect of "faithful accounts of a 'real' world" still seen as fundamental to an emancipatory science (*Simians*,

Cyborgs, and Women, p. 187). Objectivity is "positioned rationality" and rational knowledge becomes "power-sensitive conversation" (p. 196). Epistemology is redescribed as the conduct of "shared conversations" (p. 190). Foucault, Rorty, and others have written famously about the end of epistemology. But the claim to know something, along with the justificatory systems maintained by such claims, is hard to do away with, especially for scientists. So Haraway wants to hang on to epistemological functions rewritten as "shared conversations," drawing on the literary-dialogic conventions popularized by Gadamer and Habermas. Conversations are here promoted as self-revising and unpredictable, inconclusive and exploratory, while the knowledges they provide along the way are firm enough to generate objectivity effects. Situated knowledge is a compromise formation that seeks to keep its distance from the mutually annihilating and sustaining antinomic theories of knowledge as relativist and universalist. Its notion that all knowledge is potentially open to revision would hardly surprise most scientists, but it makes the stronger claim that such revision is socially embedded. Whether this and this alone is what gives it the effect of the real is a question Haraway does not entertain in any detail.

Haraway's somewhat abstract exposition of the explanatory functions of situated knowledge may startle some professional scientists into reflection on the terms of their own positionality and has some chance of polemical success in those disciplines still governed more than most (although by no means exclusively) by assumptions of impersonal, absolute, and purely rational procedures. But it does not adequately engage the argument made by much modern science for knowledges that are situation indifferent or intersituational, knowledges that are discovered by situated observers but whose reality claim is not thereby exhausted. Meanwhile, the appeal to situatedness in political theory and "political science" runs into trouble because the phenomena of group and person behavior that it purports to explain or justify hardly ever have even the appearance of an uncontested empirical existence in the first place. Here the appeal to situatedness works well enough as a negative argument against the much-berated (and somewhat reified) Cartesian subject, but much less well as an account of what might actually be the case for personal or social identity. The confusions attendant on an overconfidence in situatedness as describing anything critically specific are fully evident in Seyla Benhabib's *Situating the Self*, where the avowed goal is "to situate reason and the moral self more decisively in contexts of gender and community, while insisting upon the discursive power of individuals to challenge such situatedness in the name of universalistic principles, future identities and as yet undiscovered communities."[5] This avowal is symptomatic of where many of us think we are coming from. It reflects, in its first ambition, that moment in the history of feminism (attributed by Teresa de Lauretis to the 1980s[6]) when it was felt to be inadequate to speak simply of *women* and not of the multiply differentiated categories of race, class, occupation, and so forth—in other words all the referents of the *azza* sentence. And it reflects also the assumption that once one has done so one has said something decisive and sufficient, although that assumption cannot survive the invocation of such slippery terms as "community" and "context," which are as far as I can see not at all open to being deployed "decisively." Benhabib's emphasis then passes beyond situatedness, which has been pseudoacknowledged only in order to be pseudosubsumed in a kind of parody of the whole Sartrean investigation: we have the "power to challenge" the situatedness that has significantly made us what we are. But the power is "discursive" (real or not? real as language? as praxis?). The sentence is a model of familiar affirmations: it says "situate yourself and move on." The Cartesian subject is indeed critiqued in Benhabib's model of an "embodied and embedded human self" (p. 6), but that same subject or something very like it reappears as the authorizing principle in a challenge to those elements of one's "situatedness" that one does not like. And although the individual as single subject is displaced, the "community" or some such equivalent collective appears to have the same consolidating function once attributed to the individual: it becomes a new form of the self, from which and for which one can speak. Benhabib indeed confesses that she wishes to endorse only a "weak version" of the death-of-the-subject thesis (p. 213). She therefore makes a pitch only for a "less mystified" version of the "philosophical subject of the West," one whose "traditional attributes," including "some form of autonomy and rationality," need only be "reformulated" (rather than destroyed) by taking account of its "radical situatedness" (p. 214). The individual is weakened as essence or identity but preserved as agent acting on behalf of groups in time and place. Above all the individual (and the critic) is restored to a confidence in the adequacy of self-affiliation gestures.

Benhabib's position reveals many of the problems facing those who want to acknowledge something beyond atomic individualism without giving up on the things that individualism has mostly carried along with it to soften its harsher potential: rationalism, constructive agency, and a "normative criticism" (p. 213). Her predicament suggests that there may be no language for carrying out this project in a convincing way, and she is explicit about the appeal of *situatedness* (her term as well as mine) for a "weak version" of the "death of the subject" thesis. To be situated is to be embedded in impersonal systems but *not to the point where agency is redundant*. A "weak" version of "radical situatedness" (p. 214) tells us simply that we are not independent of social and historical affiliations and that we cannot think of ourselves *as* selves without them. This is the war cry of present-day communitarians, and it has been heard many times before. It has polemical force as a counterargument to unhindered self-interest and sometimes to the impersonal functions of what is often called "the state." But its outcome is gestural, and is descriptive only in the loosest sense. It cannot resolve problems; it can only dramatize them. Hence the appeal of the "literary turn" discussed in a chapter 4, which can present the fact of our being situated without aspiring to any scientific account of exactly how. Benhabib is fully behind the literary turn in her preference for "dialogue" over "consensus" and in her emphasis on "reversibility of perspectives" carried out through listening to or actively imagining oneself as the other (pp. 52, 54). She comes close to admitting aporia in proposing the "infinite revisability and indeterminacy of meaning" (p. 198); but what allows her to convert this possibility into a progressive model of social benefit is the imagined scene of differently situated selves of roughly equal expressive ability conducting earnest conversations in some relatively unconstrained space with enough time to wait until some sort of mutual understanding is forthcoming. This I think is the fantasy allowing "radical situatedness" to look like a positive principle that has only to be admitted to guarantee that moral progress and epistemological clarification will follow. What we have here is an elaborately academic version of the "let me tell you where I'm coming from" encounter, with a built-in assurance that the speaker will know from whence she or he comes, and be believed by everyone else. It all sounds rather like a rewritten principle of Cartesian community: "We are, therefore I think."

To her credit Benhabib herself raises some objections to the rhetoric of situatedness. She exposes the tendency of some "situated criticism" to assume that there are single sets of evident "criteria" for social analysis that are simply found rather than made, and that these categories are sufficient to justify the invocation of a "desirable future" (p. 226). She distinguishes herself from the "situated criticism" of those whose affiliation is to local narratives and little stories. And she wonders whether the whole tendency to declarations of situatedness might not emanate from a post-modern "nostalgia for home, for the certitudes of one's own culture and society" in a detraditionalized world (p. 227). Her own response to the situatedness of everything is to insist on the continued need for normative philosophical justification (p. 228); situatedness cannot be the first and last word in providing adequate accountability. Proclaiming one's affiliations is not enough. And yet situatedness continues to function in Benhabib's own rhetoric as a critical legitimating term whose precise application cannot be specified: so her own "interactive universalism" is the "situated criticism" for a "global community" (p. 228). *Situating the Self* is finally a title that cannot be interpreted as describing anything beyond an ongoing engagement with everything and everyone, in theory.

The promise of solutions is far more uninhibited in Richard Bernstein's *Beyond Objectivism and Relativism* (one should beware of all "beyonds" on this topic), which intends to take us to that point by describing "a new pattern in the conversation concerning human rationality," one that will (once again) exorcize the "Cartesian Anxiety."[7] What we get is a tour through the arguments of Gadamer and others according to which being situated is a source not of puzzlement or constraint but of new knowledge and empowerment. Bernstein's preference for local practice over grand theory leads to little more than a make-it-up-as-you-go-along policy of temporary consensus building that is subject to all the limits of such localisms, every one of which requires numerous preconditions if we are indeed to get "new, and frequently unpredictable, forms of solidarity" (p. 228) rather than just conflict and misunderstanding or the localized self-approval of the "group." There may still be for some of us a usefully therapeutic function to being reminded that our rational faculties are very much in the world, in place and time, rather than floating somewhere up above and possessed of impeccable disinterest. But this has become the common sense of late modernity and/or postmodernity and its reiteration risks becoming completely formulaic and merely ideological. One could say that the reminder is useful in calling for an operational modesty about all sorts of declarations and is likely to remain timely as long as we continue to inhabit complex societies in which some always will end up speaking for others; the more one can slow down this process by imposing some sort of circumspection, the likelier it may be that some damages may be avoided. And it is hard to dispute the case that in pursuing our construction of social groups and the standards they establish for communication between their members, we should remain attentive to questions of situatedness so that we do not fall into habitual assumptions about the authority of abstract reason, single-group standards, or atomic individualism. But the theorization of that situatedness still remains gestural, a form of politeness: whenever an empirical application of "radical situatedness" is called for—when I or you have to declare who we are and where we are coming from—there arises the need for some more exact analysis of coordinates than the rhetoric of situatedness itself can provide.

The habit of invoking situatedness as an affirmative or explanatory principle rather than as an unignorable but imprecise field of forces that raises more questions than it answers is deeply rooted and shows up in various humanistic and hermeneutic disciplines. It is a symptom of life without epistemology, without a faith in any agreed-on categories for describing and defining our place in the world, for expressing the terms of an embeddedness that we nonetheless continue to insist on as a formative and even *the* formative element of subjectivity and experience. Invoking situatedness then becomes a sort of placeholder, providing a rhetoric of knowledge that is persuasive, when it is persuasive, only because it cannot be itemized, cashed out, or rationalized. *Situatedness* and its cognates are therefore appealing as they imply or gesture toward a clear knowledge that they cannot possibly provide and as they stand in for a range of other terms that are similarly uncontainable and, as Kenneth Burke showed, interchangeable without significant loss or gain in meaning. (Christopher Herbert makes a similar argument for *culture* in his important *Culture and Anomie*.) We are mostly unwilling to admit to a critical ignorance, and to turn our ignorance to critical uses. We prefer to speak and write as if we are saying something positive and constructive about what *is*, while we are in fact only saying something about what is not: most often the much-berated Cartesian subject.

It is not uncommon to see some versions of arguments from situatedness disavowed while others are given credit without any apparent awareness of or reckoning with the degree to which they are the same argument. We continue to employ and exploit the rhetoric of situatedness as a means of fudging or obscuring possible causalities as well as invoking it for false resolutions. One can find everything along the scale from apparently good faith misuses to apparently conscious opportunisms: those who do not know that they are lost for words, and those who are shrewdly aware that everyone else is. It is not always possible to tell the difference. Daniel Jonah Goldhagen's best-selling account of the origins of genocidal anti-Semitism in Germany, *Hitler's Willing Executioners*, argues opportunistically both for and against the explanatory power of situatedness. Goldhagen takes aim at the kinds of "situational explanations" that privilege limited and self-contained institutional or psychological pressures—the urge to obey orders, to look dutiful, to belong to an elite, to please one's peers—as explaining why people were so willing to kill Jews.[8] He also rejects the explanatory power of bureaucratic rationalization as providing any sufficient account of the Holocaust. Critical action is not caused by "structures" (p. 20) but by people deciding to carry it out. To do so they need a motive. Goldhagen finds this in the ideology of (German) anti-Semitism, the "central causal agent" (p. 9) of the genocide, which he describes as historical (and so not inevitable or essential) but still generically national and not limited to subgroups such as the s s or the state bureaucrats. Consciousness, he argues, did indeed determine being (p. 455), and it did so on a grand and general scale.

But the disavowal of "situational explanations" is followed by an endorsement of a general form of situatedness. The first—local, group based, sectarian—is disallowed; the second, that of a comprehensive national ideology, is endorsed as primary cause. Goldhagen is not just making a familiar point about the power of ideology and the social construction of knowledge. Even as he is making that point, he wants to redescribe ideology as free will and he sustains both rhetorics simultaneously. He proposes that those who killed Jews did so because they wanted to, not because they were forced to act against their natures by some persuasively immediate pressure. He proposes that there were in fact no clearly adverse consequences for those who refused to kill, so that those who did the killing did so out of desire. There was strong ideological pressure, but the ideology was not unambiguously coercive: it left room for choice—to kill or not to kill. That so many chose to kill is evidence of the power of that ideology, which was able to reproduce itself as "voluntarism" (p. 17). It was a situated voluntarism, one unique to Germany (so Goldhagen says) yet still historical, and therefore not essentially and forever German. But in its time it was pervasive enough to determine the behavior of almost all Germans.

I have none of the qualifications that would permit me to hold a view on the adequacy of Goldhagen as a historian of the Holocaust, and I intend no comment on that topic and therefore no approval or dismissal of the book. It has however been critiqued by almost all historians in the field, while becoming a best-seller among the nonspecialist public—most notably among the modern German public.[9] Some of the disquiet and outrage that the book has generated surely has to do with its confused and confusing use of arguments from situatedness. Conventionally we are offered the option to decide for freedom *or* determination, unencumbered choice *or* enforced behavior. Goldhagen proposes that the power of genocidal anti-Semitic ideology was such as to make determination reproduce itself *as* free choice. If true, this explanation completely destroys any belief in a residual core of human response that is immune to being reprogrammed by social and historical conditions. So fully embedded and hegemonic was this national culture, Goldhagen suggests, that it probably enabled the Nazis to take and hold on to power in a uniquely German way. Nazism did not create genocidal anti-Semitism, in other words, but exploited what was already there. It is possible, then, that successfully established belief systems can allow people to believe that killing Jews by any means at hand is not just not inhumane but may even be an act of virtue. We cannot, says Goldhagen, go on persuading ourselves that people killed Jews because they were forced to or because of the operations of some bureaucratic mentality that conditioned all human agents into obedient automata. He wants to say that the will itself was at work.

But there are at least two problems here. First, Goldhagen admits that full scientific proof of the thesis must remain unavailable. Analysis "cannot be definitive. The proper data simply do not exist." He can suggest only a "*dominant cognitive thread*" and its "probable societal scope" (p. 47). This is an honest admission, and it invokes the probability clause so important to Bentham and Mill as a way of limiting the claims that social science can make; but its full recognition would totally refigure the rhetoric of Goldhagen's own exposition, committing it to a constant invocation of the hypothetical and the plausible rather than of the assertive and the affirmative. It is of course much harder for a scholar to achieve any kind of popular hearing for his or her case if it is made in the language of "maybe" and "might have been": the language of ignorance. So, in this book, the Holocaust has to have a "principal cause" (p. 455) and the Germans are presented "as human agents, as people with wills" (p. 13), even though there are attendant qualifications about the reliability of the data and about the ideological formation of the will itself. That is the second problem. After all, if the heroism of exigent choice itself is part of ideology, then *will* ceases to be will in the traditional sense. If Germans were trained and encouraged to do and rewarded for acts of will against the grain of what they well knew to be normal human standards, can one call this "will" in the sense of implying free choice between equally available options, and then sit in judgment over those who make the wrong choice? And what about the circumstances, whereby a generally anti-Semitic ideology might have been made more critical, active, and rewarding for those persons affiliated with particular subcultures (party, military, *Einsatzgruppen*)? At this point there are no "ordinary" Germans and there is no uncontestable, single national situation. Goldhagen simultaneously recognizes the aporia of situatedness and then goes on to write as if it were not there. Situatedness is denied explanatory power at one level and accorded the same power at another. There is no epistemological mechanism offered (how could there be?) for showing where one begins and the other ends. That the book has been more popular in Germany than anywhere else can only signify an appetite for some massive simplification and obfuscation of the duties of national memory and moral adjudication. The strategy of simultaneously affirming and negating situatedness conditions, as if one sort could be kept neatly apart from other sorts, is symptomatic of an analytical culture within which the whole matter of situatedness is mired in confusion and, moreover, acceptable to many of us *because* of the confusion.

A very similar confusion about situatedness also figured in the debate (or dispute) over the 1992 publication of national standards for the teaching of history in America's public schools: but here it was the effort to preserve some sort of complexity rather than to reduce it that offended many who responded. The collectively authored *Lessons from History* was very much a document of intellectual compromise between all of the emphases and methods that go into the writing and teaching of history in the contemporary world. A world history section that gamely tries to mention everything at least briefly forms a large part of the text, but it is slightly shorter than the section given over to U.S. history. The message is one of multiple and complex causes and interests at work in the world. Traditional political and military history is not ignored, but space is made for social and economic determinations. There is some acknowledgment of the issues that make up what the educational Right likes to call "political correctness," but the clash of cultures that marked the making of "America" is decorously nominated "the Great Convergence" — not a melting pot, but certainly not genocidal imperialism either.[10] The events of 1492 are referred to as a consequence of "multi-causal relationships" (p. 53) rather than being attributed to the ravages of a manic Eurocentrism or the expansion of a benevolent western civilization. There is throughout the document a commitment to the cultivation of historical empathy, to putting ourselves in the position of the other, in the spirit of the contemporary literary turn evident across all the nonscientific disciplines (for example, p. 106). This obtains even when the other is widely regarded as morally inadequate (for example, the southern slaveholder). Individualism is contextualized and explained as a historical and local (western) priority rather than the property of all persons in all places (p. 32), but it is also given full play as both a rhetorical and moral priority when the authors recommend a belief in "human agency and individual action" as an essential safeguard against "civic apathy, cynicism, and resignation" (p. 20). The will is given ample space as a response to evidence that should make students "make moral choices again and again" (p. 22), although this is not at all a history built simply around the achievements of great men and their moral decisions.

In short, the document had something to please everyone. And, judging by the hostile reactions from both (so-called) Left and Right, something to offend everyone in the grip of what Todd Gitlin has called a national "identity panic." [11] The very emphasis on the complex causes of historical events, and thus on the complex nature of human situatedness itself, an emphasis that might have been thought of as disarming extreme criticism by disarming extreme hypotheses, seems to have been itself a cause for offense. The implication that the model of complex causes holds out is that we might not be in a position to know, finally and without the shadow of a doubt, what makes history happen, what makes people do what they do. The authors of *Lessons from History* thus touch on the aporetic features of this kind of knowledge seeking—hence perhaps their emphasis on the making of moral judgments as some sort of supplement to the nonfinality of "facts"; but they also tend to present the options as all equally true and thus all equally not true. It is as if the gestural politeness of acknowledging the complexity of situatedness conditions has preempted the credibility of any judgment that is not based merely on one's moral preference: everything is affirmed, nothing is denied. Thus individual agency and social determination are both acknowledged but not set into any kind of conflict or tension. All factors seem to be equally in play all of the time; the importance of everything is affirmed. The authors' nervousness about confessing ignorance (or making clear judgments) is understandable given the nature and occasion of the document, and many of their critics seem to have wanted something that could be taken to guarantee the polemical battle between so-called Left and Right over the narration of the national past. The model of subjectivity that such a polemic requires is one made up of victims and aggressors (for the so-called Left) or heroes and inert masses (for the so-called Right), each requiring simple constructions of agency and nonagency. But in avoiding this kind of simplification the authors of the standards may have condoned another: the notion that causes are always complex in exactly the same way and never ever reducible to simple description is just as reductive as the position it displaces. The history lessons were crafted to address each constituency by meeting it part way, as well as to model a challenging version of doing history itself. The lesson learned by the authors was that many around them did not accept their efforts as a paradigm for teaching the history of the United States. The availability of a firm and clear delineation of the "facts" about human situatedness and the history it generates is still a powerful belief for a lot of people. So too is the alternative that the authors recommend, the making of moral choices "again and again" (p. 22). What is not apparently acceptable is any declaration of critical ignorance or incomplete knowledge that is un-accompanied by a rush to some other form of making decisions, in this case to "morality." Goldhagen made headlines by offering a single expla-nation of what had been (and has remained) a notoriously difficult ar-ray of complex possible causes; Lessons from History stirred up comparable passions because it approved all forms of situatedness without choosing between them or suggesting that such choices could ever be other than matters of personal preference.

Another notorious national debate accompanied the appearance of The Bell Curve by Richard Herrnstein and Charles Murray, the study of "intelligence" that proposed, once and for all, not to complicate the rhetoric of situatedness (as the historians were said to have done) but to simplify it, to sort out what is "innate" from what is the result of "en-vironment," and to produce (yet one more time) the very epistemology that the rhetoric of situatedness is designed both to proffer and to refuse. This book was so widely discussed that there is no need to offer here any extended summary of its claims and the responses they generated.[12] The authors have various targets, not all mutually integrated, including (what they see as) a proliferating "cognitive elite," a declining "cognitive capital," and a national overemphasis on treating people "as members of groups" rather than as "individuals" equal before the law.[13] It thus played a role in the movement against affirmative action that began in Texas and California and is currently seeking to expand its influence in other states. What concerns us here is the book's treatment of situatedness, which is variously obscure and highly polemical (and by current consensus quite unscientific), and above all unwilling, once again, to stay within the limits of what can be said and to accept the obligation to work through our igno-rance rather than to translate it into positive-seeming knowledge. The conventional claim for the mutuality of "heredity" and "environment" is made and reiterated at regular intervals, and an appropriately vague range of influence for each is proposed. This is given quantitative form as the authors try to mathematicize the anatomy of situatedness: heritable IQ, for instance, is "quantified" at somewhere between 40 percent and 80 percent (p. 105), leaving 20 percent to 60 percent for the environment. The extreme flexibility of this range (if we accept it as defensible at all) might suggest a high degree of circumspection; nonetheless the authors' aim is quite bluntly to "disentangle the comparative roles of cognitive ability and socioeconomic background in explaining poverty" (p. 132).

Here once again there appears the ongoing dream of objectivist social science, the dream of precipitating out what we "are" or can become from what we have been "made." There has long been serious evidence that we cannot do this, and those best qualified to respond to Murray and Herrnstein have generally agreed that we still cannot do it, and that the science of genetics is nowhere near being in a position to address this sort of question: indeed, that same science looks more like proving once and for all that the question cannot be resolved in this particular vocabulary. But perhaps there is to be no once and for all. The social energies that flow through and around The Bell Curve and that ensured that it would gain such widespread attention seem to be themselves more decisive than the book's actual content, which has earned few if any professional vindications. It seems as if situatedness, for and against, is too popular and effective as a polemical tool to be addressed in the terms that I have been arguing that it deserves: aporetic and antinomic instead of affirmative and unambiguous. There seems to be no immediate prospect of these aggressive simplifications going away as long as they continue to perform the function of encouraging us to maintain the debate in terms that guarantee that it will never be resolved. They are, one must suppose, a licensed distraction, a collection of traditional red herrings working to prevent us from following other trails and trains of thought. The aim of my study here is to appeal for an understanding of the prescribed dead ends that result from taking the rhetoric of situatedness at face value, without giving way to the reactive frustration that wants to accord it no value at all.

The arguments around Goldhagen's book, the history standards, and The Bell Curve are all instances of vaguely academic controversies that have gained urgent public attention because they speak to matters that are of clear public concern; their notoriety indicates how deeply the antinomies of situatedness are implicated in the rhetoric with which we address and think we can solve our collective problems and frame our collective prospects. Because they also self-destruct and thus rise from the ashes as continually repeatable, these antinomies would appear to be functioning ideologically: the very fact that they are insoluble keeps us going at the task as if, like Fermat's last theorem, they might one day yield to proof or analysis. But they are not like Fermat's theorem because they are set up as by definition without agreed parameters. Because nothing can be excluded, nothing can be conclusively affirmed. And when limited but significant claims can be made, as they are, for example, by responsible social science, the risk is that the demonstrably inconclusive nature of the general rhetoric of situatedness can be exploited to discredit all attempts at informing social and political policy. Going back to the list that Dershowitz comes up with in *The Abuse Excuse*, for example, one would have to be concerned that the implausibility of the "Twinkie defense" and of such things as "meek mate syndrome" could also work to discredit more serious kinds of situatedness conditions such as fetal alcohol syndrome. Because we spend much of our energy arguing about the middle ground, where there is some credibility to the arguments both for and against the power of situatedness, this built-in volatility to situatedness arguments should be cause for concerned attention.

My next example is a "real life" case. I am writing about a month after the most destructive of the high school shooting tragedies of recent years, that of April 20, 1999, at Columbine High School in Littleton, Colorado. The violent death of fifteen young people, including the two perpetrators, has sponsored the usual range of monocausal explanations about why two teenage boys killed their schoolmates: violence on television, violence in rock music, unmonitored access to the Internet, loss of faith in God, the breakdown of the nuclear family, the anomie of the affluent white suburbs, the stultifying subculture of American high schools, the failure of counseling and medical services, and so forth. Because the murderers are dead there will be no trial. Had there been a trial, we would have had some version of a rerun of Loeb-Leopold. The same issues are now being aired mostly in the media and outside the criminal justice system (although some peripheral prosecutions are pending or projected). Here every vested interest has said its piece, and everyone who is for or against some specific kind of situatedness has weighed in with an explanation. Only very rarely has anyone written about our ignorance.[14] The Littleton case offers something for everyone, in a riot of democratic opinion making. Those who favor reining in the media and bringing our children back to God were embarrassed by a copycat crime in Georgia committed one month later (May 20) by a churchgoing Boy Scout from an apparently normal family. A prominent component of the Littleton debate is the discussion of gun control. The easy availability of lethal weapons is the item that most simply distinguishes American high school students from those in the rest of the affluent world who suffer some of the same tensions and rituals, as the foreign press persistently and the American press occasionally points out. And at the time I am writing this, support for serious gun control legislation has made small progress in Washington.

The specific event I want to bring up for its symptomatic interest is the presidential one-day summit set up by Bill Clinton on May 10, 1999. There the explicit agenda and result of the discussion was *not* to apportion blame on specific situatedness conditions but to *diffuse* it. Mr. Clinton declared himself delighted that "no one was pointing the finger of blame . . . this was exactly the kind of session I had hoped for." The reporter for the *New York Times*, Katharine Seelye, wrote that "so many factors were identified—the Internet, movies, parental responsibility, domestic violence, lack of religious faith, a coarsening of the culture—that guns were lost in the shuffle." So it was agreed that we are facing here "a vastly complex societal problem."[15] It would be nice to think that this is evidence of the positive dissemination of a critical culture of skepticism or ignorance. But it is more likely a case of the other side of the rhetoric of situatedness, its (always available) indecisiveness, being cynically exploited to avoid offending any of the key lobbying organizations and vested interests who fund the political process. Indeed, the *New York Times* reported the day *before* the meeting that nothing would come of it. The gun lobby, Hollywood, and the Internet all announced before the event that they would not tolerate being blamed: music industry representative David Geffen echoed Clarence Darrow (consciously or otherwise) in saying "why not blame the libraries? They're full of violent books."[16] The meeting was stage managed to display concern and not much more. I suspect that everyone except the president introduced him or herself "as a" something or other; and even the president might have spoken as a concerned parent.

Acknowledging the inconclusive nature of arguments from situatedness, in other words, is not in and of itself a good or adequate thing. It is as subject to abuse and appropriation as its opposite. Clarence Darrow used the shadow of a doubt that is thrown by situatedness arguments to argue against a death penalty that would have ended all debate about appropriate punishments for Loeb and Leopold. Implicitly he was arguing against all death penalties and he was right to do so, because irrevocable punishment can never fit with incomplete information about crimes: there is no chance to use new information. The Littleton summit shows another use for the same "shadow of a doubt" strategy for diffusing responsibility, this time working to preserve the *likelihood* of irrevocable actions (more deaths by shooting). One has to worry then not just about overaffirmative uses of the rhetoric of situatedness—those who think they know where they or you are coming from—but also its dissemination into meaningless ubiquity, its equal applicability to everything. The clear and simple difference between the world of American high schools and that of others is the easy availability of guns: no one knows what the schools would be like without that condition. One does not have to believe in guns as an exclusive, monocausal factor to make the case for trying the experiment of doing without them. But the managed multiplicity of alternative arguments from various other conditions making up our situatedness makes it harder to create the consensus for any such experiment. There are always other places to lay the blame.

The ultimately efficient strategy of containment, ensuring that there never will be any conclusive decision about selves and groups in relation to environments, may well be this very reiteration of alternatives, this constant oscillation between one extreme simplification and its opposite (which is thus of course not at all its opposite but its necessary partner): this is what Burdeau called "the institutionalisation of ambiguity." So what happens happens, and when it happens a series of antithetical justifications for it will be ready and waiting. Either there is a single category put up for inspection, which is then open to a cycle of affirmation and disproof (*race* has been a favorite of both Left and Right, and has been affirmed and disproved by both in different spheres); or we all get to pick our candidate for "most influential kind of situatedness" because there will be enough candidates to make the ballot papers unmanageable. High theory has exemplified the same syndrome by way of the antinomic parallelism of theorizing the human subject as alternately a desituated or agential individual and an externally constructed, hypersituated entity. The much-discussed "death of the subject" associated with a number of important French theorists (among them Althusser, Foucault, and Derrida, in their different ways) has never gained complete credibility in the anglophone liberal democracies; it has been countered at almost all points by the commitment to individual will and agency. A common middle ground has emerged in much "Left" theory, one that designates the individual not as an atomic self making free choices but as the nexus of a series of "subject positions" derived from and/or addressed to external conditions. This has sometimes been understood to involve a series of incommensurable and divergent formations that cannot be integrated into a wholeness of self or of the external world, a wholeness that can only ever appear as "the *wish* for a fullness that is permanently deferred," so that no invocation of "the dispersion of subject positions" can amount to any "solution" or "totality." [17] But more often, in less exigent theoretical contexts than the one provided by Laclau and Mouffe from which I have just quoted, it is assimilated back into some or other version of the traditional alternatives, as it was by Seyla Benhabib (self as community) and by Alan Dershowitz (in his plea for a return to personal responsibility).

Laclau and Mouffe make a strong case against the political meanings of groups and movements ever being "given from the beginning" (*Hegemony and Socialist Strategy*, p. 87) and ever being determined by fantasies of foundational identities.[18] They also seek to restrain the slippage whereby any model of indeterminate and in-process subjectification of the sort that they regard as fundamental to a radical democracy tends to get rewritten as an uncritical mandate to "be all that you can be." The pressures encouraging this slippage are, however, very strong indeed, especially in the United States where the antinomies of freedom and determination are managed with particular intensity. Thus David Hollinger's *Postethnic America* converts the model of subject positionality into a category of free choice, resurrecting the voluntarist subject out of its own ashes. Here the approved "postethnic" spirit is that which allows for "voluntary over involuntary affiliations." [19] Given that the five traditional categories of the "ethno-racial pentagon" (p. 12) have broken down in the face of a bewildering number of ethnic part-identities and mixtures, Hollinger proposes a replacement of imposed or interpellated subjectivities by "communities of consent" (p. 7). The consent is "revocable" (p. 13) in order to appear to stay in tune with the individual's "life-project," which must "entail a shifting division of labor between the overlapping 'we's' of which he or she is a part" (p. 12), a formulation that Hollinger cares enough about to repeat (p. 106) but that reads suspiciously like an affirmative rationalization of a social condition that is as much imposed as elected. As I have said before, the economy of short-term contracts and flexible task distribution, along with the erosion of the benefits that have often accompanied long-term or permanent employment, as well as the short-term emotional contracts governing personal intimacies between people that Anthony Giddens describes in *Modernity and Self-Identity*, are hardly matters of choice. Even if we do not assert absolute economic determination, these circumstances should at least be produced to sharpen the discussion of any approval of what Hollinger calls a "process of consciously and critically locating oneself amid these layers of 'we's'" (p. 106) that make up individual life experience. Hollinger is looking for a new way of describing and sharing around economic and civil rights in a diverse society facing the negative demise of affirmative action in California and Texas and potentially in the nation at large. But his preferred model of a "postethnic perspective" that "challenges the right of one's grandfather or grandmother to determine primary identity" (p. 116) sounds very traditional, very like John Locke writing against patriarchy or the founding fathers of the United States defending the cause of independence. To be able to "choose" one's affiliations according to descent or "nondescent" may be a utopian prescription for making people be "more free than they are now from social distinctions visited upon them by others" (pp. 116, 118). But it does nothing to assist the problems of redistributing either wealth or the opportunity to acquire it in a society now more divided than in the recent past by quantifiable inequalities reflected in group designations. Nor does it address the difficult decisions that the criminal justice

216

system must make as it processes those incompetently affiliated figures we call criminals—and they are many—by attributing degrees of blame and responsibility for aberrant behavior. Being free to choose the terms of one's situatedness, in other words, does none of the most critical work that arguments affirming or denying attributed situatedness had tried, albeit inconclusively, to do.

What then can be done, or said? It is often said that we live a social and individual life that does not have the sorts of epistemological guarantees that were once thought to exist: Nietzsche, Foucault, and others have shown us why this has to be so. But Foucault, above all, has also shown the historicality of this very condition of being permeated by temporality and finitude, and at one point in his career he projected that it might be coming to an end. One could suppose that the preeminence of the rhetoric of situatedness in our current self-descriptions is a form of nostalgia for the imagined lost world of metaphysical and epistemological assurance, for a time when we knew who we were and where we were coming from. Or one could suppose that the visible inefficiency of this same rhetoric speaks for a new formation that has yet to be born, something that will refigure the opposition between mobility and locatedness. But it must also be said, as I have said now many times, that the very inadequacy of the claim to situatedness is fulfilling something in the cultural logic of late capitalism (to pirate Jameson's subtitle to *Postmodernism*). It fills the gap of subject specification but does so only in a hortatory or approximate way and to a degree that can be indefinitely extended or diminished as it is challenged or subsumed by new circumstances. It is a rhetoric of knowledge signifying a predicament of ignorance, but it does not confess itself as such. It is self-interpellation claiming to be a reclaimed epistemology, even as its very stridency indicates that we are not supposed to be deploying epistemology at all. It is an identity function for a time in which identity has supposedly been discredited. And above all it is a gesture aimed at the rhetorical reconstitution of our bonds with others, with nature, or with locality (for all of this is in our *situation*) that have arguably disappeared or at least been placed under unprecedented stress. The existence of those bonds may be a reasonable desire, but it is hardly an adequate account of how things *are*. To get any sense of that we are going to have to try harder to stay within the limits of what can be said about situatedness, and be a lot less willing than we usually are to situate ourselves. The rhetorical discomfort following from this effort (for how then do we introduce ourselves?) might well be rewarded in ways that we cannot yet predict.

The Persistence of Ethics The assertions of belonging that inform declarations of situatedness can then be read partly as wish fulfillments — for how else could their reiteration be so effectively ensured? Michael Sandel has specified the potential of the "multiply-situated" selves that he sees us to be to collapse into "formless, protean, storyless selves, unable to weave the various strands of their identity into a coherent whole" (*Democracy's Discontent*, p. 350). The maximizing of personal opportunities for some is shadowed by the melancholy of a lost or vanishing community even among those able to profit from flexible subjectification procedures. Others are presumably consigned to pure insecurity or to the imagined consolations of residual traditional groups of the sort that tend to go by the name of *communities*. Such groups as we do belong to or affiliate with are themselves insecure both as experienced and in their relation to anything identifiable as a general history. Lukács may have been one of the last to believe that the "self-understanding" of a group, which was in this case a class, the proletariat, could also be "simultaneously the objective understanding of the nature of society," so that all conscious furtherance of class-specific aims was also the truth of history (*History and Class Consciousness*, p. 149). A more common contemporary experience is the declaration of group interests as . . . group interests, and those of groups to which one only partly or temporarily belongs anyway. So the debate over the feminist "standpoint epistemology" that was derived from Lukács rapidly acknowledged the problem of there being no visibly coherent groups, or too many of them, to belong to.[20] Postmodern theory can sometimes declare itself comfortable enough with the predicament of fractured identity as itself a source of knowledge and oppositional energy, making a virtue of the condition that so concerns Michael Sandel. But there are still many of us who punctuate the narrative with regular declarations of situatedness, obeying an ethical mandate not to be a mere individual by way of a hoped-for connection with some interpersonal or impersonal identity-forming principle.

218

Which leads us, at last, to the matter of ethics, and to a discussion I have withheld until now. What is at work in these assertions of the determining power of situatedness—positive for Benhabib and Sandel, and also for Hollinger when rendered subject to revocable consent—seems to be an instance of what Glen Newey has described as "the major project in modern liberalism . . . to use ethics to contain the political." [21] What is actually going on in these addresses to the current condition, in other words, is an ethics, or an exhortation to certain sorts of ethical behavior, largely on the part of individuals. What is being said is not that I *am* in some clearly explicable sense situated here or there or then or now, but that I *should or should not be* so situated, in order to authorize what I am saying as the property of something beyond just myself. And that in being thus situated I am not responsible for what I am saying or doing: the responsibility is collective. And that in challenging or denying me in what I affirm or desire, you are opposing not just me but a group that I represent, which is an unethical thing for you to do. The claims and assumptions are muddled, even to the point of appearing by some definitions quite unethical (for this is hardly the Kantian subject doing rigorous justice on itself): notice that it is mostly a virtue to situate oneself but a sort of diminishment or accusation to ask someone else to do the same. But it is ethical argument that often pops up to fill the space abandoned by epistemology: what we cannot know for sure is supplanted by what we ought to be or do. So in the Goldhagen case the central hypothesis is about choice: how the Germans could have refused (without fear of reprisal) to kill Jews, but killed them anyway. In the exposition of the history standards, the gaps in our knowledge that come from the sheer proliferation of possible knowledges are filled by encouraging students to make moral choices. The scientism of *The Bell Curve* hardly conceals its address to the question of whether we *should* be in the business of maintaining (racial) preferences. And the Littleton summit and its ongoing rehearsal have a good deal to do with what we call in the last commonplace instance *family values* and *community standards*. It is for good reasons that Alain Touraine has characterized us as giving up on "scientism" in favor of a "return to moralism." [22]

Touraine himself seems quite happy with this. Notwithstanding his rigorous critique of identity crisis as a social-historical phenomenon, it is to another such category, that of the creative subject, to which he turns for solace: "If we are to defend democracy, we must recenter our social and political life on the personal subject . . . hence the growing importance of ethics, which is a secularized form of the appeal to the subject."[23] It is now twenty years since Fredric Jameson wrote about ethics as a "historically outmoded system of positioning the individual subject" and as "the sign of an intent to mystify" by way of the "comfortable simplifications of a binary myth."[24] These remarks are even more timely now than when they were first recorded, and Jameson himself has again recently reminded us that ethical speculation is "irredeemably locked into categories of the individual" and that "the situations in which it seems to hold sway are necessarily those of homogeneous relations within a single class."[25] This need not be always and in principle the case, and one would hardly wish to discourage attention to questions that are ethical in the broadest sense: questions about how one should act, how one might best live one's life, how one might limit the damages one does to others. But my very use of the impersonal pronoun here indicates the problem: that ethics for most of us most of the time means subjective meditation.[26] The return to or persistence of ethics is a form of what Jameson has called "pastiche," which is "the blank and non-parodic reprise of older discourse and older conceptuality, the performing of the older philosophical moves as though they still had a content, the ritual resolution of 'problems' that have themselves long since become simulacra, the somnambulistic speech of a subject long since extinct" (p. 99). This could be said too of the "problem" of the subject that the rhetoric of situatedness is designed both to repackage and to "resolve." Those of us in the habit of situating ourselves on a regular basis might stop to investigate the peculiar feeling of virtue we have as we do so, and ponder whether we have deserved it by any active connection with anything (some of us of course can pass this test, but not all of us). Niklas Luhmann has written of the tendency whereby ethical prescriptions apply to others rather than to oneself: "One can formally subject oneself to them, but self-application is not an option because of the lack of any consequential authority for action." He sees them as symptoms of an "irritation" in the social sphere that can only take the form of pure "communication"

(*Observations on Modernity*, p. 78). In its turning from "cognitive to normative" ethics then becomes itself "an unethical kind of doping" (pp. 91, 94) whereby one confesses one's own limits—itself a form of authority ("let me tell you where I am coming from")—only in order to expose everyone else's. The imperative to situate oneself is perceived as ethical even as (or perhaps because) it is usually devoid of critical content and without consequences beyond the moment of utterance. Meanwhile the ethics of situatedness promises to restore to the individual a satisfaction that in its profound loneliness it can no longer derive from the metaphysics of individuality itself.

What follows from my willingness to situate myself and to allow others to do so in my presence? I might agree to respect my friend's declarations of situatedness as they succeed one another or accumulate—as a gay man, a Native American, a Chicano, a lawyer (and as many identities as he chooses for however long he chooses)—but that is exactly where the process stops, with a gesture of respect. Such respect might work to prevent adverse discrimination, although it probably works best among those already least likely to practice such discrimination, those who already belong to the class-group configuration that the proclamation of affiliations is itself supposed to transcend. (The absurdity of the moment may perhaps be captured by my asking you to envisage a location in which a speaker introduces himself "as a militant neo-Nazi exponent of violence against immigrants.") The process is one of recognition or interpellation rather than description: it will be useless to me if I am trying to assess my friend's eligibility for some kind of restricted benefit or his personal responsibility for some sort of crime. It is also useless as a description or analysis of any kinds of situatedness to which my friend does not admit and of which he may not be conscious, and it is very difficult to employ as a way of assessing the degrees to which his variously attributed forms of situatedness affect his behavior. These models of the self can work as incentives to forgiveness ("he did x because he is a y living in z") in that they specify conditions that are plausibly and even obviously of some relevance to the self's disposition and behavior. But they cannot work as positive prescriptions or predictions ("any p living in condition q will behave r") or as unambiguous justifications ("he could only have done b

because he is a member of ɛ group and for no other reason"). They can encompass few if any of the problems that a politics or a jurisprudence must decide.

It is perhaps inevitable that the current discrediting of epistemology should open up a space to be occupied by ethics, which comes on to the scene to take up the slack in the exposition of a rhetoric of situatedness that has not after all ceased to be a major part of late modernity's self-descriptions. Situatedness is deemed mostly pertinent to decisions about degrees of choice and compulsion, and these have been significantly carried through under the sign of ethics. Cause for concern here is the tendency to a reciprocal discrediting of the entire social science project, and not just of its extreme objectivist claims, which have always been relatively rare and which were, in the exemplary paradigms devised by Bentham and Mill, from the beginning made subject to strict self-imposed limits. Benhabib and Sandel recommend recognition of one's place in communities, Hollinger proposes voluntary affiliation, while the reaction to the killings in Littleton has sponsored an orgy of amateur social science of such range and variety that it threatens to overwhelm any careful version of the argument for the importance of some kinds of situatedness over others. The ethical emphasis risks a disavowal of the potential of any impersonal and general conditions as at all relevant to the prospect for human knowledge and human happiness. Alasdair MacIntyre's *After Virtue*, first published in 1981, was a symptomatic and widely applauded effort at reassessing moral theory and many other kinds of theory in relation to the terms of human situatedness, and it took a very aggressive position on the adequacy of the social sciences for describing or predicting human behavior. The book begins by pointing to the empirical dominance of moral dissensus, a condition widely attributed to the rhetorical dependence of each morally coherent subgroup on where it is coming from, which is assumed to be a place different from where anyone else is coming from. MacIntyre does not deny the power of situatedness in hopes of coming up with some new version of a universal standard. Quite the opposite: it is the historical and cultural variability of moral behavior through the ages that most interests him and that seems to him to provide the best hope for a rethinking of the assumption that relativism itself must now be taken as a universal standard. He sees the contemporary moment as dominated by "emotivism," which is "the doctrine that all evaluative judgments and more specifically all moral judgments are *nothing but* expressions of preference, expressions of attitude or feeling, insofar as they are moral and evaluative in character."[27] (This was, it will be remembered, the same concern that Husserl sought to allay by recourse to ontology.) Here there are no "rational criteria for evaluation," so that "everything may be criticized from whatever standpoint the self has adopted" (p. 31). In this climate of preference the task of criticism becomes (as Luhmann too has noticed) one of "unmasking" the operations of other people's wills and desires as they seek to pass themselves off as general standards (p. 72).

This surely describes something easily recognized as a contemporary orthodoxy, one that makes every utterance or preference the result of coming from some one place rather than another, often to be found supported by the language of self-affiliation with its peculiar blending of the overaffirmative and the tentative or temporary. MacIntyre's point is not to deny positionality and its importance, but to show that positionality is never just individual: virtuous acts can only be claimed as such within a tradition that extends back into history and not just out into communal space (p. 127). We "are" significantly what the past has made us, and we carry forth that past in ourselves when we live in a tradition (p. 130). Traditions, moreover, are highly enduring, and history is a great conserver: even the heroic values of preclassical Greece have remained a vital part of our moral culture (p. 130). To try to dispel the past is to "deform" the present. We are all the "bearers" of a tradition, like it or not, and vital tradition is an embodiment of "continuities of conflict," not the inert (Edmund) Burkean fantasy that is merely the counterformation of a reified individualism (pp. 221–22).

MacIntyre thus seeks to counter the divisive results of situatedness claims with a broader notion of situatedness itself, one that is both historical and spatial. The group to which we say we belong itself belongs in a long-durational matrix: we bring things with us from the past, even as we experience the world in an evolving and unpredictable present in which any action can be situated in a variety of ways. The varieties would indeed be infinite were it not for the ordering functions of narrative histories, which make things intelligible both to ourselves and to others (p. 211).

The puzzles of personal identity can be addressed by seeing ourselves as "characters in enacted narratives" (p. 217)—our unity of selfhood is like that of the character in a novel, one not based on psychological states but still one that requires accountability and continuity in one's own story. So the ethical argument is shored up by the turn to literature that remains, as we have seen, itself a prominent component of the effort to analyze and legitimate the forms of situatedness. Any one act (MacIntyre picks, in a rather Heideggerian way, digging the garden) can be interpreted in a wide range of ways—the pertinent forms of situatedness are various— and the way to decide among them is to place the act in the context of a narrative in which it may be "situated" (p. 206). One important form of such situating is ethical—asking questions about what is good, and doing so within a "historically extended, socially embodied argument" that is a "living tradition" (p. 222). This is all very well, but what happens when people disagree radically about what the narratives are, or when some have power over others with whom they disagree? Embedding oneself in narratives can only be comfortable as long as one's right and opportunity to do so is unchallenged, in other words as long as we inhabit a world without critical scarcity where everyone can afford others the same options as they permit themselves. As an ethical standpoint for secure individuals who have the luxury of understanding their own positions as contingent albeit deeply held, this may be an admirable doctrine (although it seems to me to be very close to the very liberalism that MacIntyre intends to dispute). But it does not handle much beyond the sphere of strictly doctrinal disagreements, and it seems a nostalgic prescription for a postmodern world in which narratives are so often imaged as incoherent, bewilderingly complex, and beyond the scope of mere self-description or self-discovery. MacIntyre seems to admit as much in his final imperative toward "the construction of local forms of community within which civility and the intellectual and moral life can be sustained through the new dark ages which are already upon us" (p. 263). Those who can convince themselves that they have working traditions, in other words, should hang on to them and conduct themselves in the spirit of that other great pastiche creation, "civil society."

MacIntyre is clear that these narratives for life allow for a high degree of unpredictability even as they are rooted in living traditions. It is this that is most threatened, he thinks, by the overextended claims of a social science kind (which he attributes to Marx). We are allowed "statistical regularities" (p. 102) and some causal explanations for events in social life. But these must always be balanced by recognition of unpredictability; they can never generate "law-like generalizations" on the model of the natural sciences, which is what "two hundred years" of social science has, according to MacIntyre, tried to do (p. 88). I have argued that this is one side of the institutional and intellectual profile of social science, and one only. MacIntyre finds the objectivist tendency to be dominant because of its associations with the conventions of "bureaucratic managerial expertise": the professional credibility of social scientists must be threatened by any admission of the "permanent unpredictability of human life" (p. 106). Clearly, one result of this critique might be a better social science, one more fully credible because it has limited its own claims before others start to limit or disavow them. With this implication in MacIntyre's argument I am very much in sympathy (and so, I think, was Mill). But his own chosen emphasis is ethical—the elaboration of a new recognition of the enabling powers of traditions and moral choices that, if they were ever to be efficient, would render our dependence on the social sciences relatively slight. These conventions may indeed govern the "lives of certain communities whose historical ties with their past remain strong" (p. 252)—some Irish, some Greeks, some Jews in the United States—but these are hardly possible models for either nation-state or global behavior, and are indeed notoriously under stress as they themselves adapt to a culture in which boundaries are increasingly unapparent or indefensible. Their appearance here as a model for imitation and extension can only be seen as nostalgia for a time before modernity, or before the wheel.

MacIntyre does, it must be said, diagnose the limitations of bourgeois liberalism in ways that complement my own analysis. He sees that there can be no internal resolution of moral dissensus (typified for example by the debate between Rawls and Nozick discussed on pp. 246–52) and that the predicament of the atomic self is one of seeking to remain *"opaque and unpredictable"* in the face of the threats offered by the "predictive practices of others" (p. 104). He also understands that entrepreneurial culture requires these complexities, and that effective (managerial) organization must seek to tolerate and even stimulate a high degree of unpredictability (p. 106). Indeed, his invocation of traditions that are as familiar as they are dubious (outside the strictly academic sphere) will likely ensure that his diagnosis will remain more appealing than any I can put forward to a world that is, as the sociologists like to put it, increasingly detraditionalized. His case for an academy that should be more tolerant of its own conservative subcultures will also probably continue to find an audience. MacIntyre continues his argument in the 1988 follow-up volume *Whose Justice? Which Rationality?*, where he sets out to develop further the attempt at moving beyond the antinomic structure of modernity, the "assertion and counterassertion of alternative and incompatible sets of premises."[28] Again it is embeddedness in traditions that comes to the rescue of a culture in which the denial of "any overall theory of human good" can otherwise only consign all conflict resolution to its legal system (p. 344). The hope is that the "fundamental and radical crisis" of our culture may now be so advanced as to necessitate a serious encounter with "rival" traditions, either latent in our collective history or new to it (p. 364). It is again the "literary" imagination that is called on to enact such an encounter, by way of "a work of the imagination whereby the individual is able to place him or herself imaginatively within the scheme of belief inhabited by those whose allegiance is to the rival tradition" (p. 394), and thus to take part in "a conversation between the traditions" (p. 398). So I would say that there is nothing new here, nothing that stretches the problem beyond the dialogic model that governs so much "political" speculation within the mandate of ethical thinking. MacIntyre does not, in other words, give space to the possibility that his solutions are nothing more than repetitions of the problems they are designed to solve, or ever seriously doubt that the tools that we need to address dissensus are already at hand in the language that we have, that they are just waiting to be called into service.

Charles Taylor's *Sources of the Self* (1989) also takes the position favorable to situatedness arguments: that "one cannot be a self on one's own."[29] Taylor's work too is part of the turn against the "belief in the deliverances of unsituated reason" (p. 324) that we have seen in a number of other writers, part of the turn against what is often referred to in shorthand as "Descartes," that figure whose appeal and persistence is now mostly signaled by way of the energies of strenuous negation, although it is a negation that indicates the power of the antinomy generated by the articulation of modernity itself. Like MacIntyre, Taylor makes an argument against liberalism's inherited and insufficient vocabularies for describing and recommending the forms and varieties of human affiliation.[30] Above all he makes the case that the best understanding of the self is to be had by "enlarging our range of moral descriptions" and in terms of a history of "how our pictures of the good have evolved" (p. 1). Ethics, again, is front and center to the inquiry into situatedness, and it provides an alternative to what Taylor has elsewhere called "the dead hand of the epistemological tradition" and its reduction of the ethical.[31] He finds the beginnings of the "punctual self"—the self that "gains control through disengagement" (p. 160) with an aim to radical self-"remaking" (p. 171)—in Augustine's "inwardness of radical reflexivity" (p. 131) before it is in Descartes, after whom it becomes the model for modernity's "unsituated" self (p. 514). He also notes the power of the alternative presented by Montaigne (p. 182), and the way in which subjectivism and anti-subjectivity belong together and emerge out of the same model (p. 456). Taylor's preferred alternative to the aporetic experience of thinking about subjectivity is (like Augustine's) a spiritual and religious one, although he is well aware that the symptoms of confusion are not going to disappear overnight as a result of any purely philosophical argument: they are rooted in what he elsewhere calls the demands of the "market and bureaucratic state" in which we are likely to remain embedded for some time yet.[32] Along with modernity's affirmation of ordinary life as ethically and philosophically significant (*Sources of the Self*, p. 23) there came an inevitable confusion, of exactly the sort that MacIntyre has described, in pointing out the conveniences of imagining an unsituated self for ourselves and a situated self for others. The project of social science is for Taylor caught within this confusion, assuming an unsituated position from which the analyst can plot the terms of others' situatedness.

As soon as one agrees to understand the whole matter of human self-description as hermeneutic rather than rational, then the chances of a convincing epistemology seem to disappear, and it can begin to look as if only ethics or religion, which compose so much of what we are given to think with, can provide the assurances that Enlightenment faith in epistemology (and objectivist social science) once promised. *Situatedness* is a sort of placeholder offering an epistemological promise that it mostly cannot fulfill; that is I suspect why its invocation is so often shadowed by ethical imperatives and why so many of the mainstream academic efforts (at least in the humanities) to refine arguments based on acknowledging situatedness now tend to occur in ethics. Working through ethics, rhetoric, and theology, Paul Ricoeur, for example, has produced major studies of the necessary degree to which the modern self is all over the place, or nowhere: "Exalted subject, humiliated subject: it seems that it is always through a complete reversal of this sort that one approaches the subject; one could thus conclude that the "I" of the philosophies of the subject is *atopos*, without any assured place in discourse" (*Oneself as Another*, p. 16). So the "I" that we speak of can be and should be "revealed in all its strangeness in relation to every entity capable of being placed in a class, characterized, or described" (p. 45). It has only an "occasional" meaning in time and place (p. 50). Its provisionality only defeats those ethical systems premised on the unsituated self: for Ricoeur this same provisionality enables a new model of interactive behavior that accepts a higher level of dispersion and obscurity than the atomic self would have permitted. In so doing, however, it inevitably risks (or invites) the recuperation of Luhmann's "ecology of ignorance" within the tried-and-true terms of the loyal opposition to Enlightenment and modernity, religion itself, whose modeling of unknowing as holy folly can only remystify any secular effort at plotting the terms and implications of an incrementally dislocated and stressed subjectivity-effect.[33] The equivalent form for much of the discipline of ethics is the recommendation of a strenuous modesty, an individual effort to be maximally aware of where someone else might be coming from.

It is easy to find this turn against epistemology across a range of writings that set out to produce situatedness as an essential but always imprecise component of selfhood. It is easy to see why, because in terms of exact knowledge about the terms of being in the world we are still very much where we were in the eighteenth century, where the materialists pointed out that no two persons can possibly share exactly the same situation, and where Adam Ferguson, in a passage I quoted in chapter 2, lamented our ignorance, perhaps never to be corrected, of "the structure of those finer organs with which the operations of the soul are connected" (*An*

Essay on the History of Civil Society, p. 118). This recurring impasse has not, however, prevented situatedness from being invoked as a firm knowledge rather than as a space not open to such knowledge or at best one imaginable as open to a perhaps possible knowledge in a world yet to come into being. Or it has been fully admitted as undecidable, as it was by John Rawls, who reiterated eighteenth-century materialist doctrine in finding that no two persons could ever share exactly the same situation and that no general method could ever take account of the "endless variety of circumstances and the changing relative positions of particular persons," only to find himself under attack as a universalist insensitive to the real-life conditions of those same particular persons.[34] Richard Rorty, who has been enormously influential in his account of the dead ends of epistemological inquiry, takes situatedness as a given — "*We* can only start from where *we* are" — and sets out from this position to justify liberalism as the most committed among the forms of situatedness to the continual testing out and revision of its own assumptions by way of a tolerant encounter with the other.[35] Liberalism is indeed encumbered with a "concrete historical situation" (p. 93) but it is one that compulsively seeks to revise itself governed by the imperative to avoid causing pain. Whatever potential this ethic might hold for public policy is discouraged by Rorty's own insistence that justice and self-creation, public and private, are distinct spheres of attention and should remain so (unless one is a novelist). This is a neat move, because it is only in the public domain that the condition of situatedness becomes a knowledge problem, requiring knowledge models for its application (as in the social sciences) rather than an ethical precondition that can be admitted and passed beyond.

Rorty's ingenious explanation of how to accept situatedness without getting too anxious about it may well be missing the point: that anxiety is itself the point. Looking at the history of arguments about situatedness suggests, as I began by saying, that the aim of the collective inquiry into situatedness is not to "solve" the questions it sets itself but to go on reproducing the terms of the antinomy and the experience of aporia as themselves the goals of late capitalism's cultural configuration. This pattern requires that hyperassertive solutions appear from time to time in order to occasion equally assertive refutations. The history of the syndrome shows that there has been no shortage of either position. The questions that now need airing are at least these, once again: why do "we" go on repeating the terms of this debate about situatedness, and what options are left for referring to it once we understand that precise knowledge is not and is not likely to become available to us? Why are so many of us content with an ethical rehearsal of a problem that matters critically to epistemology, where it cannot be satisfied simply by an exhortation to civility and good manners?

Democracy in America? Much of the field of attention required for understanding our apparently compulsive rehearsal of antinomies was laid out in chapter 1 and repeatedly signaled in later chapters: the disciplinary, administrative, and descriptive priorities of western modernity have required that the individual be opportunistically described as both unencumbered, free, atomic, and *at the same time* as situated, contextualized, constrained, and determined. Late modernity and/or postmodernity have if anything intensified these contradictions and rendered them even more exigent and perplexing, which is perhaps what is sponsoring the efflorescence of ethical adaptations of the sort that can be "handled" (few of us doubt the absolute propriety and adequacy of situating ourselves). The erosion of "traditional" forms of solidarity is an argument one should only make if one is very sure that traditional life was ever solid in the first place. But even without a reification of the past into some idyllic world in which everyone knew his or her own and everyone else's place, it is still possible to suggest from the rhetorical record that our sense of situatedness has been placed under particular stress for describable reasons in place and time. One of these is certainly the long-term social experience of "democracy." Tocqueville made the brilliant and startling suggestion that the United States is one of the countries where "the precepts of Descartes are least studied and best applied" —least studied because of a bias against "speculative thought" and best applied because the breakdown of the class system puts every man on his own feet: "Everyone shuts himself up tightly within himself and insists upon judging the world from there." [36] Democracy produces a "sort of incessant jostling of men" and a world wherein decisions are made not by careful meditation (or by disinterested selves) but by "the accidents of the moment, and the art of turning them to account" (2: 44). It not only detraditionalizes, making "every man forget his ancestors," but it "hides his descendants and separates his contemporaries from him," threatening to confine him "entirely within the solitude of his own heart" (2: 106). Such barriers as exist between people are "almost invisible," and even then they are "constantly broken or moved from place to place" (2: 227), so that "all stations appear doubtful" (2: 228). Short-term contracts are the rule in a society where "the prevailing notion is that nothing abides" (2: 198). Everything is in motion: "Neither laws nor customs retain any person in his place" (2: 145). Democracy also alters the language. Because there is no forum for the adjudication of exact or exclusive meanings, and because all meanings need to be held as no more than provisional, there is a strong preference for general and abstract terms, terms that can be applied to anything and thus not falsified. (Again, this has something to do with the revivial of ethics.) Such terms promise clarity but produce confusion: "They render the mode of speech more succinct and the idea contained in it less clear" (2: 74). Kenneth Burke wrote of much the same world in A Rhetoric of Motives, as we saw in chapter 1, and I have argued that *situatedness* and its cognates are exactly such terms.

As is so often the case, Tocqueville's analysis of nineteenth-century life in the United States is remarkably prescient of what appear to be its current conditions, and of the confusions that continue to govern the articulation of human situatedness as long as our humanity is experienced under something like these same conditions. The panic that Todd Gitlin called "identity panic" (The Twilight of Common Dreams, p. 122) does indeed seem to be incumbent on the inhabitants of a culture within which personal and professional roles are felt as temporary and vulnerable, even as they inhibit the development of other and more enduring self-images. The demands of professionalism within democracy undoubtedly constitute a particular longer-durational motivation for the complexities of situatedness arguments on into the present moment. Harold Perkin has described professionalism as replacing "the horizontal connection of class" by a "vertical career hierarchy," one in which one is always looking up and down, forward and backward, simply as part of any effort to stay in place.[37] One is, in other words, very unsure of one's situation, not least in a world where the significance of and dependence on professionalism is marked most visibly by the habit of attacking it. Today the idea of nationality, already unstable enough in a collective such as "the United States," has been brought into further crisis; a crisis caused by the global developments in industry and communications whose critical moment was perhaps symbolized by what is often called the end of the "American century" with the oil crisis of 1973 (a "century" that began only in 1945), and by the emergence of alternative and "minority" voices inside the nation that vigorously claim to be coming from a place of their own that is not shared by others. Atomic selfhood and its aspirations to a desituated reason may now survive most intelligibly as reactions to an irreversible loss of personal decision-making power that is still enshrined in the rhetoric of daily life and in the legal system while it is being massively eroded in ways that no group of "we" or "us" can hope to control.

Ulrich Beck's *Risk Society*, which can usefully be read along with Giddens's *Modernity and Self-Identity* (both discussed in chapter 1 and elsewhere) for the beginnings of a powerful analysis of the way we live now, in the moment that may be called late modernity or postmodernity, suggests that the poor old Cartesian subject has now taken such a drubbing (and it continues to suffer at the hands of many of us who are up-to-date thinkers) that the real problems are only being masked by exhuming it for regular reburial. Beck finds us experiencing a world in which *nothing* that is felt to be ultimately pertinent to our lives can be known through the experience of our lives. What most requires being known is now outside the individual: that which is "devoid of personal experience becomes the central determinant of personal experience," leading to a sense of "imperceptible and yet omnipresent latent causality" (*Risk Society*, p. 72). The assumed roles of class and family, visible even if never simply stable, are replaced by a host of "secondary agencies" too numerous to track and too mutable to hold on to (p. 131). Along with this there arise "risk conflicts" that cannot possibly be managed by individuals and that are in their scope nothing less than global and comprehensive, potentially removing all inherited protections possessed by the haves and withheld from the have nots. This complete breakdown of familiar patterns of cause and effect has, says Beck, produced a bizarre hyperbole, a placing of all decision-making language (certainly not power) back in the mouths (certainly not hands) of individuals. So we are presented with "construction kits of biographical combination possibilities" (p. 135), offered the chance to be all that we can be in a world where we can affect almost nothing that most matters to who we are and what we might become. Biography, as it had been for Sartre, becomes again the site of "systemic contradictions" that are experienced as choices (p. 137): "The floodgates are opened wide for the subjectivization and individualization of risks and contradictions produced by institutions and society" (p. 136).

Beck's account (with Giddens's) asks to be read alongside Hollinger's to my mind far too affirmative recommendation of the lifestyle of making choices presented in *Postethnic America*. Beck's *Risk Society* finds that it is indeed a matter of choosing "between different options, including as to which group or subculture one wants to be identified with," but also that we have to "take the risks in doing so" (p. 88). These risks are substantial indeed, so that the language of self-determination covers over a predicament of near-powerlessness. Those alert to the dishonesties enshrined in the culture of empowerment will find much to identify with in Beck's analysis of the way in which "experts dump their contradictions and conflicts at the feet of the individual and leave him or her with the well intentioned invitation to judge all of this critically on the basis of his or her own notions" (p. 137). The pressures are unbearable: the individual is invited to take "a continual stand" on almost everything, and is "elevated to the apparent throne of a world-shaper" at the same time "as he or she sinks into insignificance" (p. 137). The effort to describe "individual situations" becomes more impossible than ever before owing to the proliferation of possible determinations needing to be accounted for (p. 138). Meanwhile, "handling fear and insecurity becomes an *essential cultural qualification*, and the cultivation of the abilities demanded for it becomes an essential mission of pedagogical institutions" (p. 76).

This last observation contains another clue as to why it is that we (in the academy) so often go on speaking as if situatedness were a firm knowledge-producing concept, either by unanalyzed epistemological gestures or by recourse to an ethical vocabulary in which no epistemology need ever be tested. Pedagogical institutions, including not only the schools and universities, with their monotonous rhetoric of self-fashioning, but also the popular media and the manipulators of common sense, have a powerful interest in presenting imposed predicaments as matters of choice, while those who resist this message find themselves driven to equally unambiguous alternatives, whereby situatedness precludes all significant choice whatsoever. Because neither position is tenable in the abstract, the debate between them is endless: it simply has no language in which it could possibly conclude anything. Beck suggests that we in fact live with neither kind of certitude, but with the experience of muddle and confusion in a state of considerable psychological stress: the sort of stress that I have argued is apparent in the rhetoric of self-affiliation with its awkward oscillation between hyperaffirmative and hypertentative declarations. (Common sense, and common usage, may then reveal more about the nature of our situatedness than many of those manning the "pedagogical institutions" would be prepared to admit.) Happy situatedness was probably always no more than a fantasy. Think of Heidegger with his hammer, hammering away happily because the act has subsumed the "equipment" in a way that "could not possibly be more suitable" because it calls up no theorization or reflection. The more purposive the action, the more "primordial" we become. Exchanging one hammer for another more suitable one embodies the way in which "interpretation is carried out primordially not in a theoretical statement but in an action of circumspective concern," with no "wasting words" (*Being and Time*, pp. 98, 200). Or recall Malinowski's picture of the tribal fishermen, each totally absorbed in carrying out his part of the general task at hand, confident in the habits of "old tribal tradition" and "lifelong experience" ("The Problem of Meaning in Primitive Language," p. 311). This is (or was), perhaps, happy situatedness, wherein one is connected to an environment in a manner that does not call for reflection and where what are otherwise thought of as self and other fulfill themselves in perfect purpose. But where now are the primitive fishermen, and what would we do to them if we found them? How long can one go on hammering without hitting one's thumb? While hammering, no one has to answer Adorno's question, "who are you?" Unless of course the hammering is going on in a lumberyard governed by divided labor instead of in some idyllic do-it-yourself situation with no one else around. Modernity has mostly been a condition of having others around; hence its reactive valuation of privacy and solitude. Late modernity is experienced as a sense of having far too many others around, and takes the nightmare form of a doomsday population explosion or (in the more decorously affluent locations) a building-out of green spaces. According to Beck and Giddens, and to many other analysts of late modernity, privacy itself is now so thoroughly permeated by choice-making obligations and exterior determinations ranging from the local and microorganic to the global that the word hardly has meaning. Total situatedness, total panic. Perhaps the old false certainties of both kinds, the ones that claim self-determination (I can make my situation) and the ones that refuse all responsibility (I am a creature of my situatedness) are now all the more marketable because of the extent of this panic.

So much for the first question: why do we keep on replaying the antinomies of situatedness? This whole book has been an account of just this syndrome, and I have meant to show that it has been a long-durational condition whose recent incarnations may be taking on a special urgency thanks to the conditions that are commonly called postmodern. This leaves the second question: what does one do with this understanding? What kinds of judgments, if any, can it sustain? The first task, I think, is relatively academic and calls for the refinement of the language in which we discuss and debate the matter of situatedness. This will take the form of refining and exploring rather than sidestepping the aporia, which is to be understood not as the result of some failure of method—so that we can imagine getting it right and getting rid of the aporia, in the manner of the dream of high-objectivist social science (which has been even more often the staged nightmare of its critics)—but as the intrinsic condition of stating the question of situatedness in the way that we do. J. L. Austin's wonderful essay "A Plea for Excuses" provides a model for refining the aporetic without assuming either that it will disappear or that it must be maintained in exactly the same form in which one first conceives it. Austin shows, very much in the spirit of Kenneth Burke, that in the slippage between justification and excuse, which different arguments often use as if they are the same, and in the "miscellany of even less clear terms" that creeps in between them because of that slippage, there are implications for some of the more consequential social languages, for instance that of the law.[38] Areas in which the common language is especially "rich and subtle," says Austin (p. 182), call for careful attention, both for their traditional discriminations, which are to be taken seriously as having solved expressive and descriptive problems, and for their obscurities, which are often the source of false solutions (p. 185). Austin advises special attention to words that seem to be rapidly reproducing themselves, appearing in places where they were not previously found and coming to describe things either not previously described or described differently: "It must be remembered that there is no necessity whatsoever that the various models used in creating our vocabulary, primitive or recent, should all fit together neatly as parts into one single, total model or scheme of, for instance, the doing of actions. It is possible, and indeed highly likely, that our assortment of models will include some, or many, that are overlapping, conflicting, or more generally simply *disparate*" (p. 203). The term *situatedness*, I have been suggesting, is a term that now requires special inspection as it spreads through the human sciences and claims to describe something important. I do not think that it can be defended as part of any precise descriptive language. But I do think that it calls attention to an aspect of our being in the world in the late twentieth century in the western democracies, and especially in the United States, that must be recognized and that cannot be ignored. Just because the complexities of situatedness are literally and theoretically imponderable in any exact way and to any precise degree we should not send ourselves back either to the language of free will and unencumbered personal responsibility or to an endorsement of total determination and reproduction. Both are stridently apparent in the rhetoric of daily life and its pseudosolutions to the problem of accounting for who we are in terms of where we are coming from. What then ought we to do or say?

First, I suspect that we are not going to find a new language or rhetoric, or at least not yet, or not simply by virtue of pointing out the limitations of what we have. Compound phrases such as *subject positionality* are apparently more tentative, but they still imply a conscious, knowledge-based control, a clear insight into where one is coming from. The *azza* sentence is, after all, a version of just this, although it is often (however inadvertently) more honest about its confusions. Nothing in the present disposition of attentions suggests a clear and clean paradigm shift within which the whole matter of subjective and objective is going to be refigured in terms other than themselves. What Beck and Giddens call "risk culture" depends on maintaining the illusion of freedom of choice, and thus of the subject-object relation that undergirds such a model. When we go to trial or sign a contract, we do so as individuals. And much of what constitutes pleasure or satisfaction still comes and is offered to us in individualized forms. But if there were about to be a paradigm shift, it is in the nature of things that we would be unlikely to see it coming before it happens, and there is no reason to suspend all speculation about alternatives until it does happen. Dewey offered a glimpse of a way to live with the predicament of having to answer questions whose solutions are preempted by definition because of the language in which they are asked. He called for some hard thinking about "altered distributions" yielding more "desirable consequences" than those currently on offer (*The Public and Its Problems*, pp. 192–93).

This much I think we can hope for. I have argued over and over again that arguments specifying our situatedness do not fully explain what they assert, do not produce clear and distinct knowledges. They do, however, produce fuzzy information — information that is important to consider even though it cannot be called knowledge in any uncontested sense — as well as statistics describing general trends or conditions. As such, they work to remind us of what we do *not know* but can *suspect* or *imagine* at moments when we would rather be making decisions based on knowledge; or they remind us of what has been the case in a significant number of past instances. Their use is thus often negative, not affirmative. Clarence Darrow seems to have sensed this in devising all those ingeniously reductive explanations for the murderous behavior of Loeb and Leopold. He could not of course prove that it was all the result of reading Nietzsche and of the teacher who introduced them to Nietzsche (and so on back to Adam and Eve), but he could and did introduce the shadow of a doubt. That is, he was able to convince the jury that they were not absolutely sure that a murder conviction, and hence the death penalty, was a justifiable outcome to the case. Some of the latest thinking about the free will problem emphasizes the point that all assertions of freedom can be rewritten as determination unless one thinks of oneself as *causa sui* — which most of us do not, most of the time.[39] There is then no point at which one can be absolutely sure that to pronounce ourselves or anyone else responsible or not for an action or predicament is a fully justifiable thing to do. That we do so all the time should not lead us to forget the process of approximation that informs all such judgments; and it might lead us to avoid judgments in circumstances that are not critical but merely habitual, but that help to maintain the cloud of unknowing that mostly surrounds these matters.

One current and highly polemicized instance that reflects, in Austin's terms, a disparate assortment of models, is the debate about affirmative action. The various perspectives in play here include those of individual and group rights, deserts and outcomes, all quite different priorities. Any one of them taken as primary will refigure and disturb the claims of the others. To claim rights is to propose a desituated standard applicable to all individuals; to claim merit is to advance a measure that is taken by some to be desituated while being understood by many others as a context-based standard, a result of specific kinds of situatedness; to look to outcomes is to direct the debate away from the issues of individual or group categories to more general benefits.[40] It could well be that some clearer thinking about this might come out of asking what consequences are desired, for example income redistribution across different ethnic groups, increased toleration of nonmajority subcultures, a wider distribution of the opportunities for higher education, "minority" representation in particular workplaces, and so on. These are not the same things, although some of them may overlap. And it is not clear that they can be best discussed in a rhetoric that is by definition antinomic, a rhetoric wherein the rights of individuals subsist along with claims made for groups, and where groups themselves are not always organically coherent. Many of the arguments made about affirmative action policies are arguments for and against the importance of situatedness. Putting these arguments into question should not result in an abandonment of the goals sought by the policies, but it might usefully disambiguate those goals and offer us different paths for achieving them. (Bowen and Bok's The Shape of the River, for example, is explicit about their sense of the purpose of affirmative action: it is to increase the representation of minorities in the professional middle class and the leader class, and not to solve the poverty problem.) It might also offer different kinds of consensus than those that currently emerge from the debate. Arguments made from situatedness do, I think, remain critically significant for what they can tell us about group conditions (for example, unemployment figures in the inner cities), as Bentham claimed long ago, even if they do not predict the exact patterns

238

of individual lives. To dismiss such arguments for failing to perform what they were never devised to perform in the first place is a great mistake. Right now it is important to limit the claims made by social science in order to maximize their real usefulness and to head off the conflict with individualist rhetorics in which one or the other will always be the loser, according to the particular dispositions of time and place.

Here and now, in the United States at the beginning of the twenty-first century, it seems fairly clear that the rhetoric of individualism is riding high, along with a relatively unanalyzed assertion of the significance of group identities. It then becomes all the more important to maintain the credibility of group-based or context-based arguments (kinds of situatedness) in their nonreductive, nonhyperbolic, nonparodic forms. The two kinds of argument and information are, as J. L. Austin might have said, *disparate*. They are not different enough that the one can refute the other, and not enough alike that the one can replace the other. So it is seldom clear in any propositional way exactly how to weigh each against the other. Dershowitz's regression in *The Abuse Excuse* toward normative standards of individual responsibility, while it may seem appealing enough in the face of some of the more visibly absurd situatedness defenses, is nothing more than a symptom of the recurring extremes generated by an antinomic system that is not being critically monitored or understood for what it is. Indeed, it may be significant that the willingness of juries to entertain or defense lawyers to propose mitigation or exculpation arguments based on arguments from kinds of situatedness that seem absurd to many of us (meek mate syndrome, the "Twinkie defense," and so on) registers a more general crisis in the relations between the state and its dependents. The credibility of these various accounts of individual nonresponsibility does after all seem to have increased at a time when the state itself is questioning or withdrawing some of the traditional postwar mechanisms for caring and support and throwing us all more and more visibly on our own "personal" resources. One would expect these pressures to register on a legal system that is after all the one sphere in which ordinary citizens have (as jurors) direct and determining contact with the state apparatus. The more the forms of inequality are tolerated or stimulated by the various mechanisms available to our political and economic system, the more anxious and urgent debates about situatedness are likely to become: they are a licensed testing ground for our evalua-tions of ourselves and others. To understand this is to recognize that the fate of these arguments is closely tied in with the question of what is lost and gained in a late capitalist, entrepreneurial culture dependent on flex-ible and opportunistic definitions of the relations between agency and responsibility.

Thus, a stricter adherence to the limits of arguments made from claims about situatedness also and simultaneously requires a stricter attitude to those made from desituated subjectivity in the language of atomic individualism. An example is the death penalty, which is invoked much more commonly now than in the recent past, and is invoked in this way in the United States at a time when many otherwise comparable west-ern democracies have given it up or are moving toward so doing. I can-not here fully rehearse the debates around this question, but I can say that there can be, by definition, no point at which absolute responsibility can be attributed to any criminal agent, without the shadow of a doubt. Death is not reversible, whereas new information has quite commonly come to light (and is doing so now more than ever) about the diminished or non-existent culpability of individuals convicted of capital offenses. There must always remain the shadow of a doubt about criminal intent (given the complex nature of "intention" in situated lives) as well as about agency (who really did it). This does not argue for exculpation; but it does argue clearly and, I think, unambiguously against nonrevocable punish-ments, of which the death penalty is the clearest example. Some (I am not among them) may wish to propose quite other grounds for keeping it in place; but the complex fuzziness of our efforts at refining the limits and nature of situatedness (and thus of freedom) does not allow for a jus-tification of the death penalty in these particular terms, and least of all when the statistics really do make clear that its imposition is radically differential among different ethnic groups.

Or take a less exigent but probably more frequently encountered cir-cumstance, one where those who possess something (like affluence) claim that it is the result of effort and deserving—a good use made of op-portunities open to all—while those who are relatively deprived claim that their group identity (for example inner-city unemployed and/or black) operates against their ever having such opportunities. Much of the discussion of this sort of difference becomes highly inflamed not least because of the category confusions that occur when a single method or informational norm is presumed to govern the terms of the question. It is in the interests of the affluent to deny that they are part of a group; it is in the interests of the nonaffluent to claim group status as an explanation for what they do not have. The imposition of a single category of free effort and choice must make the poor look like personal failures, while the extension of group status to the affluent threatens them with seeming not to deserve (also in personal terms) what they have. It might prove helpful to recognize the potential for opportunistic manipulation of this antinomic system not just by individuals caught up in it but by others with access to the rhetoric of social discipline from which it emanates. It might be useful to redirect the whole argument away from declaring absolutely for or against the power of situatedness, away from claims that cannot be fully resolved and therefore serve to distract any discussion that assumes that they can or that gives up because they cannot. We might then have the energy for some fresh attention to the nature of the goals desired (although we would still have to do battle with a prevailing bias against the utilitarian tradition as well as with the reductive rhetoric of *outcomes* that has been so prominent in contemporary managerial speech). If, for example (and I am of course presenting a hypothetical case), it were ever to be agreed on by a significant number of people that a narrowing of the gap between wealth and poverty were a policy worth pursuing, for reasons that do not depend on judgments made about the relative states of *deserving* individuals or groups, then arguments based on assumptions about the power or impotence of situatedness would become less inhibiting than they are bound to be when rehearsed almost entirely in the restricted and contentious sphere of criminality. There will certainly be those who will wish to use the inconclusiveness of any effort at a precise description of individual situatedness to deny the place of situatedness itself. They should be reminded that the same aporetic blockages govern arguments depending on the will. It is the entire dialectic of free choice and determined response that is discredited by the obscurity of situatedness.

A further result of admitting the complex inadequacies of arguments based in or against situatedness might be an attention to the nonmentalist components of human life. Often the most unnegotiable way in which we have a sense of our situatedness consists in our conscious relationship to our bodies. Because mind is traditionally lodged in body (the very terms signal the extent of the problem), that body becomes a separable and detachable item and, with the current popular awareness of the "cyborg" paradigm, the level of detachment is probably increasing (although the cybernetic modeling of brain functions goes the other way and is in tension with the common understanding of mental integrity). Bodies, indeed, have commonly become part of the lifestyle project; one "works" on one's body in order to shape it and present it in certain chosen ways. Disabled, seriously ill, and radically aging persons often have a more fatalistic attitude to the body as that which has or may be about to let "them" down. But in many cases, and certainly in many policymaking contexts, the body is ignored as the condition of situatedness is made to refer to a mind in a world, in situations offering it a menu of freedoms and constraints. The dominant form of post-Enlightenment situatedness, and thus the principal topic of my analysis, has been the relation of self to world, and especially to the social-cultural world (how quaint many of us now find it that Montesquieu and his contemporaries took climate seriously as an influence on character). Because the self has been located principally if not entirely in the mind, this has meant that the constraints and opportunities affecting the body have been relatively undiscussed.

Marx and those of his predecessors who analyzed the effects of divided labor systems were very aware of the physiological consequences of different kinds of work; over time we have come to be much more interested in its mental and "ideological" functions. The bodily emphasis is indeed not the least of the challenges that Marx continues to present; and the feminist project has done a great deal since Marx to restore the body to a dignity that commands attention. Recent awareness of various workplace syndromes has so far been least apparent in the places where they are most needed—increasingly, the factories and production sectors of the "third" world. But the general reimagining (it can hardly be a concept) of nature itself, and bodily nature, now involves so much more than making it a site for sustaining our tortured spirits in the inherited modern masculinist sense. Thus Beck's Risk Society images the body as the site of untraceable and proliferating threats to well being, threats that entirely escape the attentions of consciousness, while genetic science holds out images of both perfectibility and disaster depending on how and to whom and by whom its findings are to be applied. Recent emphasis on the body as something more than just a lodging place for mind or soul has produced some good arguments for increasing attention to such primary needs as food, shelter, and healthcare.[41]

Bodies, of course, do not speak: they do not have the language of self-affiliation open to them (imagine "as a hard-working leg with a long-standing loyalty to the rest of the body"), nor can they be included within the dialogic and conversational models by which our contemporary "politics" is increasingly being described. So there arise some obvious tensions in any culture pressuring its members to include health and physical well-being within their own choice-based lifestyles. The obscurity of the form of situatedness that is the body—not only a form in itself but also a site of import-export relations to an unpredictable world—is such as to allow for radical confusions about what the conscious, mental self can and cannot control about the physical self, a confusion further compounded by the ubiquity of the workout gyms and the fashion industry, which invite us to work on our own body presentation, and the plastic and other surgeries for which we can pay someone else to do so. The rhetoric goes both ways, as in the common phrases "he has let himself go" (conscious decision about the body) and "I feel like a prisoner in my own body" (attack on consciousness by the body). In ordinary life many people handle quite well the ranges of ambiguities and uncertainties about bodies and body parts, accepting that there are some things they can do and others that may be beyond control. And many use the ambiguity in an effort to gain some control (for example, those who want to try to "beat" cancer) that may prove beneficial in other ways as well as or instead of repairing the body. But the more general, social-political (and therefore rhetorical) level of concern is underdeveloped in comparison with how much is left to personal "choice": it is always "I" who does or does not "like my body." Again, the obscurity and uncertainty of exactly how this kind of situatedness matters (a body whose parts are in different relations to different models of the "self") does nothing to detract from a strong sense that it does matter. The ambiguities are an argument not for ignoring or arguing away the body's claim to attention but for expanding the provision of not just visible but also possible goods in a more comprehensive and better maintained model of "welfare" than the one we have; it should arguably be a model that goes beyond the boundaries of the nation-state to take account of the dispersed labor pool that works for our benefit and contributes its hidden life to our own bodily situatedness. There is a trend in this direction among many feminist and other socially conscious thinkers, and it is one that the fuzziness of human situatedness should support rather than discredit, owing to the incalculable number of possible goods that might ensue, and to the absence of any clear proof that they will not.

I have tried to show in this chapter that the implausible claims made for and against the power and nature of situatedness need not stand in the way of more specific and perhaps even more useful arguments made from a recognition of their fuzziness. A shared culture of ignorance and skepticism about situatedness has positive potential, although it is not of itself and on principle positive (hence the manipulation of fuzziness at the White House conference on Littleton). I think that there is a need for a different use of the information we have about situatedness, and a use for its obscurities, for its status as not clear knowledge. The social science project has, in its alliances with government and its compliance with an ideology of perfectibility, undoubtedly at times overreached itself and appeared to promise what it could not possibly deliver. It may also have had something to do with encouraging the dubious affirmations announced by a host of individuals as they situate themselves. But the contributions of social scientific information are not to be disregarded just because they have been overextended or metaphorized into new and strange forms, any more than they are to be worshipped when they are produced as cogs in the disciplinary machinery of social control. If we are now at a moment when the very real complexities of situatedness arguments are prone to radical reduction as simply new versions of identity, as I think that we are, then it is important to insist on the limitations and to attempt to see through to the ideological functions of that reduction. I am suggesting that the complexities and confusions are useful, partly in themselves and partly as symptoms whose analysis can tell us something about the conditions of our world. But the confusions can only be useful, and used in good faith, if they are known as such. So confusing are they, indeed, that I do not think it important to try to pronounce an absolute commitment to either the aporia or the antinomy as describing their structural logic. The antinomy may appear as a way out of aporia, a way of proceeding to a clear contradiction that then makes clear the need for a new beginning of some sort. And that is one way of untangling the problems in the rhetoric of situatedness and perhaps of leading us to other ways of asking the questions that references to situatedness have been thought to illuminate or resolve. At the same time, insofar as we are expecting a resolution of situatedness in its own terms, it is the aporia that will continue to confront us. Both of these results seem to me to be helpful and important ones — they are just different ways of telling us what we do not know for sure. In expanding the territory of what we do not or cannot know for sure, they should make us find different kinds of reasons for doing what we want to do, involving different uses of the information we have about situatedness. But they should not lead us to abandon the effort at knowledge in favor of reposing within an ethical vocabulary that is itself a symptom rather than a solution of the obscurities of situatedness.

Before I conclude I must point out one awkward and even logical confusion that I am myself risking. On the one hand I have argued steadily for the syndrome of situatedness as an instance of the governing rhetoric of late capitalist entrepreneurial culture. This is a position of critique (and I have explained why I think it can be offered in reference to a perhaps transformative "irritation," as Luhmann might call it, in the historical as well as the communicative condition), and as such it gestures toward a different or more desirable world in which the forms of inequality are less extreme and the rhetorical irritations consequently less significant and functional. On the other hand I have also argued for the positive uses of a "better" understanding of the implications of situatedness arguments, which could be taken to imply a basic comfort with the terms of our culture, which only need to be twiddled around and polished up to produce positive outcomes. Perhaps it is only my own generational formation that leads me to worry about saying where I stand on this question; for to do so would of course be to situate myself and to encounter all the problems of so doing, the problems about which I have been writing. It may indeed be the case that the apparent contradiction here, which, put melodramatically, is that between reform and revolution, cannot be expressed (at least by me) in any other way than that of a contradiction. And it may be that the mechanics of a better world really do lie latent in the world that we have, if only they could be put to use. It is not mere modesty that prevents me from proposing an answer to these questions, because their intransigence is itself the signature of where we are coming from. But their incidence does suggest that the analysis of antinomy and aporia, even if it is not directly productive of a new world order, is something more than the rehearsal of predetermined dead ends. Nothing I write here can of itself change the direction of the prevailing rhetoric of identification; but if those who read this are made more unsure about situating themselves and others, and more curious about alternatives, then I will feel that I have been useful. Pascal wrote against Jesuit casuistry and its artful manipulation of antinomic logic to justify whatever needed justification, so that "we have perfect freedom of conscience to adopt any one of these conflicting judgments which pleases us best."[42] Anything can be made right or wrong, according to the needs of the moment. The rhetoric of situatedness is a modern form of casuistry that we deploy not only at the expense of others but on ourselves, as long as the invocation of the power of circumstances continues to invite and even require an antithetical claim on behalf of the individual will.

Let me end with a recent and typical, although small and far from global, example of what I take to be a misunderstanding of how we can acquire and use information about situatedness. Perhaps the bathos of the commonplace is the appropriate place and mood to end with: it is after all where I began and where we should expect to see signs of any future changes in the rhetoric. In a well-intentioned although hasty response to the end of affirmative action programs in the state sector of higher education, the University of California invited applicants to its graduate schools to submit statements describing any hardships they might have encountered on their way to higher education. These statements are still, at the time of this writing, used as the basis for graduate fellowship decisions. The goal is one that many approve of—maintaining a diverse student population and putting the money where it is most needed. This is, to be sure, a hasty political strategy, a quick response to the abolition of affirmative action policies, and it is imperfect in the ways that such strategies often are. But it is worth pondering the difficulties that the policy itself creates, not least by the way in which it deploys certain assumptions about how to describe situatedness. The message received by the applicants is that they can be rewarded for suffering, indeed that they are to take part in a competition in which the quality and extent of their suffering will be judged. Many students of all kinds, sufferers or not, have found and will continue to find this process demeaning. They may also find it intellectually fraudulent. Despite the surge in the rhetoric of all kinds of identity politics, many people know that they do *not* know how their situatedness affects their lives in any exact way. They will also not share any standards for a definition of hardship. Most important, they are in the position of having to decide in the first person about conditions that are best described in the third person, but that are often not open to third-person inspection and that remain terribly problematic even when they are. In this process the analysis of determination (hardship) is to be carried out as a matter of choice (willingness or ability to tell). Means testing is time-consuming and complex, cannot prevent deceit, and is widely considered demeaning. The confessional alternative is all of these except time-consuming, at least for the institution; it is of course massively so for the individuals filling out the applications. We know from experience that some of the most profound hardships leave the survivors unable or unwilling to tell, often because they cannot bear to tell themselves what has happened. And in less exigent circumstances, there are still a lot of modest people (and ethnically inflected forms of modesty) in the world. It may then be unsurprising that many applicants, for presumably all sorts of reasons, are not cooperating and not telling their hardship stories. Many persons of clear good will are doing their best to evaluate this information as generously as possible. But they cannot evaluate what they do not have, and they do not have it even when they think they do. It seems that we still have a long way to go in figuring out what information is appropriate to the distribution of scarce resources as well as how we might go about getting it. A long way to go, that is, in coming to terms with situatedness as imprecise albeit essential information for the adjudication and prediction of human needs and human futures.

Notes

Introduction

1 Inga Clendinnen, *Reading the Holocaust* (Cambridge: Cambridge University Press, 1999), p. 17.

2 Kenneth Burke, *The Philosophy of Literary Form: Studies in Symbolic Action*, rev. ed. (New York: Random House, 1957), pp. 5, 8.

3 Michel Foucault, *The Order of Things: An Archaeology of the Human Sciences* (New York: Random House, 1973).

4 See Jerome H. Barkow, Leda Cosmides, and John Tooby, eds., *The Adapted Mind: Evolutionary Psychology and the Generation of Culture* (New York: Oxford University Press, 1995).

5 Homi K. Bhabha, *The Location of Culture* (London: Routledge, 1994), pp. 25, 89.

6 Manuel Castells, *The Information Age: Economy, Society, and Culture* (Oxford: Blackwell, 1999), 2: 276, 310.

7 See Jerome Bruner, *Acts of Meaning* (Cambridge, Mass.: Harvard University Press, 1990), on the recent turn against agency (pp. 9, 15). As he puts it: "It is plain that people can describe correctly neither the basis of their choices nor the biases that skew the distribution of those choices" (p. 17).

8 Ulrich Beck, *Risk Society: Towards a New Modernity*, trans. Mark Ritter (London: Sage, 1992).

1. Self-Affiliation and the Management of Confusion

1 *The Dictionary of South African English on Historical Principles* (Oxford: Oxford University Press, 1996). I owe this observation to Rob Nixon, *Homelands, Harlem, and Hollywood: South African Culture and the World Beyond* (New York: Routledge, 1994), p. 23.

2 Kenneth G. Wilson, *The Columbia Guide to Standard American English* (New York: Columbia University Press, 1993).

3 Ken Knabb, ed. and trans., *Situationist International Anthology* (Berkeley: Bureau of Public Secrets, 1981), p. 22.

4 This was principally a theological initiative; see Joseph Fletcher, *Situation Ethics: The New Morality* (Philadelphia: Westminster Press, 1966).

5 Jon Barwise and John Perry, *Situations and Attitudes* (Cambridge, Mass.: MIT Press, 1983), p. x.

6 Jerry Seligman, "Perspectives in Situation Theory," in *Situation Theory and Its Applications*, ed. Robin Cooper et al., vol. 1 (Stanford: Center for the Study of Language and Information, 1990), p. 147.

7   John R. Perry, "Semantics, Situation," in *Routledge Encyclopedia of Philosophy*, ed. Edward Craig (London: Routledge, 1998), 8: 669.

8   Edward S. Casey, *The Fate of Place: A Philosophical History* (Berkeley and Los Angeles: University of California Press, 1998), pp. xii, 340.

9   Significantly it is a geographer, a student of place, who has made the only other effort I know of at situating situatedness; see David Harvey in his *Justice, Nature, and the Geography of Difference* (Oxford: Blackwell, 1996), pp. 354–58. Harvey identifies a "vulgar" situatedness that refers to "wooden" identity, and a more dialectical version that stops far enough short of complete fluidity to make "political action" possible. The detailed coordinates of this are, however, asserted ("there has to be . . .") rather than explored or exposed. But Harvey's four pages cited here, and indeed the rest of his book, engage with many of the questions that I address in this volume.

10 Donna J. Haraway, "Situated Knowledges: The Science Question in Feminism and the Privilege of Partial Perspective," in *Simians, Cyborgs, and Women: The Reinvention of Nature* (New York: Routledge, 1991), pp. 183–201.

11 Jürgen Habermas, *The Theory of Communicative Action. Volume 1: Reason and the Rationalization of Society*, trans. Thomas McCarthy (Boston: Beacon, 1984), pp. 69, 119.

12 Louise Lamphere, Helena Ragone, and Patricia Zavella, eds., *Situated Lives: Gender and Culture in Everyday Life* (New York: Routledge, 1997), p. 5.

13 Dominick LaCapra, *Representing the Holocaust: History, Theory, Trauma* (Ithaca: Cornell University Press, 1994), p. 46. My thanks to Kevis Goodman for directing me to this passage.

14 Jacques Derrida, *Specters of Marx: The State of the Debt, the Work of Mourning, and the New International*, trans. Peggy Kamuf (London: Routledge, 1994), p. 82.

15 Elspeth Probyn, "Travels in the Postmodern: Making Sense of the Local," in *Feminism/Postmodernism*, ed. Linda J. Nicholson (New York: Routledge, 1990), p. 177.

16 Gayatri Chakravorty Spivak, *A Critique of Postcolonial Reason: Toward a History of the Vanishing Present* (Cambridge, Mass.: Harvard University Press, 1999), pp. 247–49.

17 Gayatri Chakravorty Spivak, *Outside in the Teaching Machine* (New York: Routledge, 1993), p. 3.

18 Nancy Hartsock, "Rethinking Modernism: Minority vs. Majority Theories," *Cultural Critique*, 7 (1987), p. 196.

19 Caren Kaplan, *Questions of Travel: Postmodern Discourses of Displacement* (Durham: Duke University Press, 1996), p. 159. See also Indepal Grewal and Caren Kaplan, eds., *Scattered Hegemonies: Postmodernity and Transnational Feminist Practices* (Minneapolis: University of Minnesota Press, 1994); this volume contains an exemplary declaration of situatedness, by Fred Pfeil (p. 197),

which reproduces, at length and perhaps to the point of parody, almost every feature of the syndrome I am analyzing.

20 Doreen Massey, *Space, Place and Gender* (Minneapolis: University of Minnesota Press, 1994).

21 James Clifford, "Notes on Theory and Travel," *Inscriptions*, 5 (1989), p. 179.

22 Louis Althusser, *Lenin and Philosophy and Other Essays*, trans. Ben Brewster (New York: Monthly Review Press, 1971), p. 175.

23 *Immanuel Kant's Critique of Pure Reason*, trans. Norman Kemp Smith (London: Macmillan, 1933), p. 394 (A 422).

24 Stanley Fish, *Doing What Comes Naturally: Change, Rhetoric, and the Practice of Theory in Literary and Legal Studies* (Durham: Duke University Press, 1989), p. 437.

25 Anthony J. Cascardi, *The Subject of Modernity* (Cambridge, Eng.: Cambridge University Press, 1992), pp. 26, 35. The next step is to discover Nietzsche within Descartes. See below, chapter 5.

26 Fredric Jameson, *The Seeds of Time* (New York: Columbia University Press, 1994), pp. 1–71.

27 Georg Lukács, *History and Class Consciousness: Studies in Marxist Dialectics*, trans. Rodney Livingstone (Cambridge, Mass.: MIT Press, 1972), p. 128.

28 Jacques Derrida, "*Ousia* and *Gramme*: Note on a Note from *Being and Time*," in *Margins of Philosophy*, trans. Alan Bass (Chicago: University of Chicago Press, 1982), pp. 29–67.

29 Jacques Derrida, *Aporias*, trans. Thomas Dutoit (Stanford: Stanford University Press, 1993), p. 12.

30 Kenneth Burke, *A Grammar of Motives* (Berkeley and Los Angeles: University of California Press, 1969), pp. xviii–xix.

31 Frank Lentricchia, *Criticism and Social Change* (Chicago and London: University of Chicago Press, 1985), p. 25.

32 Apparently the *azza* locution is just as rampant in Britain. Andrew Sullivan, "London Diarist," *The New Republic*, November 20, 1995, p. 50, has beaten me into print with his notice of the *azza* designation. I owe this reference to Alan Grob.

33 Charles Darwin, *The Origin of Species*, ed. J. W. Burrow (Harmondsworth: Penguin, 1986), p. 65.

34 Mary Wollstonecraft, *A Vindication of the Rights of Woman*, ed. Carol H. Poston, 2nd ed. (New York: Norton, 1988), p. 35.

35 Mary Cholmondeley, *Red Pottage*, ed. Elaine Showalter (1899; New York: Virago-Penguin, 1985), pp. 135–36. This example came to me from Helena Michie.

36 Anthony Giddens, *Modernity and Self-Identity: Self and Society in the Late Modern Age* (Stanford: Stanford University Press, 1991), p. 28; Beck, *Risk Society*.

37 Erving Goffman, *The Presentation of Self in Everyday Life*, rev. ed. (New York: Doubleday, 1959), p. 21. Goffman's work has been important for Habermas; see, for example, *The Theory of Communicative Action*, vol. 1, pp. 90–95.

38 Thomas J. Peters and Robert H. Waterman Jr., *In Search of Excellence: Lessons from America's Best-Run Companies* (1982; London: HarperCollins, 1995), pp. xxiv, 56, 58.

39 Tom Peters, *Liberation Management: Necessary Disorganization for the Nanosecond Nineties* (New York: Fawcett Columbine, 1992), pp. 10, 12, 15.

40 Arif Dirlik, *The Postcolonial Aura: Third World Criticism in the Age of Global Capitalism* (Boulder: Westview Press, 1997), p. 209.

41 F. J. Roethlisberger and William J. Dickson, *Management and the Worker: An Account of a Research Program Conducted by the Western Electric Company, Hawthorne Works, Chicago* (1939; Cambridge, Mass.: Harvard University Press, 1950), pp. 292, 320, 322, 409, 448.

42 Richard Sennett and Jonathan Cobb, *The Hidden Injuries of Class* (New York: Random House, 1973), p. 196.

43 Richard Sennett, *The Fall of Public Man: On the Social Psychology of Capitalism* (New York: Random House, 1978), p. 331.

44 Samuel Taylor Coleridge, *Biographia Literaria*, ed. James Engell and W. Jackson Bate (Princeton: Princeton University Press, 1983), 1: 72.

45 Bronislaw Malinowski, "The Problem of Meaning in Primitive Languages," supplement to C. K. Ogden and I. A. Richards, *The Meaning of Meaning: A Study of the Influence of Language upon Thought and of the Science of Symbolism* (London: Routledge and Kegan Paul, 1966), p. 307.

46 Emile Durkheim, *The Division of Labor in Society*, trans. George Simpson (New York: Free Press, 1964), p. 42.

47 Alain Touraine, *Return of the Actor: Social Theory in Postindustrial Society*, trans. Myrna Godzich (Minneapolis: University of Minnesota Press, 1988), pp. xxiii, 6.

48 Thomas Nagel, *The View from Nowhere* (New York: Oxford University Press, 1986), p. 4.

49 Fredric Jameson, *Postmodernism, or, The Cultural Logic of Late Capitalism* (Durham: Duke University Press, 1991), p. ix.

2. Mitigating Circumstances: Secular Situatedness and the Law

1 M. Helvétius, *A Treatise on Man: His Intellectual Faculties and his Education. A New and Improved Edition*, trans. W. Hooper (London: Vernor, Hood and Sharp etc., 1810), 1: 12, 16.

2 See John C. O'Neal, *The Authority of Experience: Sensationist Theory in the French Enlightenment* (University Park: Pennsylavnia State University Press, 1996), pp. 173–95. O'Neal identifies Helvétius as strictly a sensationist rather than a materialist, but the distinction is not important to my argument here.

3   Jeremy Bentham, "Essay on the Influence of Time and Place in Matters of Legislation," in *The Works of Jeremy Bentham*, ed. John Bowring (Edinburgh: William Tait, 1838–43), 1: 180–81.

4   Jeremy Bentham, *An Introduction to the Principles of Morals and Legislation*, ed. Laurence J. Lafleur (New York: Hafner, 1963), pp. 43–69.

5   Adam Ferguson, *An Essay on the History of Civil Society* (1767), ed. Duncan Forbes (Edinburgh: Edinburgh University Press, 1978), p. 117.

6   Alan M. Dershowitz, *The Abuse Excuse: and Other Cop-Outs, Sob Stories, and Evasions of Responsibility* (Boston: Little, Brown, 1994), p. 10.

7   Ian Hacking, *The Social Construction of What?* (Cambridge, Mass.: Harvard University Press, 1999), pp. 100–62.

8   Barbara J. Shapiro, in *"Beyond Reasonable Doubt" and "Probable Cause": Historical Perspectives on the Anglo-American Law of Evidence* (Berkeley and Los Angeles: University of California Press, 1991), has described the proliferation of eighteenth-century treatises that attempt to decide the place of reasonable doubt and probable cause. See especially pp. 25–41.

9   Bentham, *An Introduction to the Principles of Morals and of Legislation*, p. 79n.

10 *The Basic Works of Aristotle*, ed. Richard McKeon (New York: Random House, 1941), p. 964.

11 Thomas Hobbes, *Leviathan*, ed. Michael Oakeshott (Oxford: Basil Blackwell, 1955) p. 107.

12 John Locke, *An Essay Concerning Human Understanding*, ed. Peter H. Nidditch (Oxford: Clarendon Press, 1979), pp. 342–43.

13 William Blackstone, *Commentaries on the Laws of England* (1765–69; Chicago: University of Chicago Press, 1979), 4: 18.

14 Sir Robert Chambers, *A Course of Lectures on the English Law, Delivered at the University of Oxford, 1767–73*, ed. Thomas M. Curley (Madison: University of Wisconsin Press; Oxford: Oxford University Press, 1986), 1: 327–36. The same exemptions appear in *Mr. Serjeant Stephen's New Commentaries on the Laws of England*, rev. and modernized by Edward Jenks, 14th ed. (London: Butterworth, 1903), 4: 17–29.

15 See Theodore F. T. Plucknett, *A Concise History of the Common Law*, 4th ed. (London: Butterworth, 1948), p. 437.

16 M. de Mirabaud [Baron d'Holbach], *Nature and Her Laws; as Applicable to the Happiness of Man Living in Society; Contrasted with Superstition and Imaginary Systems* (London: W. Hodgson, 1816), 1: 130, 112, 253.

17 William Paley, *The Principles of Moral and Political Philosophy*, 20th ed. (London: printed for J. Faulder etc., 1814), 2: 266–67.

18 Immanuel Kant, *Lectures on Ethics*, trans. Louis Infield (New York: Harper and Row, 1963), p. 66.

19 J. G. Fichte, *The Science of Rights*, trans. A. E. Kroeger (London: Routledge and Kegan Paul, 1970), pp. 19–21.

20 *Hegel's Philosophy of Right*, trans. T. M. Knox (London: Oxford University Press, 1975), pp. 88–89.

21 The fear is probably exaggerated given the complexity of the sentencing and appeals processes which, for example, often work against the awards or decisions rendered by particular juries.

22 Morton J. Horwitz, *The Transformation of American Law, 1780–1860* (Cambridge, Mass.: Harvard University Press, 1977), p. 30.

23 On this subject, see also Nan Goodman, *Shifting the Blame: Literature, Law, and the Theory of Accidents in Nineteenth-Century America* (Princeton: Princeton University Press, 1998).

24 Oliver Wendell Holmes, *The Common Law*, ed. Mark De Wolfe Howe (Cambridge, Mass.: Harvard University Press, Belknap Press, 1963), p. 41.

25 Adam Smith, *Lectures on Jurisprudence*, ed. R. L. Meek, D. D. Raphael, and P. G. Stein (Oxford: Clarendon Press, 1978), for example, p. 104. The impartial spectator plays an important role in Smith's *Theory of Moral Sentiments*, ed. D. D. Raphael and A. L. Macfie (Oxford: Clarendon Press, 1976).

26 Morton J. Horwitz, *The Transformation of American Law, 1870–1960: The Crisis of Legal Orthodoxy* (New York: Oxford University Press, 1992), pp. 109–43.

27 Oliver Wendell Holmes, "The Path of the Law," in *Collected Legal Papers* (London: Constable and Co., 1920), pp. 173, 180, 186–87.

28 Horwitz, *The Transformation of American Law, 1870–1960*, p. 117.

29 Ibid., pp. 53–56.

30 Clarence S. Darrow, *Resist Not Evil* (1903; Montclair, N.J.: Patterson Smith, 1972), pp. 85–87.

31 For an elegant argument in favor of the traditionally restrictive excuse conditions (insanity, infancy, diminished responsibility, etc.) as *contributing to* rather than removing an individual's critical decision-making role, see H. L. A. Hart, "Legal Responsibility and Excuses," in *Determinism and Freedom in the Age of Modern Science*, ed. Sidney Hook (New York: Collier, 1961), pp. 95–117.

32 Clarence Darrow, "Plea in Defense of Richard Loeb and Nathan Leopold," in *Clarence Darrow on the Death Penalty* (Evanston, Ill.: Chicago Historical Bookworks, 1991), p. 30.

33 *Basic Writings of Nietzsche*, ed. and trans. Walter Kaufmann (New York: Random House, 1968), p. 516.

34 Clarence S. Darrow, *The Story of My Life* (New York: Grosset and Dunlap, 1932), pp. 214–42.

35 Clarence S. Darrow, *An Eye for an Eye* (New York: Fox, Duffield and Co., 1905), p. 27.

36 Meyer Levin, *Compulsion* (New York: Simon and Schuster, 1956). Levin defends his novel as "poetically valid" even if not historically correct (p. x), and as not intending strict or mere justice.

37 See Horwitz, *The Transformation of American Law, 1870–1960*, pp. 169–246. Horwitz describes legal realism as a collection of opinions contesting the idea of the law as neutral doctrine, and operating out of a general cognitive relativism.

38 Michael J. Sandel, *Democracy's Discontent: America in Search of a Public Philosophy* (Cambridge, Mass.: Harvard University Press, Belknap Press, 1996), p. 55.

39 A similar trend has been observed in the expansion of First Amendment doctrine to cover a whole range of forms of personal expression arguably not anticipated in 1791; see the essays in T. Daniel Shumate, ed., *The First Amendment: The Legacy of George Mason* (Fairfax, Va.: George Mason University Press, 1987). The subject is, of course, contested. For a different view defending the case for unrestrained individualism, see Steven H. Shiffrin, *The First Amendment: Democracy and Romance* (Cambridge, Mass.: Harvard University Press, 1990).

40 John Dewey, *The Public and Its Problems* (Athens: Ohio University Press, The Swallow Press, 1991), pp. 95, 97.

41 Charles Horton Cooley, *Human Nature and the Social Order*, in *The Two Major Works of Charles H. Cooley*, ed. Robert Cooley Angell (Glencoe, Ill.: The Free Press, 1956), p. 420.

3. With God on Our Side? The Science of Character

1 Alain Touraine, *Return of the Actor*, p. 6; Immanuel Wallerstein, *The End of the World as we Know It: Social Science for the Twenty-First Century* (Minneapolis: University of Minnesota Press, 1999), pp. 120, 147.

2 Hacking, *The Social Construction of What?*, p. 35; Barkow, Cosmides, and Tooby, *The Adapted Mind*, p. 40.

3 Ernesto Laclau, *New Reflections on the Revolution of Our Time* (London: Verso, 1990), p. 182.

4 Emile Durkheim, *The Rules of Sociological Method*, ed. Steven Lukes, trans. W. D. Halls (New York: The Free Press, 1982), pp. 71, 171.

5 Habermas, *The Theory of Communicative Action*, 1: 4–5.

6 Ian Hacking, *The Emergence of Probability: A Philosophical Study of Early Ideas about Probability, Induction, and Statistical Evidence* (Cambridge: Cambridge University Press, 1975), p. 176.

7 Johann Gottfried von Herder, *Reflections on the Philosophy of the History of Mankind*, ed. Frank E. Manuel (Chicago: University of Chicago Press, 1968), p. 4.

8 *Condorcet: Selected Writings*, ed. Keith Michael Baker (Indianapolis: Bobbs-Merrill, 1976), p. 186.

9 There is a good deal of important scholarship that supports such a position. See, among others, and besides Hacking (note 6 above), Theodore M. Porter, *The Rise of Statistical Thinking, 1820–1900* (Princeton: Princeton Univer-

sity Press, 1985), and his *Trust in Numbers: The Pursuit of Objectivity in Science and Public Life* (Princeton: Princeton University Press, 1995); and Stephen M. Stigler, *The History of Statistics: The Measurement of Uncertainty before 1900* (Cambridge, Mass.: Harvard University Press, Belknap Press, 1986).

10 Baron de Montesquieu, *The Spirit of the Laws*, trans. Thomas Nugent (London: Macmillan, 1949), pp. lxvii–lxviii.

11 *The Works of the Late William Robertson, D.D.* (London: printed for Cowie, Low etc., 1826), 5: 276, 278.

12 Max Horkheimer and Theodor W. Adorno, *Dialectic of Enlightenment*, trans. John Cumming (New York: Continuum, 1986), pp. xi–xiii.

13 T. W. Adorno, Else Frenkel-Brunswik, Daniel J. Levinson, and R. Nevitt Sanford, *The Authoritarian Personality* (New York: Harper, 1950), pp. vii, 10.

14 Bronislaw Malinowski, *Freedom and Civilization* (New York: Roy Publishers, 1944), p. 13.

15 John Locke, "Some Thoughts Concerning Education," in *The Educational Writings of John Locke*, ed. James L. Axtell (Cambridge: Cambridge University Press, 1968), p. 148.

16 Peter Novick, *That Noble Dream: The "Objectivity Question" and the American Historical Profession* (Cambridge, Eng.: Cambridge University Press, 1988), pp. 16, 281.

17 Benjamin Rush, *Thoughts on the Mode of Education Proper in a Republic* (1786), in *Essays on Education in the Early Republic*, ed. Frederick Rudolph (Cambridge, Mass.: Harvard University Press, Belknap Press, 1965), pp. 17, 15.

18 Wolf Lepenies, *Between Literature and Science: The Rise of Sociology*, trans. R. J. Hollingdale (Cambridge, Eng.: Cambridge University Press, 1992), pp. 1–15.

19 Carl N. Degler, *In Search of Human Nature: The Decline and Revival of Darwinism in American Social Thought* (New York: Oxford University Press, 1991), chaps. 1, 3, 5.

20 Christopher Herbert, *Culture and Anomie: Ethnographic Imagination in the Nineteenth Century* (Chicago: University of Chicago Press, 1991), pp. 17, 24. Another term that comes close to fulfilling the role that Herbert describes for culture is milieu. According to Paul Rabinow, *French Modern: Norms and Forms of the Social Environment* (Chicago: University of Chicago Press, 1995), pp. 126–67, the Comte de Buffon was instrumental in giving currency to this term and imparting to it a Lamarckian spin whereby persons are imagined to be able to adapt actively to what they find in place in the world. They can, in other words, affect or control their situations. The appeal of this model later to Sartre and others will be discussed in chapter 5.

21 John Stuart Mill, *A System of Logic, Ratiocinative and Inductive*, 8th ed. (London: Longmans, Green, Reader, and Dyer, 1872), 2: 422. Porter, *The Rise of Statistical Thinking*, pp. 82–83, describes a strong attack on classical probability's

disregard for empirical evidence in the 1843 first edition of *A System of Logic*, which Mill modified thereafter.

22   John Stuart Mill, *On Liberty*, ed. Currin V. Shields (Indianapolis: Bobbs-Merrill, 1956), p. 7.

23   Herbert, *Culture and Anomie*, p. 53, notes a "persistent collapsing together in nineteenth-century writing of the two antithetical terms, freedom and control," whereby each can appear as the other.

24   Darwinism strictly interpreted gave little credit to the interventionist agendas of social science because the all-important mechanisms of natural selection took effect only over long periods and depended on coincidence rather than effort or intent. Herbert Spencer's *The Principles of Psychology* (London: Longman, Brown, Green, and Longmans, 1855), with its materialist weighting of the relation of organism to environment, giving priority to physiology and biology over external, "immediate impressions" (p. 619), is close to the Darwinian model. But despite Darwin's apparent inapplicability to the social sciences, evolutionary metaphors were used to justify and affirm accounts of what William Graham Sumner and Albert Galloway Keller, in *The Science of Society* (New Haven: Yale University Press; Oxford: Oxford University Press, 1927), p. 3, called "the adjustment of life to life-conditions." Darwin's emphasis on long-durational patterns and arbitrary outcomes is here invoked to justify ignoring "conscious, reasoned and purposeful action on the part of the individual" (p. 41).

25   William James, *Pragmatism; and Four Essays from "The Meaning of Truth"* (Cleveland: World Publishing Company, 1970), pp. 45, 46.

26   And perhaps it is also a harbinger of a postmodern social science. In his description of pragmatism as feminine, as something that "unstiffens" theory, as willing to follow "either logic or the senses and to count the humblest and most personal experience" (p. 61), and as willing to approach totality only by way of incremental localisms, "innumerable little hangings-together of the world's parts within the larger hangings-together" (p. 94), James is remarkably prescient of the orthodoxies of the 1990s.

27   John Dewey, *Democracy and Education: An Introduction to the Philosophy of Education* (New York: Macmillan, 1916), p. 26.

28   John Dewey, *Human Nature and Conduct: An Introduction to Social Psychology* (New York: Henry Holt, 1922), p. 10.

29   Thomas L. Haskell, *The Emergence of Professional Social Science: The American Social Science Association and the Nineteenth-Century Crisis of Authority* (Urbana: University of Illinois Press, 1977), p. 40.

30   Foucault, *The Order of Things*, p. 303.

31   Talcott Parsons, "Overview," in *American Sociology: Perspectives, Problems, Methods*, ed. Talcott Parsons (New York: Basic Books, 1968), p. 320. Parsons noted

that the membership of ten thousand in the American Sociological Association in 1966 represented a doubling over the previous fifteen years.

32 Robert S. Lynd and Helen Merrell Lynd, *Middletown: A Study in Contemporary American Culture* (New York: Harcourt Brace, 1929), p. vi.

33 See Anthony Giddens, *The Consequences of Modernity* (Stanford: Stanford University Press, 1990), pp. 39–41. Sociology is described here as the most visibly reflexive among the disciplines and thus as the best attuned to the institutions of contemporary life, which are engaged in the "chronic revision of social practices in the light of knowledge about those practices" (p. 40).

34 Cooley, *Social Organization*, in *The Two Major Works of Charles H. Cooley*, pp. 210, 383.

35 George H. Mead, *Mind, Self, and Society from the Standpoint of a Social Behaviorist*, ed. Charles W. Morris (1934; Chicago: University of Chicago Press, 1952), pp. 174–75.

36 Ruth Benedict, *Patterns of Culture* (Boston: Houghton Mifflin, 1959), pp. 10–11.

37 Margaret Mead, *From the South Seas: Studies of Adolescence and Sex in Primitive Societies* (New York: William Morrow, 1939), p. x. This volume reprints three separately paginated books: *Coming of Age in Samoa*; *Growing Up in New Guinea*; and *Sex and Temperament in Three Primitive Societies*.

38 Margaret Mead, *Coming of Age in Samoa*, p. 8.

39 Margaret Mead, *Growing Up in New Guinea*, p. 5.

40 Margaret Mead, *Sex and Temperament in Three Primitive Societies*, p. 316.

41 Otto Klineberg, "Racial Psychology," in *The Science of Man in the World Crisis*, ed. Ralph Linton (New York: Columbia University Press, 1945), p. 77.

42 Ralph Linton, "The Scope and Aims of Anthropology," in Linton, ed., *The Science of Man in the World Crisis*, p. 3.

43 Clyde Kluckhohn and William H. Kelly, "The Concept of Culture," in Linton, ed., *The Science of Man in the World Crisis*, pp. 105–6.

44 *Selected Writings of Edward Sapir on Language, Culture, and Personality*, ed. David G. Mandelbaum (Berkeley and Los Angeles: University of California Press, 1958), pp. 561, 593–97.

45 Henry A. Murray and Clyde Kluckhohn, "Outline of a Conception of Personality," in *Personality in Nature, Society and Culture*, ed. Clyde Kluckhohn and Henry A. Murray (New York: Knopf, 1948), p. 5.

46 Kluckhohn and Murray, eds., *Personality in Nature*, pp. 132, 117, 84.

47 Hans Gerth and C. Wright Mills, *Character and Social Structure: The Psychology of Social Institutions* (New York: Harcourt, Brace and World, 1964), pp. xv–xvi.

48 Hook, ed., *Determinism and Freedom*, p. 9. See also Herbert Morris, ed., *Freedom and Responsibility: Readings in Philosophy and Law* (Stanford: Stanford University Press, 1961).

49 Werner Heisenberg, *Physics and Philosophy: The Revolution in Modern Science* (New York: Harper and Row, 1962), pp. 17–18. The book first appeared in 1958, a year after Sputnik and when, perhaps, there was increased anxiety about the credibility, ability, and truth to nature of liberal-democratic culture. The next scientific book to make a comparable impact was Thomas Kuhn's *The Structure of Scientific Revolutions* (Chicago: University of Chicago Press, 1962), which was taken as a vindication of the socialized nature of all significant knowledge. Perhaps Kuhn should be read as the "revenge" of the social sciences on the metaphor of indeterminacy.

50 Barkow, Cosmides, and Tooby, *The Adapted Mind*, pp. 3–5.

51 George Orwell, *Nineteen Eighty-Four* (New York: Harcourt, Brace and World, 1949), p. 272.

52 See David Simpson, "Prospects for Global English: Back to BASIC?" *Yale Journal of Criticism* 11, no. 1 (1998): 301–7.

53 Any thorough history of the postwar social sciences would include a discussion of linguistics, which subsisted as a highly politicized discipline in its waverings between sociolinguistic and general grammar paradigms. For a short history, see Frederick J. Newmeyer, *The Politics of Linguistics* (Chicago: University of Chicago Press, 1986), esp. pp. 29–126.

54 Giddens, *The Consequences of Modernity*, p. 39; Herbert, *Culture and Anomie*, pp. 13–16, 105.

4. Literary Situations, Novel Solutions

1 Durkheim, *The Division of Labor in Society*, p. 37.

2 William Wordsworth, *The Prelude: 1799, 1805, 1850*, ed. Jonathan Wordsworth, M. H. Abrams, and Stephen Gill (New York: Norton, 1979), p. 432.

3 A classic statement of the case is J. C. F. von Schiller's "On Naive and Sentimental Poetry," trans. Daniel O. Dahlstrom, in *Friedrich Schiller: Essays*, ed. Walter Hinderer and Daniel O. Dahlstrom (New York: Continuum, 1995) pp. 179–260. See also David Simpson, *Irony and Authority in Romantic Poetry* (London: Macmillan, 1979).

4 See Lepenies, *Between Literature and Science*, p. 152. Christopher Herbert makes a persuasive case for Trollope as a "social science" novelist in *Culture and Anomie*, pp. 253–99.

5 James Chandler, *England in 1819: The Politics of Literary Culture and the Case of Romantic Historicism* (Chicago: University of Chicago Press, 1998), p. 305.

6 Sir Walter Scott, *Waverley*, ed. Andrew Hook (Harmondsworth: Penguin, 1982), pp. 45–49.

7 Smith, *The Theory of Moral Sentiments*, pp. 9–26.

8 Coleridge, *Biographia Literaria*, 2: 126, 136.

9 Bruner, *Acts of Meaning*, p. 55; Burke, *The Philosophy of Literary Form*, p. 8.

10 Ian Watt takes Crusoe as one of the four foundational heroes of modernity,

one of the key figures representing the transformation of individuality from being a punishment to being an enabling condition; see *Myths of Modern Individualism: Faust, Don Quixote, Don Juan, Robinson Crusoe* (Cambridge, Eng.: Cambridge University Press, 1996).

11 William Godwin, *Things as They Are, or the Adventures of Caleb Williams*, ed. Maurice Hindle (Harmondsworth: Penguin, 1988), p. 3.

12 Mary Hays, *Memoirs of Emma Courtney* (London: Pandora, 1987), p. 6.

13 Thomas Carlyle, "Signs of the Times," in *The Works of Thomas Carlyle*, Centenary Edition ed. H. D. Traill (London: Chapman and Hall, 1896–99), 27: 60, 67, 63.

14 Charles Dickens, *Oliver Twist*, ed. Peter Fairclough (Harmondsworth: Penguin, 1985), p. 244.

15 Jane Austen, *Persuasion*, ed. Linda Bree (Peterborough, Ont.: Broadview Press, 1998), pp. 185–86, 207.

16 Jean-Paul Sartre, *The Family Idiot: Gustave Flaubert, 1821–1857*, trans. Carol Cosman (Chicago: University of Chicago Press, 1981–93), 3: 446–47.

17 Douglas Lane Patey, *Probability and Literary Form: Philosophic Theory and Literary Practice in the Augustan Age* (Cambridge: Cambridge University Press, 1984), p. 89. Patey's discussion of casuistry is to be found on pp. 50–62.

18 Jane Austen, *Emma*, ed. Fiona Stafford (London: Penguin, 1996), p. 121.

19 Jane Austen, *Mansfield Park*, ed. Tony Tanner (London: Penguin, 1985), p. 454.

20 George Eliot, *Adam Bede*, in *The Cabinet Edition of the Novels of George Eliot* (Blackwood, 1878–85), 1: 259.

21 George Eliot, *Middlemarch*, in *The Cabinet Edition of the Novels of George Eliot* (Edinburgh: Blackwood, 1878–85), 1: 1–2.

22 Alexander Welsh, *Strong Representations: Narrative and Circumstantial Evidence in England* (Baltimore: Johns Hopkins University Press, 1992).

23 See Gillian Beer, *Darwin's Plots: Evolutionary Narrative in Darwin, George Eliot, and Nineteenth-Century Fiction* (London: Routledge and Kegan Paul, 1983), pp. 149–80, for an account of Eliot's interest in depicting "individual diversity beneath ascribed typologies" (p. 154) within the "web of affinities" (p. 167) wherein everything may be connected, temporally or spatially, with everything else. Darwin might well be taken to adumbrate the features of an emergent "risk culture" in which causal relations are definitive but unpredictable.

24 Arnold's *Culture and Anarchy* and his essay "The Function of Criticism at the Present Time," as well as Richards's *Science and Poetry* and F. R. Leavis and Denys Thompson's *Culture and Environment* all make claims for the salvific power of literary language.

25 Martha C. Nussbaum, *Poetic Justice: The Literary Imagination and Public Life* (Boston: Beacon Press, 1995), pp. 2, 5.

26 Martha C. Nussbaum, *Love's Knowledge: Essays on Philosophy and Literature* (New York: Oxford University Press, 1990), pp. 23, 37.

27 Cleanth Brooks, "Irony as a Principle of Structure" (1948), in The Critical Tradition: Classic Texts and Contemporary Trends, ed. David H. Richter, 2nd ed. (Boston: Bedford Books, 1998), p. 765.

28 Lepenies, Between Literature and Science, pp. 154, 195; Perry Anderson, "Components of the National Culture," in English Questions (London: Verso, 1992), pp. 48–104.

29 For a very recent claim about the positive functions of a specifically Wordsworthian attitude to language and culture in British life, see Geoffrey H. Hartman, The Fateful Question of Culture (New York: Columbia University Press, 1997).

30 Sir Henry Newbolt, The Idea of an English Association, pamphlet no. 70 (London: The English Association, 1928), p. 10.

31 Roy Harvey Pearce, Historicism Once More: Problems and Occasions for the American Scholar (Princeton: Princeton University Press, 1969), pp. 17, 19, 41.

32 Paul Ricoeur, Oneself as Another, trans. Kathleen Blamey (Chicago: University of Chicago Press, 1992), pp. 148–49.

33 Regenia Gagnier, Subjectivities: A History of Self-Representation in Britain, 1832–1920 (New York: Oxford University Press, 1991), pp. 31, 141, 148.

34 Arthur Schopenhauer, The World as Will and Representation, trans. E. F. J. Payne (New York: Dover, 1969), 2: 433.

35 Jean-Jacques Rousseau, The "Confessions" and Correspondence, Including the Letters to Malherbes, ed. Christopher Kelly, Roger D. Masters, and Peter G. Stillman (Hanover, N.H.: University Press of New England, 1995), p. 9.

36 The Miscellaneous Works of Mr. J.J. Rousseau (London: Becket and De Hondt, 1767), 3: 35.

37 See Susan D. Moeller, Compassion Fatigue: How the Media Sell Disease, Famine, War, and Death (New York: Routledge, 1999), for some Rousseauvian thoughts on the effects of the mass media.

38 Richard Rorty, "The Inspirational Value of Great Works of Literature," Raritan 16, no. 1 (summer 1996): 8–17.

39 This was the general argument I made in The Academic Postmodern and the Rule of Literature: A Report on Half-Knowledge (Chicago: University of Chicago Press, 1995).

40 William Empson, Seven Types of Ambiguity, 2nd ed. (Harmondsworth: Penguin, 1965), p. 243.

5. Reasonable Situations: Philosophy, Biography, & Private Life

1 St. Augustine, Confessions, trans. R. S. Pine-Coffin (Harmondsworth: Penguin, 1984), p. 212.

2 Niklas Luhmann, "Individuality and the Individual: Historical Meanings and Contemporary Problems," in Essays on Self-Reference (New York: Columbia University Press, 1990), p. 109.

3   *The Philosophical Writings of Descartes*, trans. John Cottingham, Robert Stoothoff, and Dugald Murdoch (Cambridge, Eng.: Cambridge University Press, 1993), 1: 116.

4   Susan Bordo, *The Flight to Objectivity: Essays on Cartesianism and Culture* (Albany: SUNY Press, 1987), p. 62.

5   See, for example, Dalia Judovitz, *Subjectivity and Representation in Descartes: The Origins of Modernity* (Cambridge, Eng.: Cambridge University Press, 1988), which proposes the Cartesian subject as an "autobiographical, historical and narrative entity" (p. 3) engendering an inevitable confusion between metaphysical and empirical selves within a "single self-contradictory structure" (p. 183). See also various essays in Amelie Oksenberg Rorty, ed., *Essays on Descartes' "Meditations"* (Berkeley and Los Angeles: University of California Press, 1986); and Bernard Williams, *Descartes: The Project of Pure Inquiry* (Hassocks, Sussex: Harvester Press, 1978), which argues for the Cartesian maxims as calling to be embedded in "actual exposure to intellectual problems" in order to "gain meaning" (p. 33). All of these approaches (among others) work to put the cogito back into the very condition of situatedness from which Descartes has been so often taken to have extracted it.

6   See Ermanno Bencivenga, *The Discipline of Subjectivity: An Essay on Montaigne* (Princeton: Princeton University Press, 1990), for a persuasive rehearsal of the case.

7   C. B. Macpherson, *The Political Theory of Possessive Individualism: Hobbes to Locke* (1962; Oxford: Oxford University Press, 1983), p. 3.

8   *The Philosophical Writings of Descartes*, 1: 118; *Friedrich Schlegel's "Lucinde" and the Fragments*, trans. Peter Firchow (Minneapolis: University of Minnesota Press, 1971), p. 256; Ludwig Wittgenstein, *Philosophical Investigations*, trans. G. E. M. Anscombe, 3rd ed. (New York: Macmillan, 1958), p. 3.

9   Friedrich Nietzsche, *The Will to Power*, ed. Walter Kaufmann, trans. Walter Kaufmann and R. J. Hollingdale (New York: Random House, 1968), p. 283.

10 Schopenhauer, *The World as Will and Representation*, 1: 99–101, 115.

11 Arthur Schopenhauer, *Parerga and Paralipomena: Short Philosophical Essays*, trans. E.F.J. Payne, 2 vols. (Oxford: Clarendon Press, 1974), 1: 204.

12 Schopenhauer, *The World as Will and Representation*, 1: 344–48.

13 Nietzsche, *The Will to Power*, pp. 422, 427, 434.

14 Friedrich Nietzsche, *Untimely Meditations*, trans. R. J. Hollingdale (Cambridge, Eng.: Cambridge University Press, 1983), p. 101.

15 Edmund Husserl, *The Crisis of European Sciences and Transcendental Phenomenology*, trans. David Carr (Evanston, Ill.: Northwestern University Press, 1970), p. 196.

16 Hans-Georg Gadamer, *Philosophical Hermeneutics*, trans. David E. Linge (Berkeley and Los Angeles: University of California Press, 1977), p. 196.

17 A telling example of the latter occurs in Hitler's autobiography, where the

origins of the self are embedded in a highly localized small Austro-German town, Braunau, rather than in any pan-European situation: "In this little town on the river Inn, Bavarian by blood and Austrian by nationality, gilded by the light of German martyrdom, there lived, at the end of the eighties of the last century, my parents." *Mein Kampf* (New York: Reynal and Hitchcock, 1940), p. 5.

18 Martin Heidegger, *Being and Time*, trans. John Macquarrie and Edward Robinson, 7th ed. (London: SCM Press, 1962), p. 233. Not-being-at-home is being *unheimlich*, uncanny but also unhomed.

19 Martin Heidegger, *Poetry, Language, Thought*, trans. Albert Hofstadter (New York: Harper and Row, 1975), p. 161.

20 See Charles B. Guignon, "Introduction," in *The Cambridge Companion to Heidegger*, ed. Charles B. Guignon (Cambridge, Eng.: Cambridge University Press, 1993), pp. 29, 31. I have found this essay, and others in the volume, to be very helpful in attempting to write about Heidegger.

21 Charles Taylor, "Engaged Agency and Background in Heidegger," in Charles B. Guignon, ed., *The Cambridge Companion to Heidegger*, pp. 317–36.

22 The connections between the early Heidegger and the later Wittgenstein are explored by Richard Rorty, "Wittgenstein, Heidegger, and the Reification of Language," in Charles B. Guignon, ed., *The Cambridge Companion to Heidegger*, pp. 337–57.

23 Wittgenstein, *Philosophical Investigations*, p. 192. Compare Heidegger on "seeing as" in *Being and Time*, pp. 189–93.

24 Karl Jaspers, *Allgemeine Psychopathologie: Ein Leitfaden für Studierende, Ärtze und Psychologen* (Berlin: Springer Verlag, 1913), pp. 208, 295.

25 See Karl Jaspers, *Psychologie der Weltanschauungen*, 4th ed. (Berlin: Springer Verlag, 1954), p. 229. Jaspers claims to have reprinted the original text unaltered.

26 Karl Jaspers, *General Psychopathology*, trans. J. Hoenig and Marion W. Hamilton (Chicago: University of Chicago Press, 1963), p. 325. This is a translation of the text completely rewritten by Jaspers for republication in 1942.

27 Hoenig and Hamilton's "marginal situations" does not seem to be the best translation of *Grenzsituationen*, so I have followed others. The term is rendered as "boundary situations" in Jaspers's *Philosophy*, trans. E. B. Ashton, vol. 2 (Chicago: University of Chicago Press, 1970), p. 177.

28 Karl Jaspers, *Man in the Modern Age*, trans. Eden Paul and Cedar Paul (London: Routledge and Kegan Paul, 1951), pp. 28, 30–31.

29 Karl Jaspers, *Philosophy*, trans. E. B. Ashton, 3 vols. (Chicago: University of Chicago Press, 1969–70), 2: 178.

30 Jaspers also discusses the insolubility of antinomies in his *Psychologie der Weltanschauungen*, p. 232.

31 Compare Hans-Georg Gadamer's adaptation of Husserlian "horizons" in

Truth and Method (New York: Seabury Press, 1975), pp. 26–74. For Gadamer the empirical experience of being completely within "situations" can subsist along with "the attainment of a higher universality" (p. 272).

32 Jean-Paul Sartre, Being and Nothingness, trans. Hazel E. Barnes (London: Methuen, 1957), pp. 85–90.

33 A more thorough historical account of the career of the situation than I attempt here would have to make room for a discussion of the work of Maurice Merleau-Ponty, whose use of the term is both indubitably and perhaps polemically related to Sartre's. Samuel B. Mallin, in Merleau-Ponty's Philosophy (New Haven: Yale University Press, 1979), takes the situation as the core of his work, the "ground or source of every form of existence" (p. 17) and the fundamental instance of the "essential inseparability of the subject-side and object-side" (p. 34). In his Phenomenology of Perception, trans. Colin Smith (London: Routledge and Kegan Paul, 1962), Merleau-Ponty invokes the opacity of the situation to explain why "our contact with ourselves is necessarily achieved only in the sphere of ambiguity" (p. 381). To be able to "thematize every motive" would be to cease to be in a situation (p. 395), which cannot happen. Situational components are at once bodily and environmental. Freedom is never absolute but arises within the situation that produces or is "geared" to it (p. 442). Also significant is the work of Simone de Beauvoir on the "situation," which offers a feminist inflection and critique of Sartre by emphasizing the passivity of certain situations — gender roles, the physical body — which can be historically modified but are not spheres of mere human freedom. See Eva Lundgren-Gothlin, Sex and Existence: Simone de Beauvoir's "The Second Sex," trans. Linda Schenk (Hanover, N.H.: Wesleyan University Press and University Press of New England, 1996), pp. 93–95, 154–83.

34 Jeremy Bentham, The Panopticon Writings, ed. Miran Bozovic (London and New York: Verso, 1995), p. 34.

35 Jean-Paul Sartre, Critique of Dialectical Reason. Volume 1: Theory of Practical Ensembles, ed. Jonathan Ree, trans. Alan Sheridan-Smith (London: Verso, 1982), p. 69. The matter of totality and totalization has of course been one of the critical pressure points for critiques of marxist theory in the late twentieth century, and Sartre is a central figure in the discussion. See Martin Jay, Marxism and Totality: The Adventures of a Concept from Lukács to Habermas (Berkeley and Los Angeles: University of California Press, 1984), pp. 331–60, for a good account of Sartre's relations to Heidegger, phenomenology, and marxism, and for an argument that Sartre's own attempts at fixing on a plausible model of totalization were not finally coherent.

36 This raises the question of whether dialectical reason is categorically different from analytical reason; of whether it might not be, as Lévi-Strauss

put it, nothing more or less than "analytical reason in action." See Claude
Lévi-Strauss, *The Savage Mind* (Chicago: University of Chicago Press, 1970),
p. 251.

37 Fredric Jameson, *Marxism and Form: Twentieth-Century Dialectical Theories of Literature* (Princeton: Princeton University Press, 1974), p. 256. Jameson's long
discussion of Sartre (pp. 206–305) is an invaluable introduction to the first
volume of the *Critique of Dialectical Reason.*

38 Fredric Jameson, *Postmodernism*, pp. 346–47.

39 Fredric Jameson, *Sartre: The Origins of a Style* (New York: Columbia University
Press, 1984), p. 223. See also Jameson, *Marxism and Form*, p. 210.

40 David Hume, *A Treatise of Human Nature*, ed. L. A. Selby-Bigge (Oxford: Clarendon Press, 1973), pp. xv–xvi.

41 Wilhelm Dilthey, *Introduction to the Human Sciences*, ed. Rudolf A. Makkreel and
Frithjof Rodi (Princeton: Princeton University Press, 1989), p. 85.

42 Georgi Plekhanov, "On the Individual's Role in History," in *Selected Philosophical Works* (Moscow: Progress Publishers, 1976), 2: 300.

43 Jean-Paul Sartre, *Critique of Dialectical Reason. Volume 2 (unfinished): The Intelligibility of History*, ed. Arlette Elkaim-Sartre, trans. Quintin Hoare (London:
Verso, 1991), pp. 207, 209.

44 Jean-Paul Sartre, *Search for a Method*, trans. Hazel E. Barnes (New York: Random House, 1963), pp. 36, 99.

45 Hazel E. Barnes, *Sartre and Flaubert* (Chicago: University of Chicago Press,
1982), pp. 340–87, offers an account of the "Bovary" case assembled from
notes and other comments and supposes it implicit in what we already have
of the published work on Flaubert.

46 See Jean-Paul Sartre, *Situations, X: Politique et autobiographie* (Paris: Gallimard,
1976), p. 106, where he announces that the goal of *The Family Idiot* is to prove
that "every man is perfectly knowable provided that the appropriate method
is employed and one has the necessary documents" (my translation).

47 Douglas Collins, *Sartre as Biographer* (Cambridge, Mass.: Harvard University
Press, 1980), p. 22.

48 Lucien Sève, *Man in Marxist Theory; and the Psychology of Personality*, trans. John
McGreal (Sussex: Harvester Press, 1978), p. 146.

49 Georges Burdeau, *Traité de science politique* (Paris, 1956), 6: 42; my translation.

50 Jürgen Habermas, *The Structural Transformation of the Public Sphere: An Inquiry into
a Category of Bourgeois Society*, trans. Thomas Berger and Frederick Lawrence
(Cambridge, Mass.: MIT Press, 1989), pp. 171–72.

51 Compare Sebastiano Timpanaro, *The Freudian Slip: Psychoanalysis and Textual
Criticism*, trans. Kate Soper (London: Verso, 1985), p. 13, who complains that
Freud made a "mistake in taking a psychological situation associated with
monogamy and paternal authority as an absolute condition."

52   Compare Nietzsche, *The Will to Power*, p. 344: "The influence of 'external circumstances' is overestimated by Darwin to a ridiculous extent: the essential thing in the life process is precisely the tremendous, shaping form-creating force working from within which *utilizes* and *exploits* 'external circumstances.'"

53   Sève, *Man in Marxist Theory*, e.g., pp. 150, 384; Timpanaro, *The Freudian Slip*, p. 114.

54   Sigmund Freud, *The Psychopathology of Everyday Life*, trans. Alan Tyson (Harmondsworth: Pelican, 1976), pp. 333–35.

55   Sigmund Freud, *The Interpretation of Dreams*, trans. James Strachey, rev. by Angela Richards (Harmondsworth: Pelican, 1976), pp. 105, 169, 315–38.

56   Paul Ricoeur, *Freud and Philosophy: An Essay on Interpretation*, trans. Denis Savage (New Haven: Yale University Press, 1977), p. 65.

57   Sigmund Freud, *Beyond the Pleasure Principle*, trans. James Strachey (New York: Norton, 1961), p. 31.

58   Sigmund Freud, *Civilization and Its Discontents*, trans. James Strachey (New York: Norton, 1962), pp. 23–24, 33.

59   Freud, *The Interpretation of Dreams*, p. 735.

60   Sapir, *Selected Writings*, p. 513, is especially critical in noting that "what passes for individual psychology is little more than an ill-assorted melange of bits of physiology and of studies of highly fragmentary modes of behavior which have been artificially induced by the psychologist. This abortive discipline seems to be able to arrive at no integral conceptions of either individual or society and one can only hope that it will eventually surrender all its problems to physiology and social psychology." But of course it is individual psychology that attempts to take account of the idiosyncrasies that make social psychology, as Mill and others had admitted, never more than probability based.

61   *The Complete Essays of Montaigne*, trans. Donald M. Frame (Stanford: Stanford University Press, 1965), p. 629 (bk. 3, ch. 3).

62   G. E. Moore, *Principia Ethica*, ed. Thomas Baldwin, rev. ed. (Cambridge, Eng.: Cambridge University Press, 1993), p. 238.

63   Charles Taylor, *Sources of the Self: The Making of the Modern Identity* (Cambridge, Mass.: Harvard University Press, 1989), pp. 23, 131, 140, 188–89.

64   Norbert Elias, *The Civilizing Process*, trans. Edmund Jephcott (Oxford: Blackwell, 1994), p. 443.

65   Lawrence Stone, *The Family, Sex, and Marriage in England, 1500–1800* (New York: Harper and Row, 1977), pp. 3–10.

66   Roger Chartier, ed. *A History of Private Life. Volume 3: Passions of the Renaissance*, trans. Arthur Goldhammer (Cambridge, Mass.: Harvard University Press, Belknap Press, 1989), p. 2. See also Francis Barker, *The Tremulous Private Body: Essays on Subjection* (London: Methuen, 1984).

67 Jean-François Lyotard, *Political Writings*, trans. Bill Readings and Kevin Paul Geiman (Minneapolis: University of Minnesota Press, 1993), pp. 112–13.

68 Knabb, *Situationist International Anthology*, p. 22.

69 Guy Debord, in *ibid.* p. 25.

6. Lost for Words: Can We Stop Situating Ourselves?

1 Jacques Derrida, "Structure, Sign, and Play in the Discourse of the Human Sciences," in *The Structuralist Controversy: The Languages of Criticism and the Sciences of Man*, ed. Richard Macksey and Eugenio Donato (Baltimore: Johns Hopkins University Press, 1972), p. 271.

2 Lauren Berlant, *The Queen of America Goes to Washington City: Essays on Sex and Citizenship* (Durham: Duke University Press, 1997), pp. 14, 1.

3 Niklas Luhmann, *Observations on Modernity*, trans. William Whobrey (Stanford: Stanford University Press, 1998), pp. 77, 78, 81.

4 Clifford Geertz, " 'Local Knowledge' and Its Limits: Some Obiter Dicta," *Yale Journal of Criticism* 5, no. 2 (spring 1992): 132.

5 Seyla Benhabib, *Situating the Self: Gender, Community, and Postmodernism in Contemporary Ethics* (New York: Routledge, 1992), p. 8.

6 Teresa de Lauretis, *Technologies of Gender: Essays on Theory, Film, and Fiction* (Bloomington: Indiana University Press, 1987), p. 2.

7 Richard J. Bernstein, *Beyond Objectivism and Relativism: Science, Hermeneutics, and Praxis* (Philadelphia: University of Pennsylvania Press, 1983), pp. 48, 225.

8 Daniel Jonah Goldhagen, *Hitler's Willing Executioners: Ordinary Germans and the Holocaust* (New York: Random House, 1997), p. 7.

9 For some brief and trenchant thoughts on this matter, see Raul Hilberg, "The Goldhagen Phenomenon," *Critical Inquiry* 23 (1996–97): 721–28.

10 Charlotte Crabtree, Gary B. Nash, Paul Gagnon, and Scott Waugh, eds., *Lessons from History: Essential Understandings and Historical Perspectives Students Should Acquire* (Los Angeles: University of California, National Center for History in the Schools, 1992), p. 51.

11 Todd Gitlin, *The Twilight of Common Dreams: Why America Is Wracked by Culture Wars* (New York: Henry Holt, 1995), p. 122. Gitlin's book offers an account of the attack from the Left. Most of the headlines in the popular press covered the attack from the Right.

12 For which, a beginning may be made with Russell Jacoby and Naomi Glauberman, eds., *The Bell Curve Debate: History, Documents, Opinions* (New York: Random House, 1995); and Steven Fraser, ed., *The Bell Curve Wars* (New York: Basic Books, 1995).

13 Richard J. Herrnstein and Charles Murray, *The Bell Curve: Intelligence and Class Structure in American Life* (New York: The Free Press, 1994), pp. 25, 341, 387.

14 A notable instance here is Sheryl Gay Stolberg, "Science Looks at Littleton, and Shrugs," *New York Times*, May 9, 1999, sec. 4, pp. 1, 4.

15 Katharine Q. Seelye, "Clinton Holds Youth Violence Summit," *New York Times*, May 11, 1999, p. A14.

16 John M. Broder, "Searching for Answers after School Violence," *New York Times*, May 10, 1999, p. A16.

17 Ernesto Laclau and Chantal Mouffe, *Hegemony and Socialist Strategy: Towards a Radical Democratic Politics* (London: Verso, 1985), pp. 121–22.

18 See pp. 181–82 for important remarks on the "logic of equivalence" and its limits.

19 David A. Hollinger, *Postethnic America: Beyond Multiculturalism* (New York: Basic, 1995), p. 3.

20 For an account of this, see Sandra Harding, *The Science Question in Feminism* (Ithaca: Cornell University Press, 1986), esp. chs. 1, 6, 7.

21 Glen Newey, reviewing Quentin Skinner, *Liberty before Liberalism*, in the Times *Literary Supplement*, no. 4969, June 26, 1998, p. 29.

22 Touraine, *Return of the Actor*, p. 18.

23 Alain Touraine, *What Is Democracy?*, trans. David Macey (Boulder: Westview Press, 1997), p. 130.

24 Fredric Jameson, *Fables of Aggression: Wyndham Lewis, the Modernist as Fascist* (1979; Berkeley and Los Angeles: University of California Press, 1981), pp. 56–57.

25 Fredric Jameson, *The Cultural Turn: Selected Writings on the Postmodern, 1983–98* (London: Verso, 1998), p. 98.

26 The performative mystery and hermeneutic irony that resides at the heart of moral action was, according to Gadamer, well understood by Aristotle, for whom moral knowledge is to be distinguished from scientific knowledge in that one has to have it (or something of it) already in order to decide on its applicability to the "concrete situation" (*Truth and Method*, p. 283). All such knowledge then emerges from a "standpoint" within which morality is already embedded (p. 286). So the "situation" appears as it is because one is already within it. For a thorough history of much of the trajectory that pertains to this question, see J. B. Schneewind, *The Invention of Autonomy: A History of Modern Moral Philosophy* (Cambridge, Eng.: Cambridge University Press, 1998).

27 Alasdair MacIntyre, *After Virtue: A Study in Moral Theory*, 2nd ed. (Notre Dame, Ind.: University of Notre Dame Press, 1984), pp. 11–12.

28 Alasdair MacIntyre, *Whose Justice? Which Rationality?* (Notre Dame, Ind.: University of Notre Dame Press, 1988), p. 6.

29 Taylor, *Sources of the Self*, p. 36.

30 For an account of Sandel, MacIntyre, and Taylor in exactly this context, with specific reference to the debate initiated by John Rawls's A Theory of Justice, (Cambridge, Mass: Harvard University Press, Belknap Press, 1973), see

Stephen Mulhall and Adam Swift, *Liberals and Communitarians* (Oxford: Blackwell, 1992).

31 Charles Taylor, *Philosophy and the Human Sciences: Philosophical Papers, vol. 2* (Cambridge: Cambridge University Press, 1985), pp. 247, 243.

32 Charles Taylor, *The Ethics of Authenticity* (Cambridge, Mass.: Harvard University Press, 1992), p. III.

33 Enormously important here is of course the practice of and response to research into human DNA, which has stimulated a renewed turn to such ethically generated concepts as "dignity": see Paul Rabinow, "Severing the Ties: Fragmentation and Dignity in Late Modernity," in *Essays on the Anthropology of Reason* (Princeton: Princeton University Press, 1996), pp. 129–52; see also his *Making PCR: A Story of Biotechnology* (Chicago: University of Chicago Press, 1996).

34 Rawls, *A Theory of Justice*, pp. 74, 87. Again, see Mulhall and Swift, *Liberals and Communitarians*, for a summary of the critical responses to Rawls's book.

35 Richard Rorty, *Contingency, Irony and Solidarity* (Cambridge, Eng.: Cambridge University Press, 1989), p. 198.

36 Alexis de Tocqueville, *Democracy in America*, trans. Henry Reeve, rev. by Francis Bowen and Phillips Bradley (New York: Random House, 1945), 2: 4.

37 Harold Perkin, *The Rise of Professional Society: England since 1880* (London: Routledge, 1990), p. 9.

38 J. L. Austin, "A Plea for Excuses," in *Philosophical Papers*, ed. J. O. Urmson and G. J. Warnock, 2nd ed. (London: Oxford University Press, 1970), pp. 175–204, 177.

39 See Galen Strawson, "Free Will," in *Routledge Encyclopedia of Philosophy*, ed. Edward Craig (London: Routledge, 1998), 3: 743–53.

40 The outcomes priority is strongly argued by William G. Bowen and Derek Bok, *The Shape of the River: Long-Term Consequences of Considering Race in College and University Admissions* (Princeton: Princeton University Press, 1998). They propose that affirmative action does more good than harm as an outcome, resorting to standard utilitarian categories and methods in an effort to get away from the dead ends of arguments based on individual rights and merits. In so doing they are of course standing against the strong cultural pressures embodied in the antinomic features of individualist thinking.

41 See, for example, Gagnier, *Subjectivities*, pp. 23–24, 57 (for example), which draws on and refers to the work of Elaine Scarry, Bernard Williams, and others.

42 Blaise Pascal, *Pensées: The Provincial Letters* (New York: Random House, 1941), p. 512.

Bibliography

Adorno, T.W., Else Frenkel-Brunswik, Daniel J. Levinson, and R. Nevitt Sanford. *The Authoritarian Personality.* New York: Harper, 1950.

———. "On Lyric Poetry in Society," in *Notes to Literature*, ed. Rolf Tiedemann, trans. Shierry Weber Nicholsen (New York: Columbia University Press, 1991), 1: 37–54.

Althusser, Louis. *Lenin and Philosophy and Other Essays.* Trans. Ben Brewster. New York: Monthly Review Press, 1971.

Anderson, Perry. "Components of the National Culture." In *English Questions.* New York: Verso, 1992.

Aristotle. *The Basic Works of Aristotle.* Ed. Richard McKeon. New York: Random House, 1941.

Arnold, Matthew. *Culture and Anarchy*, ed. J. Dover Wilson. Cambridge: Cambridge University Press, 1960.

———. "The Function of Criticism at the Present Time." In *Essays in Criticism*, 2nd ed. London: Macmillan, 1869.

Augustine, St. *Confessions.* Trans. R. S. Pine-Coffin. Harmondsworth: Penguin, 1984.

Austen, Jane. *Emma.* Ed. Fiona Stafford. London: Penguin, 1996.

———. *Mansfield Park.* Ed. Tony Tanner. London: Penguin, 1985.

———. *Persuasion.* Ed. Linda Bree. Peterborough, Ont.: Broadview Press, 1998.

Austin, J. L. "A Plea for Excuses." In *Philosophical Papers*, ed. J. O. Urmston and G. J. Warnock, 2nd ed. London: Oxford University Press, 1970.

Barker, Francis. *The Tremulous Private Body: Essays on Subjection.* London: Methuen, 1984.

Barkow, Jerome H., Leda Cosmides, and John Tooby, eds. *The Adapted Mind: Evolutionary Psychology and the Generation of Culture.* New York: Oxford University Press, 1995.

Barnes, Hazel E. *Sartre and Flaubert.* Chicago: University of Chicago Press, 1982.

Barwise, Jon, and John Perry. *Situations and Attitudes.* Cambridge, Mass.: MIT Press, 1983.

Beck, Ulrich. *Risk Society: Towards a New Modernity.* Trans. Mark Ritter. London: Sage Publications, 1992.

Beer, Gillian. *Darwin's Plots: Evolutionary Narrative in Darwin, George Eliot, and Nineteenth-Century Fiction.* London: Routledge and Kegan Paul, 1983.

Bencivenga, Ermanno. *The Discipline of Subjectivity: An Essay on Montaigne.* Princeton: Princeton University Press, 1990.

Benedict, Ruth. *Patterns of Culture*. Boston: Houghton Mifflin, 1959.

Benhabib, Seyla. *Situating the Self: Gender, Community, and Postmodernism in Contemporary Ethics*. New York: Routledge, 1992.

Bentham, Jeremy. *An Introduction to the Principles of Morals and Legislation*. Ed. Laurence J. Lafleur. New York: Hafner, 1963.

—. *The Panopticon Writings*. Ed. Miran Bozovic. London: Verso, 1995.

—. *The Works of Jeremy Bentham*. Ed. John Bowring. 11 vols. Edinburgh: William Tait, 1838–43.

Berlant, Lauren. *The Queen of America Goes to Washington City: Essays on Sex and Citizenship*. Durham, NC: Duke University Press, 1997.

Bernstein, Richard J. *Beyond Objectivism and Relativism: Science, Hermeneutics, and Praxis*. Philadelphia: University of Pennsylvania Press, 1983.

Bhabha, Homi. K. *The Location of Culture*. London: Routledge, 1994.

Blackstone, William. *Commentaries on the Laws of England*. 4 vols. 1765–69; Chicago: University of Chicago Press, 1979.

Bordo, Susan. *The Flight to Objectivity: Essays on Cartesianism and Culture*. Albany: SUNY Press, 1987.

Bowen, William G., and Derek Bok. *The Shape of the River: Long-Term Consequences of Considering Race in College and University Admissions*. Princeton: Princeton University Press, 1998.

Broder, John M. "Searching for Answers after School Violence." *New York Times*, May 10, 1999, p. A16.

Brooks, Cleanth. "Irony as a Principle of Structure." In *The Critical Tradition: Classic Texts and Contemporary Trends*, ed. David H. Richter. 2nd ed. Boston: Bedford Books, 1998.

Bruner, Jerome. *Acts of Meaning*. Cambridge, Mass.: Harvard University Press, 1990.

Burdeau, Georges. *Traité de science politique*. Vol. 6. Paris, 1956.

Burke, Kenneth. *A Grammar of Motives*. Berkeley and Los Angeles: University of California Press, 1969.

—. *The Philosophy of Literary Form: Studies in Symbolic Action*. Rev. ed. New York: Random House, 1957.

Carlyle, Thomas. *The Works of Thomas Carlyle*. Centenary Edition, ed. H. D. Traill. 30 vols. London: Chapman and Hall, 1896–99.

Cascardi, Anthony J. *The Subject of Modernity*. Cambridge: Cambridge University Press, 1992.

Casey, Edward S. *The Fate of Place: A Philosophical History*. Berkeley and Los Angeles: University of California Press, 1998.

Castells, Manuel. *The Information Age: Economy, Society, and Culture*. 3 vols. Oxford: Blackwell, 1999.

Chambers, Sir Robert. *A Course of Lectures on the English Law, Delivered at the Univer-*

sity of Oxford, 1767–73. Ed. Thomas M. Curley. 2 vols. Madison: University of Wisconsin Press; Oxford: Oxford University Press, 1986.

Chandler, James. England in 1819: The Politics of Literary Culture and the Case of Romantic Historicism. Chicago: University of Chicago Press, 1998.

Chartier, Roger, ed. A History of Private Life. Volume 3: Passions of the Renaissance. Trans. Arthur Goldhammer. Cambridge, Mass.: Belknap Press, 1989.

Cholmondeley, Mary. Red Pottage. Ed. Elaine Showalter. 1899; New York: Virago-Penguin, 1985.

Clendinnen, Inga. Reading the Holocaust. Cambridge: Cambridge University Press, 1999.

Clifford, James. "Notes on Theory and Travel." Inscriptions 5 (1989): 177–88.

Coleridge, Samuel Taylor. Biographia Literaria. Ed. James Engell and W. Jackson Bate. 2 vols. Princeton: Princeton University Press, 1983.

Collins, Douglas. Sartre as Biographer. Cambridge, Mass.: Harvard University Press, 1980.

Condorcet, Marquis de. Condorcet: Selected Writings. Ed. Keith Michael Baker. Indianapolis: Bobbs-Merrill, 1976.

Cooley, Charles Horton. Social Organization and Human Nature and the Social Order. In The Two Major Works of Charles H. Cooley. Ed. Robert Cooley Angell. Glencoe, Ill.: The Free Press, 1956.

Crabtree, Charlotte, Gary B. Nash, Paul Gagnon, and Scott Waugh, eds. Lessons from History: Essential Understandings and Historical Perspectives Students Should Acquire. Los Angeles: National Center for History in the Schools, University of California at Los Angeles, 1992.

Darrow, Clarence S. Clarence Darrow on the Death Penalty. Evanston, Ill.: Chicago Historical Bookworks, 1991.

———. An Eye for an Eye. New York: Fox, Duffield and Co., 1905.

———. Resist Not Evil. 1903; rpt. Montclair, N.J.: Patterson Smith, 1972.

———. The Story of My Life. New York: Grosset and Dunlap, 1932.

Darwin, Charles. The Origin of Species. Ed. J. W. Burrow. Harmondsworth: Penguin, 1986.

Degler, Carl N. In Search of Human Nature: The Decline and Revival of Darwinism in American Social Thought. New York: Oxford University Press, 1991.

De Lauretis, Teresa. Technologies of Gender: Essays on Theory, Film, and Fiction. Bloomington: Indiana University Press, 1987.

Derrida, Jacques. Aporias. Trans. Thomas Dutoit. Stanford: Stanford University Press, 1993.

———. "Ousia and Gramme: Note on a Note from Being and Time." In Margins of Philosophy, trans. Alan Bass. Chicago: University of Chicago Press, 1982.

———. Spectres of Marx: The State of the Debt, the Work of Mourning, and the New International. Trans. Peggy Kamuf. London: Routledge, 1994.

————. "Structure, Sign, and Play in the Discourse of the Human Sciences.'" In *The Structuralist Controversy: The Languages of Criticism and the Sciences of Man*, ed. Richard Macksey and Eugenio Donato. Baltimore: Johns Hopkins University Press, 1972.

Dershowitz, Alan M. *The Abuse Excuse: and Other Cop-Outs, Sob Stories, and Evasions of Responsibility*. Boston: Little, Brown, 1994.

Descartes, René. *The Philosophical Writings of Descartes*. Trans. John Cottingham, Robert Stoothoff, and Dugald Murdoch. 3 vols. Cambridge, Eng.: Cambridge University Press, 1993.

Dewey, John. *Democracy and Education: An Introduction to the Philosophy of Education*. New York: Macmillan, 1916.

————. *Human Nature and Conduct: An Introduction to Social Psychology*. New York: Henry Holt, 1922.

————. *The Public and Its Problems*. Athens: Ohio University Press, The Swallow Press, 1991.

Dickens, Charles. *Oliver Twist*. Ed. Peter Fairclough. Harmondsworth: Penguin, 1985.

The Dictionary of South African English on Historical Principles. Oxford: Oxford University Press, 1996.

Dilthey, Wilhelm. *Introduction to the Human Sciences*. Ed. Rudolf A. Makkreel and Frithjof Rodi. Princeton: Princeton University Press, 1989.

Dirlik, Arif. *The Postcolonial Aura: Third World Criticism in the Age of Global Capitalism*. Boulder: Westview Press, 1997.

Durkheim, Emile. *The Division of Labor in Society*. Trans. George Simpson. New York: The Free Press, 1974.

————. *The Rules of Sociological Method*. Ed. Steven Lukes, trans. W. D. Halls. New York: The Free Press, 1982.

Edwards, Paul, ed. *The Encyclopedia of Philosophy*. 8 vols. New York: Macmillan and Collier Macmillan, 1972.

Elias, Norbert. *The Civilizing Process*. Trans. Edmund Jephcott. Oxford: Blackwell, 1994.

Eliot, George. *The Cabinet Edition of the Novels of George Eliot*. 24 vols. Edinburgh: Blackwood, 1878–85.

Empson, William. *Seven Types of Ambiguity*. 2nd ed. Harmondsworth: Penguin, 1965.

Ferguson, Adam. *An Essay on the History of Civil Society (1767)*. Ed. Duncan Ferguson. Edinburgh: Edinburgh University Press, 1978.

Fichte, J. G. *The Science of Rights*. Trans. A. E. Kroeger. London: Routledge and Kegan Paul, 1970.

Fish, Stanley. *Doing What Comes Naturally: Change, Rhetoric, and the Practice of Theory in Literary and Legal Studies*. Durham: Duke University Press, 1989.

Fletcher, Joseph. *Situation Ethics: The New Morality.* Philadelphia: Westminster Press, 1966.

Foucault, Michel. *The Order of Things: An Archaeology of the Human Sciences.* New York: Random House, 1973.

Fraser, Steven, ed. *The Bell Curve Wars.* New York: Basic Books, 1995.

Freud, Sigmund. *Beyond the Pleasure Principle.* Trans. James Strachey. New York: Norton, 1961.

———. *Civilization and Its Discontents.* Trans. James Strachey. New York: Norton, 1962.

———. *The Interpretation of Dreams.* Trans. James Strachey, rev. by Angela Richards. Harmondsworth: Pelican, 1976.

———. *The Psychopathology of Everyday Life.* Trans. Alan Tyson. Harmondsworth: Pelican, 1976.

Gadamer, Hans-Georg. *Philosophical Hermeneutics.* Trans. David E. Linge. Berkeley and Los Angeles: University of California Press, 1977.

———. *Truth and Method.* New York: Seabury Press, 1975.

Gagnier, Regenia. *Subjectivities: A History of Self-Representation in Britain, 1832–1920.* New York: Oxford University Press, 1991.

Geertz, Clifford. " 'Local Knowledge' and its Limits: Some *Obiter Dicta.*" *Yale Journal of Criticism* 5, no. 2 (spring 1992): 130–32.

Gerth, Hans, and C. Wright Mills. *Character and Social Structure: The Psychology of Social Institutions.* New York: Harcourt, Brace and World, 1964.

Giddens, Anthony. *The Consequences of Modernity.* Stanford: Stanford University Press, 1990.

———. *Modernity and Self-Identity: Self and Society in the Late Modern Age.* Stanford: Stanford University Press, 1991.

Gitlin, Todd. *The Twilight of Common Dreams: Why America Is Wracked by Culture Wars.* New York: Henry Holt, 1995.

Godwin, William. *Things as They Are, or the Adventures of Caleb Williams.* Ed. Maurice Hindle. Harmondsworth: Penguin, 1988.

Goffman, Erving. *The Presentation of Self in Everyday Life.* Rev. ed. New York: Doubleday, 1959.

Goldhagen, Daniel Jonah. *Hitler's Willing Executioners: Ordinary Germans and the Holocaust.* New York: Random House, 1997.

Goodman, Nan. *Shifting the Blame: Literature, Law, and the Theory of Accidents in Nineteenth-Century America.* Princeton: Princeton University Press, 1998.

Grewal, Inderpal, and Caren Kaplan. Eds. *Scattered Hegemonies: Postmodernity and Transnational Feminist Practices.* Minneapolis: University of Minnesota Press, 1994.

Guignon, Charles B. "Introduction." In *The Cambridge Companion to Heidegger,* ed. Charles B. Guignon. Cambridge, Eng.: Cambridge University Press, 1993.

Habermas, Jürgen. *The Structural Transformation of the Public Sphere: An Inquiry into* a Category of Bourgeois Society. Trans. Thomas Berger and Frederick Lawrence. Cambridge, Mass.: MIT Press, 1989.

———. The Theory of Communicative Action. Volume 1: Reason and the Rationalization of Society. Trans. Thomas McCarthy. Boston: Beacon Press, 1984.

Hacking, Ian. The Emergence of Probability: A Philosophical Study of Early Ideas about Probability, Induction, and Statistical Evidence. Cambridge, Eng.: Cambridge University Press, 1975.

———. The Social Construction of What? Cambridge, Mass.: Harvard University Press, 1999.

Haraway, Donna J. "Situated Knowledges: The Science Question in Feminism and the Privilege of Partial Perspective." In Simians, Cyborgs, and Women: The Reinvention of Nature. New York: Routledge, 1991.

Harding, Sandra. The Science Question in Feminism. Ithaca: Cornell University Press, 1986.

Hart, H. L. A. "Legal Responsibility and Excuses." In Determinism and Freedom in the Age of Modern Science, ed. Sidney Hook. New York: Collier, 1961.

Hartman, Geoffrey H. The Fateful Question of Culture. New York: Columbia University Press, 1997.

Hartsock, Nancy. "Rethinking Modernism: Minority vs. Majority Theses." Cultural Critique 7 (1987): 187–206.

Harvey, David. Justice, Nature, and the Geography of Difference. Oxford: Blackwell, 1996.

Haskell, Thomas L. The Emergence of Professional Social Science: The American Social Science Association and the Nineteenth-Century Crisis of Authority. Urbana: University of Illinois Press, 1977.

Hays, Mary. Memoirs of Emma Courtney. London: Pandora, 1987.

Hegel, Georg Wilhelm Friedrich. Hegel's Philosophy of Right. Trans. T. M. Knox. London: Oxford University Press, 1975.

Heidegger, Martin. Being and Time. Trans. John Macquarrie and Edward Robinson. 7th ed. London: SCM Press, 1962.

———. Poetry, Language, Thought. Trans. Albert Hofstadter. New York: Harper and Row, 1975.

Heisenberg, Werner. Physics and Philosophy: The Revolution in Modern Science. New York: Harper and Row, 1962.

Helvétius, M. [Claude-Adrien] A Treatise on Man: His Intellectual Faculties and his Education. A New and Improved Edition. Trans. W. Hooper. 2 vols. London: Vernor, Hood and Sharp etc., 1810.

Herbert, Christopher. Culture and Anomie: Ethnographic Imagination in the Nineteenth Century. Chicago: University of Chicago Press, 1991.

Herder, Johann Gottfried von. Reflections on the Philosophy of the History of Mankind. Ed. Frank E. Manuel. Chicago: University of Chicago Press, 1968.

Herrnstein, Richard J., and Charles Murray. The Bell Curve: Intelligence and Class Structure in American Life. New York: The Free Press, 1994.

Hilberg, Raul. "The Goldhagen Phenomenon." *Critical Inquiry* 23 (1996–97): 721–28.

Hitler, Adolf. *Mein Kampf.* New York. Reynal and Hitchcock, 1940.

Hobbes, Thomas. *Leviathan.* Ed. Michael Oakeshott. Oxford: Basil Blackwell, 1955.

———. *Man and Citizen.* Ed. Bernard Gert. New York: Humanities Press, 1978.

Holbach, Baron de. *Common Sense; or, Natural Ideas Opposed to Supernatural.* New York, 1795.

———. [as M. Mirabaud] *Nature and Her Laws; as Applicable to the Happiness of Man Living in Society; Contrasted with Superstition and Imaginary Systems.* 2 vols. London: W. Hodgson, 1816.

Hollinger, David A. *Postethnic America: Beyond Multiculturalism.* New York: Basic Books, 1995.

Holmes, Oliver Wendell. *The Common Law.* Ed. Mark De Wolfe Howe. Cambridge, Mass.: Harvard University Press, Belknap Press, 1963.

———. "The Path of the Law." In *Collected Legal Papers.* London: Constable and Co., 1920.

Hook, Sidney, ed. *Determinism and Freedom in the Age of Modern Science.* New York: Collier, 1961.

Horkheimer, Max, and Theodor W. Adorno. *Dialectic of Enlightenment.* Trans. John Cumming. New York: Continuum, 1986.

Horwitz, Morton J. *The Transformation of American Law, 1780–1860.* Cambridge, Mass.: Harvard University Press, 1977.

———. *The Transformation of American Law, 1870–1960: The Crisis of Legal Orthodoxy.* New York: Oxford University Press, 1992.

Hume, David. *A Treatise of Human Nature.* Ed. L. A. Selby-Bigge. Oxford: Clarendon Press, 1973.

Husserl, Edmund. *The Crisis of European Sciences and Transcendental Phenomenology.* Trans. David Carr. Evanston, Ill.: Northwestern University Press, 1970.

Jacoby, Russell, and Naomi Glauberman, eds. *The Bell Curve Debate: History, Documents, Opinions.* New York: Random House, 1995.

James, William. *Pragmatism; and Four Essays from "The Meaning of Truth."* Cleveland: World Publishing Company, 1970.

Jameson, Fredric. *The Cultural Turn: Selected Writings on the Postmodern, 1983–98.* London: Verso, 1998.

———. *Fables of Aggression: Wyndham Lewis, the Modernist as Fascist.* 1979; Berkeley and Los Angeles: University of California Press, 1981.

———. *Marxism and Form: Twentieth-Century Dialectical Theories of Literature.* Princeton: Princeton University Press, 1974.

———. *Postmodernism, or, The Cultural Logic of Late Capitalism.* Durham: Duke University Press, 1991.

———. *Sartre: The Origins of a Style.* New York: Columbia University Press, 1984.

————. *The Seeds of Time*. New York: Columbia University Press, 1994.

Jaspers, Karl. *Allgemeine Psychopathologie: Ein Leitfaden für Studierende, Ärtze und Psychologen*. Berlin: Springer Verlag, 1913.

————. *General Psychopathology*. Trans. J. Hoenig and Marion W. Hamilton. Chicago: University of Chicago Press, 1963.

————. *Man in the Modern Age*. Trans. Eden Paul and Cedar Paul. London: Routledge and Kegan Paul, 1951.

————. *Philosophy*. Trans. E. B. Ashton. 3 vols. Chicago: University of Chicago Press, 1969–70.

————. *Psychologie der Weltanschauungen*. 4th ed. Berlin: Springer Verlag, 1954.

Jay, Martin. *Marxism and Totality: The Adventures of a Concept from Lukács to Habermas*. Berkeley and Los Angeles: University of California Press, 1984.

Judovitz, Dalia. *Subjectivity and Representation in Descartes: The Origins of Modernity*. Cambridge, Eng.: Cambridge University Press, 1988.

Kant, Immanuel. *Immanuel Kant's Critique of Pure Reason*. Trans. Norman Kemp Smith. London: Macmillan, 1933.

————. *Lectures on Ethics*. Trans. Louis Infield. New York: Harper and Row, 1963.

Kaplan, Caren. *Questions of Travel: Postmodern Discourses of Displacement*. Durham: Duke University Press, 1996.

Klineberg, Otto. "Racial Psychology." In *The Science of Man in the World Crisis*, ed. Ralph Linton. New York: Columbia University Press, 1945.

Kluckhohn, Clyde, and William H. Kelly. "The Concept of Culture." In *The Science of Man in the World Crisis*, ed. Ralph Linton. New York: Columbia University Press, 1945.

Kluckhohn, Clyde, and Henry A. Murray, eds. *Personality in Nature, Society, and Culture*. New York: Alfred A. Knopf, 1948.

Knabb, Ken, ed. and trans. *Situationist International Anthology*. Berkeley: Bureau of Public Secrets, 1981.

Kuhn, Thomas S. *The Structure of Scientific Revolutions*. Chicago: University of Chicago Press, 1962.

La Capra, Dominick. *Representing the Holocaust: History, Theory, Trauma*. Ithaca: Cornell University Press, 1994.

Laclau, Ernesto. *New Reflections on the Revolution of Our Time*. London: Verso, 1990.

Laclau, Ernesto, and Chantal Mouffe. *Hegemony and Socialist Strategy: Towards a Radical Democratic Politics*. London: Verso, 1985.

Lamphere, Louise, Helena Ragone, and Patricia Zavella, eds. *Situated Lives: Gender and Culture in Everyday Life*. New York: Routledge, 1997.

Leavis, F.R., and Denys Thompson. *Culture and Environment: The Training of Critical Awareness*. London: Chatto and Windus, 1933.

Lentricchia, Frank. *Criticism and Social Change*. Chicago: University of Chicago Press, 1985.

Lepenies, Wolf. *Between Literature and Science: The Rise of Sociology.* Trans. R.J. Hollingdale. Cambridge, Eng.: Cambridge University Press, 1992.

Levin, Meyer. *Compulsion.* New York: Simon and Schuster, 1956.

Lévi-Strauss, Claude. *The Savage Mind.* Chicago: University of Chicago Press, 1970.

Linton, Ralph. "The Scope and Aims of Anthropology." In *The Science of Man in the World Crisis,* ed. Ralph Linton. New York: Columbia University Press, 1945.

Locke, John. *An Essay Concerning Human Understanding.* Ed. Peter H. Nidditch. Oxford: Clarendon Press, 1979.

————. "Some Thoughts Concerning Education." In *The Educational Writings of John Locke,* ed. James L. Axtell. Cambridge, Eng.: Cambridge University Press, 1968.

Luhmann, Niklas. "Individuality and the Individual: Historical Meanings and Contemporary Problems." In *Essays on Self-Reference.* New York: Columbia University Press, 1990.

————. *Observations on Modernity.* Trans. William Whobrey. Stanford: Stanford University Press, 1998.

Lukács, Georg. *History and Class Consciousness: Studies in Marxist Dialectics.* Trans. Rodney Livingstone. Cambridge, Mass.: MIT Press, 1972.

Lundgren-Gothlin, Eva. *Sex and Existence: Simone de Beauvoir's "The Second Sex."* Trans. Linda Schenk. Hanover, N.H.: Wesleyan University Press and University Press of New England, 1996.

Lynd, Robert S., and Helen Merrell Lynd. *Middletown: A Study in Contemporary American Culture.* New York: Harcourt Brace, 1929.

Lyotard, Jean-François. *Political Writings.* Trans. Bill Readings and Kevin Paul Geiman. Minneapolis: University of Minnesota Press, 1993.

MacIntyre, Alasdair. *After Virtue: A Study in Moral Theory.* 2nd ed. Notre Dame, Ind.: University of Notre Dame Press, 1984.

————. *Whose Justice? Which Rationality?* Notre Dame, Ind.: University of Notre Dame Press, 1988.

Macpherson, C. B. *The Political Theory of Possessive Individualism: Hobbes to Locke.* Oxford: Oxford University Press, 1983.

Malinowski, Bronislaw. *Freedom and Civilization.* New York: Roy Publishers, 1944.

————. "The Problem of Meaning in Primitive Language." In *The Meaning of Meaning: A Study of the Influence of Language upon Thought and of the Science of Symbolism,* ed. C. K. Ogden and I. A. Richards. London: Routledge and Kegan Paul, 1966.

Mallin, Samuel B. *Merleau-Ponty's Philosophy.* New Haven: Yale University Press, 1979.

Massey, Doreen. *Space, Place and Gender.* Minneapolis: University of Minnesota Press, 1994.

Mead, George Herbert. *Mind, Self, and Society from the Standpoint of a Social Behaviorist.* Ed. Charles W. Morris. 1934; Chicago: University of Chicago Press, 1952.

Mead, Margaret. *From the South Seas: Studies of Adolescence and Sex in Primitive Societies.* New York: William Morrow, 1939. [Complete, separately paginated texts of *Coming of Age in Samoa, Growing Up in New Guinea,* and *Sex and Temperament in Three Primitive Societies.*]

Merleau-Ponty, Maurice. *Phenomenology of Perception.* Trans. Colin Smith. London: Routledge and Kegan Paul, 1962.

Mill, John Stuart. *On Liberty.* Ed. Currin V. Shields. Indianapolis: Bobbs-Merrill, 1956.

———. *A System of Logic, Ratiocinative and Inductive,* 8th ed., 2 vols. London: Longmans, Green, Reader, and Dyer, 1872.

Mirabaud, M. (See Holbach, Baron de.)

Moeller, Susan D. *Compassion Fatigue: How the Media Sell Disease, Famine, War, and Death.* London: Routledge, 1999.

Montaigne, Michel de. *The Complete Essays of Montaigne.* Trans. Donald M. Frame. Stanford: Stanford University Press, 1965.

Montesquieu, Baron de. *The Spirit of the Laws.* Trans. Thomas Nugent. London: Macmillan, 1949.

Moore, G. E. *Principia Ethica.* Ed. Thomas Baldwin. Rev. ed. Cambridge, Eng.: Cambridge University Press, 1993.

Morris, Herbert, ed. *Freedom and Responsibility: Readings in Philosophy and Law.* Stanford: Stanford University Press, 1961.

Mulhall, Stephen, and Adam Swift. *Liberals and Communitarians.* Oxford: Blackwell, 1992.

Murray, Henry A., and Clyde Kluckhohn. "Outline of a Conception of Personality." In *Personality in Nature, Society, and Culture,* ed. Clyde Kluckhohn and Henry A. Murray. New York: Alfred A. Knopf, 1948.

Nagel, Thomas. *The View from Nowhere.* New York: Oxford University Press, 1986.

Newbolt, Sir Henry. *The Idea of an English Association.* Pamphlet no. 70. London: The English Association, 1928.

Newey, Glen. Review of Quentin Skinner, *Liberty Before Liberalism. Times Literary Supplement,* no. 4969, June 26, 1998.

Newmeyer, Frederick J. *The Politics of Linguistics.* Chicago: University of Chicago Press, 1986.

Nietzsche, Friedrich. *Basic Writings of Nietzsche.* Ed. and trans. Walter Kaufmann. New York: Random House, 1968.

———. *Untimely Meditations.* Trans. R. J. Hollingdale. Cambridge, Eng.: Cambridge University Press, 1983.

———. *The Will to Power.* Ed. Walter Kaufmann, trans. Walter Kaufmann and R. J. Hollingdale. New York: Random House, 1968.

Nixon, Rob. *Homelands, Harlem, and Hollywood: South African Culture and the World Beyond.* New York: Routledge, 1994.

Novick, Peter. *That Noble Dream: The "Objectivity Question" and the American Historical Profession.* Cambridge, Eng.: Cambridge University Press, 1988.

Nussbaum, Martha C. *Love's Knowledge: Essays on Philosophy and Literature.* New York: Oxford University Press, 1990.

———. *Poetic Justice: The Literary Imagination and Public Life.* Boston: Beacon Press, 1995.

O'Neal, John C. *The Authority of Experience: Sensationist Theory in the French Enlightenment.* University Park: Pennsylvania State University Press, 1996.

Orwell, George. *Nineteen Eighty-Four.* New York: Harcourt, Brace and World, 1949.

Paley, William. *The Principles of Moral and Political Philosophy,* 20th ed., 2 vols. London, printed for J. Faulder etc., 1814.

Parsons, Talcott. "Overview." In *American Sociology: Perspectives, Problems, Methods,* ed. Talcott Parsons. New York: Basic Books, 1968.

Pascal, Blaise. *Pensées: The Provincial Letters.* New York: Random House, 1941.

Patey, Douglas Lane. *Probability and Literary Form: Philosophic Theory and Literary Practice in the Augustan Age.* Cambridge, Eng.: Cambridge University Press, 1984.

Pearce, Roy Harvey. *Historicism Once More: Problems and Occasions for the American Scholar.* Princeton: Princeton University Press, 1969.

Perkin, Harold. *The Rise of Professional Society: England since 1880.* London: Routledge, 1990.

Perry, John R. "Semantics, Situation." In *Routledge Encyclopedia of Philosophy,* ed. Edward Craig. Vol. 8. London: Routledge, 1998.

Peters, Thomas J. *Liberation Management: Necessary Disorganization for the Nanosecond Nineties.* New York: Fawcett Columbine, 1992.

Peters, Thomas J., and Robert H. Waterman Jr. *In Search of Excellence: Lessons from America's Best-Run Companies.* 1982; London: HarperCollins, 1995.

Plekhanov, Georgi. "On the Individual's Role in History." In *Selected Philosophical Works.* Vol. 2. Moscow: Progress Publishers, 1976.

Plucknett, Theodore F. T. *A Concise History of the Common Law.* 4th ed. London: Butterworth, 1948.

Porter, Theodore M. *The Rise of Statistical Thinking, 1820–1900.* Princeton: Princeton University Press, 1985.

———. *Trust in Numbers: The Pursuit of Objectivity in Science and Public Life.* Princeton: Princeton University Press, 1995.

Probyn, Elspeth. "Travels in the Postmodern: Making Sense of the Local." In *Feminism/Postmodernism,* ed. Linda J. Nicholson. New York: Routledge, 1990.

Rabinow, Paul. *French Modern: Norms and Forms of the Social Environment.* Chicago: University of Chicago Press, 1995.

———. *Making PCR: A Story of Biotechnology.* Chicago: University of Chicago Press, 1996.

———. "Severing the Ties: Fragmentation and Dignity in Late Modernity." In *Essays on the Anthropology of Reason.* Princeton: Princeton University Press, 1996.

Rawls, John. *A Theory of Justice.* Cambridge, Mass.: Harvard University Press, Belknap Press, 1973.

Richards, I. A. *Science and Poetry.* New York: Norton, 1926.

Ricoeur, Paul. *Freud and Philosophy: An Essay on Interpretation.* Trans. Denis Savage. New Haven: Yale University Press, 1977.

———. *Oneself as Another.* Trans. Kathleen Blamey. Chicago: University of Chicago Press, 1992.

Robertson, William. *The Works of the Late William Robertson, D.D.* 6 vols. London, printed for Cowie, Low etc., 1826.

Roethlisberger, F. J., and William J. Dickson. *Management and the Worker: An Account of a Research Program Conducted by the Western Electric Company, Hawthorne Works, Chicago.* 1939; Cambridge, Mass.: Harvard University Press, 1950.

Rorty, Amelie Oksenberg, ed. *Essays on Descartes's "Meditations."* Berkeley and Los Angeles: University of California Press, 1986.

Rorty, Richard. *Contingency, Irony, and Solidarity.* Cambridge, Eng.: Cambridge University Press, 1991.

———. "The Inspirational Value of Great Works of Literature." *Raritan* 16, no. 1 (summer 1996): 8–17.

———. "Wittgenstein, Heidegger, and the Reification of Language." In *The Cambridge Companion to Heidegger,* ed. Charles B. Guignon. Cambridge, Eng.: Cambridge University Press, 1993.

Rousseau, Jean-Jacques. *The "Confessions" and Correspondence, Including the Letters to Malherbes.* Ed. Christopher Kelly, Roger D. Masters, and Peter G. Stillman. Hanover, N.H.: University Press of New England, 1995.

———. *The Miscellaneous Works of Mr. J. J. Rousseau.* 5 vols. London: Becket and De Hondt, 1767.

Routledge Encyclopedia of Philosophy. Ed. Edward Craig. 10 vols. London: Routledge, 1998.

Rush, Benjamin. *Thoughts on the Mode of Education Proper in a Republic* (1786). In *Essays on Education in the Early Republic,* ed. Frederick Rudolph. Cambridge, Mass.: Harvard University Press, Belknap Press, 1965.

Sandel, Michael J. *Democracy's Discontent: America in Search of a Public Philosophy.* Cambridge, Mass.: Harvard University Press, Belknap Press, 1996.

Sapir, Edward. *Selected Writings of Edward Sapir on Language, Culture, and Personality.* Ed. David G. Mandelbaum. Berkeley and Los Angeles: University of California Press, 1958.

Sartre, Jean-Paul. *Being and Nothingness.* Trans. Hazel E. Barnes. London: Methuen, 1957.

———. *Critique of Dialectical Reason. Volume 1: Theory of Practical Ensembles.* Ed. Jonathan Ree, trans. Alan Sheridan-Smith. London: Verso, 1982.

———. *Critique of Dialectical Reason. Volume 2 (unfinished): The Intelligibility of History.* Ed. Arlette Elkaim-Sartre, trans. Quintin Hoare. London: Verso, 1991.

———. *The Family Idiot: Gustave Flaubert, 1821–1857,* Trans. Carol Cosman. 5 vols. Chicago: University of Chicago Press, 1981–93.

———. *Search for a Method.* Trans. Hazel E. Barnes. New York: Random House, 1963.

———. *Situations, X: Politique et autobiographie.* Paris: Gallimard, 1976.

Schiller, J.C.F. von. "On Naïve and Sentimental Poetry." Trans. Daniel O. Dahlstrom. In *Friedrich Schiller: Essays,* ed. Walter Hinderer and Daniel O. Dahlstrom. New York: Continuum, 1995.

Schlegel, Friedrich. *Friedrich Schlegel's "Lucinde" and the Fragments.* Trans. Peter Firchow. Minneapolis: University of Minnesota Press, 1971.

Schneewind, Jerome. *The Invention of Autonomy: A History of Modern Moral Philosophy.* Cambridge, Eng.: Cambridge University Press, 1998.

Schopenhauer, Arthur. *Parerga and Paralipomena: Short Philosophical Essays.* Trans. E. F. J. Payne. 2 vols. Oxford: Clarendon Press, 1974.

———. *The World as Will and Representation.* Trans. E. F. J. Payne. 2 vols. New York: Dover, 1969.

Scott, Sir Walter. *Waverley.* Ed. Andrew Hook. Harmondsworth: Penguin, 1982.

Seelye, Katherine Q. "Clinton Holds Youth Violence Summit." *New York Times,* May 11, 1999, A14.

Seligman, Jerry. "Perspectives in Situation Theory." In *Situation Theory and Its Applications,* ed. Robin Cooper et al. Vol. 1. Stanford: Stanford University, Center for the Study of Language and Information, 1990.

Sennett, Richard. *The Fall of Public Man: On the Social Psychology of Capitalism.* New York: Random House, 1978.

Sennett, Richard, and Jonathan Cobb. *The Hidden Injuries of Class.* New York: Random House, 1973.

Sève, Lucien. *Man in Marxist Theory; and the Psychology of Personality.* Trans. John McGreal. Sussex: Harvester Press, 1978.

Shapiro, Barbara J. *"Beyond Reasonable Doubt" and "Probable Cause": Historical Perspectives on the Anglo-American Law of Evidence.* Berkeley and Los Angeles: University of California Press, 1991.

Shiffrin, Steven H. *The First Amendment: Democracy and Romance.* Cambridge, Mass.: Harvard University Press, 1990.

Shumate, T. Daniel, ed. *The First Amendment: The Legacy of George Mason.* Fairfax, Va.: George Mason University Press, 1987.

Simpson, David. *The Academic Postmodern and the Rule of Literature: A Report on Half Knowledge.* Chicago: University of Chicago Press, 1995.

———. *Irony and Authority in Romantic Poetry.* London: Macmillan, 1989.

———. "Prospects for Global English: Back to BASIC?" *Yale Journal of Criticism* 11, no. 1 (1998): 301–7.

Smith, Adam. *Lectures on Jurisprudence.* Eds. R. L. Meek, D. D. Raphael, and P. G. Stein. Oxford: Clarendon Press, 1978.

———. *The Theory of Moral Sentiments.* Eds. D. D. Raphael and A. L. Macfie. Oxford: Clarendon Press, 1976.

Spencer, Herbert. *The Principles of Psychology.* London: Longman, Brown, Green, and Longmans, 1855.

Spivak, Gayatri Chakravorty. *A Critique of Postcolonial Reason: Toward a History of the Vanishing Present.* Cambridge, Mass.: Harvard University Press, 1999.

———. *Outside in the Teaching Machine.* New York: Routledge, 1993.

Stephen, Serjeant Henry John. *Mr. Serjeant Stephen's New Commentaries on the Laws of England.* Revised and modernized by Edward Jenks. 14th ed., 4 vols. London: Butterworth, 1903.

Stigler, Stephen M. *The History of Statistics: The Measurement of Uncertainty before 1900.* Cambridge, Mass.: Harvard University Press, Belknap Press, 1986.

Stolberg, Sheryl Gay. "Science Looks at Littleton, and Shrugs." *New York Times,* May 9, 1999, Sec. 4, pp. 1, 4.

Stone, Lawrence. *The Family, Sex, and Marriage in England, 1500–1800.* New York: Harper and Row, 1977.

Strawson, Galen. "Free Will." In *Routledge Encyclopedia of Philosophy,* ed. Edward Craig. London: Routledge, 1998.

Sullivan, Andrew. "London Diarist." *The New Republic,* November 20, 1995, p. 50.

Sumner, William Graham, and Albert Galloway Keller. *The Science of Society.* 4 vols. New Haven: Yale University Press; Oxford: Oxford University Press, 1927.

Taylor, Charles. "Engaged Agency and Background in Heidegger." In *The Cambridge Companion to Heidegger,* ed. Charles B. Guignon. Cambridge, Eng.: Cambridge University Press, 1993.

———. *The Ethics of Authenticity.* Cambridge, Mass.: Harvard University Press, 1992.

———. *Philosophy and the Human Sciences: Philosophical Papers, vol. 2.* Cambridge, Eng.: Cambridge University Press, 1985.

———. *Sources of the Self: The Making of the Modern Identity.* Cambridge, Mass.: Harvard University Press, 1989.

Timpanaro, Sebastiano. *The Freudian Slip: Psychoanalysis and Textual Criticism.* Trans. Kate Soper. London: Verso, 1985.

Tocqueville, Alexis de. *Democracy in America.* Trans. Henry Reeve, rev. by Francis Bowen and Phillips Bradley. 2 vols. New York: Random House, 1945.

Touraine, Alain. *Return of the Actor: Social Theory in Postindustrial Society.* Trans. Myrna Godzich. Minneapolis: University of Minnesota Press, 1988.

———. *What Is Democracy?* Trans. David Macey. Boulder: Westview Press, 1997.

Wallerstein, Immanuel. *The End of the World as We Know It: Social Science for the Twenty-First Century.* Minneapolis: University of Minnesota Press, 1999.

Watt, Ian. *Myths of Modern Individualism: Faust, Don Quixote, Don Juan, Robinson Crusoe*. Cambridge, Eng.: Cambridge University Press, 1996.

Welsh, Alexander. *Strong Representations: Narrative and Circumstantial Evidence in England*. Baltimore: Johns Hopkins University Press, 1992.

Williams, Bernard. *Descartes: The Project of Pure Enquiry*. Hassocks, Sussex: Harvester Press, 1978.

Wilson, Kenneth G. *The Columbia Guide to Standard American English*. New York: Columbia University Press, 1993.

Wittgenstein, Ludwig. *Philosophical Investigations*. Trans. G. E. M. Anscombe. 3rd ed. New York: Macmillan, 1958.

Wollstonecraft, Mary. *A Vindication of the Rights of Woman*. Ed. Carol H. Poston. 2nd ed. New York: Norton, 1988.

Wordsworth, William. *The Prelude: 1799, 1805, 1850*, ed. Jonathan Wordsworth, M.H. Abrams, and Stephen Gill. New York: Norton, 1979.

Index

DAVID SIMPSON is Professor of English
at the University of California at Davis.

Library of Congress Cataloging-in-Publication Data
Simpson, David
Situatedness, or, Why we keep saying where we're
coming from / David Simpson.
p. cm. — (Post-contemporary interventions)
Includes bibliographical references (p.) and index.
ISBN 0-8223-2825-9 (cloth : alk. paper)
ISBN 0-8223-2839-9 (pbk. : alk. paper)
I. Situation (Philosophy) I. Title: Situatedness.
II. Title: Why we keep saying where we're coming from.
III. Title. IV. Series.
BD340 .S56 2002 128'.4—dc21 2001040349